Better Homes and Gardens®

THE COMPLETE
home
MAKEOVER BOOK

INDEX

THE COMPLETE
home
MAKEOVER BOOK

Contents

Planning

In planning any home improvements, the first step should be to assess what you have. Look at the whole house and consider how renovating part of it will affect the remainder. If you have recently bought the house, living in it unrenovated for at least a year, through all the seasons, is the best way of getting to know its shortcomings. Your lifestyle and the number of people occupying the house are other important factors to take into account.

Good planning for your home improvements and renovations is vitally important. Mistakes can be costly as well as depressing to live with. People often begin with a 'wish list', but it is best to consider your budget first. Many grand schemes have had to be pared back after a visit to the bank manager! So, work out what you can afford and, if you have to borrow money, make sure you can afford to pay it back over an acceptable period.

Planning the renovation of a house should be an exciting and creative process, and should not be done in a rush; ideas, not to mention fashions, change. Look for inspiration in magazines, brochures, books and home exhibitions, and keep a file of your favourite ideas. Take a stroll through your neighbourhood to see how other people have tackled renovating similar houses to yours. This can be a particularly useful method of ascertaining the sorts of changes your local authority will allow. Knowing exactly what you want will make briefing an architect, builder or suppliers much easier.

Renovating an older house usually involves opening up the living areas to the outdoors. This combined living and dining room brings in more natural light and gives easy access to the garden through the French doors. By retaining the old fire surround and using polished timber floorboards and beams, the look is warm and inviting as well as practical.

ABOVE: The same tiles used inside and outside create unity and spaciousness.

RIGHT: Existing columns support the ceiling beams and align with the island bench.

BELOW: From the kitchen out to the verandah, this kitchen-cum-family room brings the family together every day, and it's all achieved by removing the wall between the two rooms and installing a partition wall to create a cosy corner for the dining table.

Look at what you have

The list of questions to ask yourself in the initial stages of planning may seem endless, but it is important to address them all if you are to achieve the desired result.

Layout

Is the layout of your house logical? How do you use the existing space? Are you making the most of it? Which way does the house face? Do you need to create more privacy? If you have a kitchen that you can eat in, do you really need a large, formal dining room as well? How often do you have guests to stay? If it's infrequently, a spare bedroom could be more useful as a study or workroom. In an older bungalow, an out-of-date bathroom may have the best view of the back garden and might be better relocated somewhere inside. The space created could then be used as a living area that opens on to the garden in the warmer months. How far are functional areas such as the kitchen, dining room, utility room and bathroom from each other? Does the utility room have easy access to the outdoor clothes line.

If you have a two-storey house with no bathroom upstairs, you have several options. You could move the main bathroom upstairs and use the new space downstairs for a toilet and hand basin only; convert a smaller upstairs bedroom into an en suite bathroom; or, if you have plenty of space and there are five or six occupants, you may want two full bathrooms. Bear in mind that relocating plumbing can be expensive.

Urban

Older inner-city houses have become highly desirable, as they are

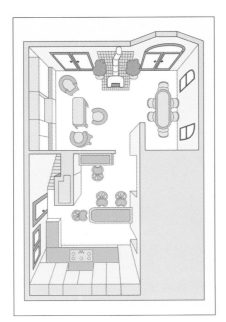

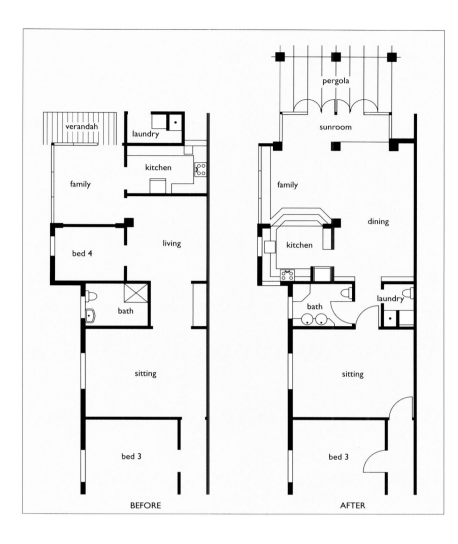

verandah
laundry
kitchen
family
bed 4
living
bath
sitting
bed 3

BEFORE

pergola
sunroom
family
dining
kitchen
bath
laundry
sitting
bed 3

AFTER

LEFT: Before renovation, the rear portion of this old bungalow was a good example of space that hadn't been used to the best advantage. For example, the kitchen was in the middle of the back section, leaving only small rooms on each side of it. The utility room was makeshift and had the best garden view of any room in the house. The bathroom's position was fine, but the room needed refurbishing. The family room was too small. The fourth bedroom was tiny and, therefore, dispensable.

BELOW: This spacious, airy bedroom makes use of waste space under the eaves for wardrobes. A bed can also be placed under a sloping ceiling where there isn't quite enough height to stand up straight, thus making use of all available space.

close to the workplace for many who, otherwise, would face long commuting journeys. Moreover, they are generally affordable for first-time buyers wishing to renovate. Victorian terraces and semi-detached houses vary in size from tiny, one-bedroom workers' cottages to three- and four-storey mansions, but they were not designed for today's lifestyle or to take advantage of the outdoors. A well-planned renovation that sometimes is only a reconfiguration of the existing space can make them attractive and functional for modern living. Some local authorities may stipulate that the facade must be retained, but an open-plan, smooth-flowing living space can easily be achieved behind that facade. In a large, two-storey house, it is often the downstairs liv-ing area that requires the most thought, as the bedroom layout will usually be retained upstairs. A work-er's cottage or a bungalow presents more of a challenge, especially if the plot is small and you cannot extend the building's area.

Suburban and rural

The advantage of living in the outer suburbs is that building plots are often larger, so renovating can involve extending the house on one or two levels. You may want to add a garage or workshop that adjoins the house so that you can come and go under cover. In rural areas, space may also be less restricted, but finding builders and suppliers of materials and fittings can be more difficult.

What you hope to achieve

Once you are familiar with all aspects of your house, you can more easily define what you hope to achieve. List your priorities in order. Think first about what you want, then consider how to achieve it. How much disruption will the renovations cause to your normal routine? In what order should the work be done? If you are planning major renovations, it may be less disruptive to arrange the work to be done in stages, although generally most builders will prefer to complete the job in one go.

ABOVE: Efficient heating and storage are essential.

BELOW: Paint is an inexpensive way to make a change.

Your ideal house

Your list of priorities should be closely related to your lifestyle. Do you want large indoor entertaining areas? How many people live in the house? Do you want to create one large living room out of two smaller rooms? Add an extra bedroom or bathroom? This is a good point at which to summarise the key features of your ideal home. It's not always possible to be specific at this stage, but you should have some general goals, such as the need for a spare bedroom, en suite bathroom or separate utility or workroom. This way, your list will develop from your 'ideals' to 'how to go about achieving them'.

ABOVE: If you need more space but don't want to encroach on your garden, you could consider an attic conversion as shown here.

RIGHT: Interior French doors prevent this green from being too sombre.

Special considerations

Although every household has its own special needs to consider when renovating a house, common aspects include the amount of space available and the number of people to accommodate and their lifestyle. By solving storage, light and room-sizing problems, you will automatically make your house more attractive.

Limited space

Space may not be a problem if you have a large house in a suburban or rural area, but inner-city residents often find a bit of lateral thinking is necessary to make the most of the available space.

Too few rooms?

If there are no longer enough rooms to go around, now that everyone requires a room of their own and you need a study as well as a second casual sitting room, there are several possible solutions. Re-allocating the existing space may be the most obvious. This may mean merely altering the functions of some rooms, requiring mainly cosmetic changes to be made, such as painting and installing or demolishing built-in furniture. You may consider converting a small utility room or scullery at the back of the house into a study and stacking the washing machine and clothes dryer

ABOVE: This library in a loft would serve equally well as a home office or parents' retreat. The wide window sill provides additional seating and the neutral colour scheme makes it an inviting space for work or reading and relaxation.

RIGHT: You may be lucky enough to find you have sufficient space under your existing roof without having to change the roofline. This is the cheapest form of attic conversion and, with a few minor structural changes to allow for windows, you can have your own secluded space such as in this charming retreat.

in a niche in the kitchen, behind louvred doors. Alternatively, if you have a large downstairs bathroom, you may be able to find space in it for these machines.

Living space too cramped?

Many older houses, and even some modern ones, have a series of small rooms that were designed neither to take advantage of the light nor to suit today's lifestyle. A small, formal sitting room at the front of the house can be opened up to an adjacent room to create a feeling of spaciousness by knocking out the wall between them. Space must be allowed to flow around the walls or partitions. If these do not reach completely to the ceiling, the latter's line will be maintained, providing an illusion of more space beyond. Some ordinary doorways can be expanded into larger openings for a flow-through effect. Opening up rooms in this way, with a timber beam or similar suitable lintel across the opening,

may be all that is needed to create an alcove off a sitting room. Such an alcove can be used to create a study

RIGHT AND BELOW: Storage can be located where you previously thought not possible: in the middle of a wall of glass or right where the bedhead is positioned, for example. In fact, the more difficult the problem, the more eye-catching the solution. Around the bed, your shelving will result in a central recess; in an expanse of windows it is an effective interruption that becomes a room's focus.

area, especially if a separate dining room or a formal sitting room is under-utilised. Space reflected in mirrors does give the illusion of a greater area. This is not a new idea and may seem obvious, but in fact it does have the effect of 'doubling' the room.

Not enough storage?

Are you making the best use of the cupboards you have? One solution is to rationalise your main storage areas so that you can leave other parts of the house uncluttered. This applies to books as well as clothes or kitchenware. Alternatively, storage can be grouped. For example, placing the television, sound system, CDs and all of your books together on one wall, or in one corner, will look better than if the various items are scattered around the room. Streamline things to achieve storage order. Where possible, always use an entire wall, lining up the different elements with continuous shelves or benches to create order. Exploit every opportunity.

Spaces that can't be used for anything else can be used for storage.

Privacy

In country and suburban areas, privacy is not usually an issue, but in high-density city areas where the houses are either very close together or joined in a terrace, privacy is an important aspect to consider when planning any renovation. If, say, you intend adding a ground-floor extension adjacent to your neighbour's patio, you will want to ensure that they cannot see directly into your rooms. While you won't want to be overlooked by neighbours, you also won't want to be overheard (or to hear them), so good wall insulation is essential to reduce noise as well as to minimise heat loss during the winter. Take some time to calculate the likely degree of exposure. Sometimes you can have uncurtained floor-to-ceiling windows in the most unexpected places, simply by arranging for them look into private outdoor spaces. Check the sight lines and decide whether you need a

screen at the window or at the boundary of your property.

Too plain?

An ordinary house with no special architectural features can be enhanced by knocking out a small window and replacing it with a larger one. Installing a shallow bay window will give a square room an extra dimension, while a window seat beneath it can be used for additional storage space. A small window over the kitchen sink can be replaced with an oriel-style window with a large sill that creates extra worktop space or an ideal position for potted herbs. By adding a glazed canopy, the traditional window over the kitchen sink can become a wonderful mini-conservatory, while an increase in ceiling height will make a room seem less oppressive. An existing window can be enhanced with a pelmet incorporating lighting at the top, shelving between the reveals and a shallow sill-height cupboard. Shutters added to a window will remove the plain look and diffuse incoming light.

The entrance to the house can also be transformed with a new floor finish, such as tiles, so that it appears separate from the house and makes a pleasing impact. It can be further separated from the interior by adding a pair of internal French doors. In older houses, the architraves are often in need of repair and, with the enormous range of mouldings available, a completely fresh look can be achieved by changing them together with cornices and skirting boards.

Not enough light?

Dark rooms that require the lights to be on during the day can have a gloomy feel. The addition of windows on the southerly aspect will make an excellent summer room that will also be comfortable in the winter sun. Glass bricks are another ideal solution, because even where privacy is a concern, the room can still be flooded with natural light. Skylights, especially above a room with a long easterly aspect and a narrow northerly one, are also a good idea. In such situations, by the time the sun reaches its summer midday intensity, the room will be in semi-shade.

ABOVE AND RIGHT: A work centre enables a usually untidy activity to fit harmoniously into any room in the house. And that is what making your home work for you is all about. Sewing, paper work or even children's hobbies can be hidden behind closed bi-folding doors. Effectively you get an extra room without losing the space.

Renovation ideas

Whether you are opening up a room with French doors, creating additional storage, putting in a staircase to the attic, or rearranging the functions and layout of your house, the possibilities are endless. The key is to make the most of the improvement opportunities your house offers; this may not mean that you need unlimited funds – an unlimited imagination is more helpful.

ABOVE: The path at the side of a house is an often under-used resource. Even if it runs along a panel fence, it still provides an opportunity for a continuous line-up of French doors. These allow the cook to be included in any garden activities.

Have you thought of this?

If you feel your home is too small or it no longer meets your family's needs, the time has come for you to consider renovating by adding to or simply updating what you have. After all, who needs the trauma of a major house move and everything associated with it? Our interesting ideas may inspire you to action on the home front. Once you've survived the renovation work, you will have a special place that you'll never want to leave.

Opening up

If you need more space without an extension, knocking down walls to create larger rooms could be the answer. The number of rooms you need depends on the make-up of your household. For families with teenagers, the emphasis will be on privacy – everybody needs their own space. But what happens when the children leave home or if the house was designed for a larger family than yours? Home owners often complain that their house

ABOVE: Knocking out a wall will make one well-proportioned living room.

RIGHT: A larger window brings more light to the new room.

LEFT: The living area flows into the kitchen/dining space.

BELOW: Before the transformation.

ABOVE: Even in a tiny
bathroom it is possible
to have a separate toilet.

LEFT: A small, well-designed
and well-ventilated bathroom.

BELOW: Before: the drawing room
of this Victorian terrace had been
restored but because it was small,
it was seldom used. The small
room on the other side of the wall
was in a similar situation.

RIGHT: After: by opening up
the dividing wall and trimming
the arch with plaster mouldings
in keeping with the Victorian
character, the entertainment
potential of these two small
rooms has been fully realised.

LEFT: Classical columns used in a large room make a grand division between dining and living areas. These are made of fibreglass and are purely decorative. The overhead steel beam, concealed in the plaster bulkhead, spans the full 3.75 m.

BELOW: French doors are a quick and effective way to give any room an extra dimension. As well as creating light, they provide easy access to the outdoors.

isn't spacious enough, but at the same time, they often have one or more rooms that are hardly used. The solution seems obvious – if you want larger spaces, you need fewer rooms. When a house needs more usable space, 'opening up' or knocking down walls between rooms and installing archways is one of the most common methods. Walls, however, don't just separate rooms; they may also support the floors and the roof above. Therefore, knocking out a wall is a job for a professional, particularly if it is made of masonry and requires the installation of a beam, or lintel, to support the structure above.

But before anybody starts knocking down walls, make sure you've thought about the new room you're creating. Will the shape of this enlarged room suit your needs? Will removing the wall deprive you of privacy or make placing furniture difficult? How will the new room affect the heating and lighting? While a professional builder

will handle the structural detail, it will be up to you to ensure that the alteration maintains the character of the house. You must make sure that the archway is trimmed to match the other doorways. Architrave profiles will vary according to the period in which your house was built, so they must be matched. For extremely contemporary interiors, plain square-set corners are the most suitable.

Look up!

Many older houses have large attics, and you will not need to seek official permission from your local authority if you want to use this area for storage only. Installing a drop-down ladder above the entry hatch will provide ease of access without the problems generated by putting in a staircase. If you want to convert the area to living space – for example, for a bedroom or a study – then the usual planning consent and compliance with the Building

Regulations will be necessary. In addition, if the building is listed, there may be further restrictions on what can be done and the way in which the work is carried out.

If you are thinking of adding an attic room, using a series of metal railings to 'close off' the staircase will maximise the feeling of spaciousness by letting light and visual space flow. The same principle applies to the ceiling in the new room – leave the pitched roofline plastered and the rafters exposed. The connecting hardware will become functional and decorative features. Windows high on the wall above the staircase will not only throw light upstairs, but also filter it down to the floor below. Plan ahead to make the most of all your building options.

ABOVE: A generous opening (3.5 m) allows the dining room to spill out into the hallway when necessary.

LEFT: Where an extension is added, the old and new spaces usually have to be opened up into one another. This three-sided kitchen bench sits right on the boundary between the two. Because the new opening is so generous, however, the two spaces merge.

Making a plan

Having organised your priorities, the next step, and probably the hardest, is to develop your plan. It is very important to take your time and make sure you are completely satisfied with it.

Measure the area to be renovated and make some rough sketches. These will give an idea of the work entailed and whether planning consent will be required. In general, planning consent is necessary for work that affects the exterior of the property, although not in all cases, so a visit to your local authority's planning department is essential. They will be able to tell you whether consent is required. Many councils have strict by-laws concerning tree removal, so it is worth checking these as well if you want to extend your house and a tree is in the way. You will also have to

approach the authority's building control department, who will tell you if the work needs to comply with the Building Regulations. In most cases it will, even if planning consent is not required.

Once you have ascertained what is allowable and decided exactly what you want, you can have a plan drawn up to submit for approval. When making your plans, consider your future as well as your present requirements. If you are middle-aged, how many years do you intend living in the house? Traipsing up and down stairs may not be so easy as you become less agile. With

ABOVE: The dining area is defined by its distinctive floor tiles.

a large plot, a granny annex or separate accommodation for teenagers is an option that can add value to the home. If you add a granny annex, it must be easily accessible for the occupant. However, a point to remember with teenagers is that they will leave home. Then you may find that you have spare bedrooms that are hardly used and could be turned into a study, workroom or TV room.

A new angle on design

Keep the 45° option in mind when you're making any changes to your home – not every corner has to be a right angle. Whether you are changing walls, doorways, or kitchen or bathroom layouts, consider incorpo-rating 45° angles into the design. Use this technique to solve some of your planning problems.

Family room + kitchen + garden = highly desirable neighbours

The best houses have the kitchen adjacent to both the outdoor living area and the family room. There's a very good reason for that. When you arrange for these three functions to keep company with one another, you immediately create a home nerve centre, which becomes the focus of family life. When planning renovations or additions, consider how you can best achieve this harmonious household triangle.

BELOW: Opening up the interior allows you to reallocate space. Without actually building on, this house was made more generous by the removal of walls, leaving a network of posts and beams. A disproportionately large utility area was then incorporated into the new open plan. The kitchen and informal sitting room are of similar size.

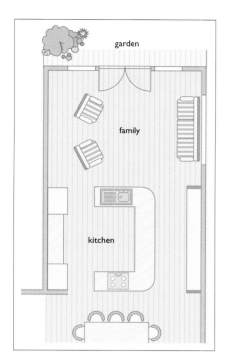

ABOVE AND RIGHT: Relocating the kitchen and family room in a new first floor addition allowed both view and aspect to be taken in. The outdoor living space takes the form of deck platforms, which connect to the garden via external stairs. The result is a light and airy high-activity kitchen/family area.

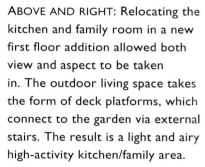

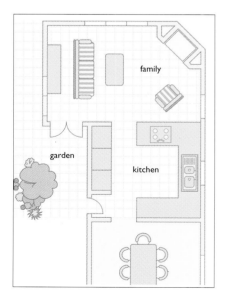

ABOVE AND LEFT: Adding on a family room made the existing kitchen internal rather than overlooking the garden. So instead of looking like a tacked-on afterthought, it was thrust into the heart of the home, surrounded by the existing structure (with its formal dining room), the new room and the garden.

ABOVE: Knocking out a wall may be all that's necessary to make a space workable. This kitchen was already in place but it was behind closed doors. By replacing a wall with a steel joist, the food preparation area was drawn out into the new, open space. It still remains in its own separate alcove but with a new island that cadges just a bit of space from the adjoining room.

ABOVE LEFT: Tightening up the plan a little may set up a chain reaction. This kitchen used to spill out to where the table is now. The breakfast table used to be where the sunny sitting corner has been positioned. Cane chairs are a compact family room solution and the table can always be moved away from the wall when it has to perform its full function.

LEFT: Here a galley kitchen is practical and doesn't encroach on living and dining space.

Turning the plan into reality

Now is the time to decide how you want the renovations or additions to be undertaken. You can do the work yourself or hire a builder to do the job for you. Whichever approach you decide on, there will be much preparation to do before work begins.

Surviving renovations

Renovating a house means mess, disruption to routine and sometimes, when major structural changes are involved, it may be necessary to move out for the duration. The prospect of finding temporary accommodation for family and pets can be daunting, but usually it means that the work will be carried out more efficiently and quickly if the builder has unrestricted access to the premises. If you are not well prepared,

turning your house into your dream home can be a nightmare.

Once you have decided exactly what you want, have had a plan drawn up and obtained any necessary planning consent from the local authority, you should obtain several quotes for carrying out the work. The draughtsperson or architect you use should supply you with enough copies of the plan so that you can distribute them simultaneously to several builders to quote from. It is very important to establish as accurate

an idea of the costs as possible to avoid blowing the budget.

The disruption that results from renovating will be easier to cope with if you remove as much clutter as possible from the house. Ensure that the working area is cleared to make the job easier and safer. If the rest of the house is also clutter-free, it will be much easier to cope with the mess of the actual building work.

Vacate the area being worked on. For example, if the kitchen is under construction, consider employing a microwave oven and a camping stove and frying pan in the utility room or dining room. Simplify your lifestyle during this period to prevent any undue stress. Now is not the time for entertaining guests. Keep your children's routine as simple and

uninterrupted as possible. Don't be surprised if they react badly to the changes and inconveniences of renovation work.

Doing the work yourself

Complete the most difficult or time-consuming aspects first, so that the remaining portion will not be as overwhelming if you begin to run out of 'steam'. Find ways to reduce interruptions. If necessary, engage a baby-sitter to look after the children away from the house, and take the phone off the hook.

If you lack motivation, write a list of all the benefits of having the job completed (for example, room for the children to play, storage space for hobbies, etc). Pin the list up on a wall in the work area. Keep reminding yourself that the

BELOW: Keeping the result uppermost in your mind will help you survive renovations. Painting and adding the finishing touches yourself can be particularly satisfying after the builder's mess has been cleaned up. Yellow is an uplifting colour, and in this room it works well on the walls with the stencilled border adding an interesting detail.

LEFT: This period house has been completely transformed with the addition of a conservatory at the back.

BELOW: This weatherboard cottage is typical of older unrenovated houses with utility rooms such as the bathroom and laundry overlooking an uninspiring backyard.

reason for the renovation work is to make life easier and more enjoyable. Try to keep the mental image of the end result uppermost in your mind.

If a project seems overwhelming, write a list of all the jobs that have to be done in smaller, more manageable portions, in the correct order. Cross them off as you complete them.

Set yourself some long- and short-term goals, along with realistic completion dates, and try hard to stick to them. Discuss with friends or family your plans for renovation so that meeting their expectations will serve as an additional incentive.

Don't allow yourself to be discouraged from starting when you only have a short time to spend on the task. Doing a little at a time is better than nothing at all.

Complete one task before starting another. Having several incomplete assignments will be too disheartening. Promise yourself a treat or reward when you have finished the job.

Employing someone to do the job

Before employing someone to do the work, make sure you know exactly what you want done. Having a vague idea of what you want the builder to do is not good enough. Unless you are in need of suggestions or advice, you should have all the details of the work to be accomplished and the materials to be used ready to give to the prospective builder so that you can obtain a fixed price. Changing your mind halfway through can be costly. If you do change your mind, obtain a new written quote from the builder before authorising him to proceed. When it comes to finding a contractor, personal recommendations are best and can come from other tradespeople, local estate agents, friends and acquaintances, local timber and hardware suppliers, or your draughtsperson or architect.

Always obtain three written quotes. Look for a professionally presented quote containing lots of detail. All quotes need to relate to the same brands and quality of materials. Make sure all aspects of the job have been covered and there are no vague areas that may cause a dispute later.

While it is desirable to stay within your budget, it is usually impossible to budget down to the last penny. Major renovation work that comes in under budget is rare.

Only give the go-ahead after:

- the types and quality of materials have been agreed;
- a fixed price has been agreed;
- a time span has been agreed, including a penalty clause for delayed completion;
- both parties understand what is to be done with old materials and appliances;
- the clean-up procedures have been agreed upon. Unless written into the specification, you could be left with a large amount of builder's rubbish to dispose of;
- agreeing that the final ten per cent of the cost will be paid 30 days after completion, to allow time for building inspector's approval;
- don't sign a contract or agreement that can be filled in later. Don't be pressured into signing a deal that only applies for that day. Give yourself plenty of time to read the contract, and make sure you read and understand the fine print! If you don't understand the jargon, ask for advice or an explanation.

Projects that go over by 20 per cent are very common, despite the best intentions of all concerned.

Use only reputable building contractors. You may wish to consult your solicitor on matters regarding the contractor's legal obligations concerning personal liability, worker's compensation and property damage. He or she may suggest looking at the contractor's insurance certificates.

If you are working directly with a builder and not through an architect, give the builder a sketched plan as reference. Also include detailed notes clearly outlining your requirements for surface materials for floors, walls and ceilings, bathroom and kitchen fixtures and appliances, as well as dimensions. You should also stipulate whether or not you wish to be consulted at every stage of the building process; if you don't con-

sider this necessary, you should still meet with the builder on a regular basis to discuss progress and any problems. Things do change as major works proceed and sometimes it is not possible to have something originally agreed to, so communication and flexibility are the keys to a successful builder-client relationship. Try to develop a friendly atmosphere, as this will make the entire experience that more pleasant, but take care that it is not misunderstood and taken as an invitation to take liberties.

Don't accept verbal promises — every detail should be clearly spelt out in writing. Don't accept materials or fittings inferior to those you have requested. The builder should check availability of all these things at the time of quoting. As the renovation progresses, keep a close check on every detail. If you are not happy with something,

RIGHT: The wall's painted finish adds to this classic look.

LEFT: Warm colour and polished floorboards often improve an older room.

speak to the contractor immediately. Any delays can make mistakes more difficult to rectify.

Finding a good tradesperson

Ask anyone about his or her last attempt to employ a tradesperson and you'll probably receive an earful. But it needn't be like that. Shop around. The best advice is: obtain a recommendation! Ask friends for the names of tradespeople they are happy with. Ask for references and inspect previous work.

If no one can give you a good recommendation, choose contractors who belong to recognised federations or associations.

Solving disputes

Discuss any complaints with your architect, tradesperson or contractor first. But when a dispute can't be resolved easily, there are several more formal procedures to pursue, including:

- arbitration, through either statutory or trade bodies. Be careful of agreements that restrict you to industry arbiters;
- small-claims court. This provides inexpensive, accessible justice. However, there is a claim limit, which may be insufficient to meet the needs of a major job;
- court. This is expensive, time consuming and exhausting. It is the last resort, but unfortunately sometimes it is the only resort.

Tips

- Obtain recommendations and testimonials, and check references. Ask trade associations for advice and the names of local members.
- Ask if it is possible to inspect previous work and consult previous employers. Satisfy yourself that the contractor has adequate insurance cover. Ask to see his insurance certificates.
- Obtain itemised quotes from at least three different contractors, and compare and contrast them.
- Once you've given the go-ahead, keep an eye on the work. Make sure the final bill is fully itemised, too. And check it!

The Framework

Walls, ceilings, floors and stairs are the framework of your house, and you should ensure that this framework is solid before you even begin renovating. Whether you are creating additional space by knocking out walls, erecting new walls, installing a staircase or merely making cosmetic changes, such as repainting walls and sanding floors, the framework will be affected to some extent.

It is important, especially in older houses, to check for any rising damp, which can affect floors and walls. This is often identified in pre-sale building surveys and usually can be treated quite easily. If you want to paint areas that have been affected by damp, preparation is especially important: use a fungicide wash before applying the paint, or an anti-mould paint, or both.

Erecting new walls and ceilings in older houses provides the opportunity to install effective insulation. In all terraced and semi-detached houses, insulation serves not only to retain heat in winter, but also to minimise noise.

There are many different types of staircase available in easy-to-assemble kit form. The one you decide on will be dictated by the amount of space you have available. In some cases, a drop-down attic ladder is a good space-saving option. These ladders are also available ready-made.

Knocking out walls, replacing floorboards, erecting ceilings and installing staircases are all major structural changes that usually require expert help. However, with a little know-how, you will be amazed at how much you can achieve yourself.

The ceiling is an important part of the framework but it is not often a decorative feature in itself. Here, however, the open beams in the ceiling enhance the feeling of space and light in the house, and complement the traditional wooden floorboards and furniture.

Walls

A new finish can make a big difference to an old wall. But before you begin any improvements involving walls, you should be aware of the potential problems and pitfalls.

Interior walls

Unless you take on a major refurbishment project, you may never have occasion to break into an interior wall. Often, though, you need to know what's inside – and where – before you can perform even simple tasks, such as hanging a heavy picture.

Interior walls may be built from masonry (bricks or concrete blocks) or they may be wood-framed. All wood-framed (stud partition) walls have a bottom plate nailed to the floor, which supports vertical studs. These, in turn, are nailed to a top plate. Generally, this framework will be built from lengths of 100 x 50 mm timber.

Around any opening, the studs may be doubled up for extra rigidity, being topped off with a horizontal head. Some walls also include horizontal noggings, usually 1.2 m above the floor. Finally, the framework may be faced with plasterboard or lath and plaster.

How to identify a loadbearing wall

Interior walls fall into two categories: loadbearing, which help support the entire house; and non-loadbearing, which support only themselves. If you remove or make a big opening in a loadbearing wall, you could literally bring down the house!

ABOVE: A section of the wall has been knocked out so that this small work area is partially open to the hallway beyond it and easily accessible to the rest of the kitchen.

RIGHT: Anatomy of a plasterboard partition.

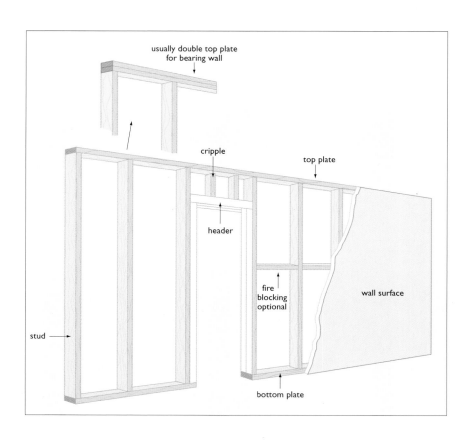

usually double top plate for bearing wall

cripple

top plate

header

fire blocking optional

wall surface

stud

bottom plate

The wall guide

	Brick	Ceramic tile	Decorative paint	Fabric
Rooms	All. Seal in wet areas.	Ideal in wet areas. Can use with other finishes.	All.	Most. Avoid wet areas.
Durability	Excellent.	Excellent if properly installed.	Shows less wear and marks because of pattern.	Fair. Depends on fabric.
DIY	Easy to seal or paint, more complex to bag, lime or plaster.	Requires skill. Walls must be dry, smooth and stable.	More time consuming than difficult.	Quite easy: staple to wall-mounted battens or hang.
Cleaning	Easy to clean: simply dust or wash.	Easy. Damp sponge and commercial cleaners.	As for paintwork.	Hard. Dust and vacuum. Test before using liquids.
Comments	Natural, clear seal, paint, plaster, bagged or lime-wash finish.	Loads of patterns, colours, sizes and styles. Machine or handmade.	Stencilling, ragging, marbling, combing, murals and more.	Many decorative fabrics. A good cover for bad walls.

	Paint	Textured plaster	Timber	Wallpaper
Rooms	All.	All.	All.	All. Water/steam proof in wet areas.
Durability	Quality acrylics: 8–10 years. Oil-based: 6 years.	Good.	Very durable, easy to maintain.	Heavyweight vinyls are harder wearing.
DIY	Painting is easy. Preparation is the hard part.	Skill required for hard plaster. Textured panels easier to install.	Can be attached to battens or used as primary facing.	Not too hard. Follow instructions carefully. Heavier papers are normally easier to handle.
Cleaning	Depends on type. Wash and wear easy, some others hard to clean without marking.	Dust, damp sponge.	Depends on the type of finish, usually easy. Natural timber can be polished.	Easy-to-clean vinyls, thin matt papers more difficult. Try using a gum eraser.
Comments	Gloss, flat/matt, low sheen, semi-gloss.	Paint or mix in coloured oxides to hard plaster. Panel finishes vary.	Warm, natural look. Can be limed, stained or painted.	Vast range of colours and styles. Helps hide bad walls.

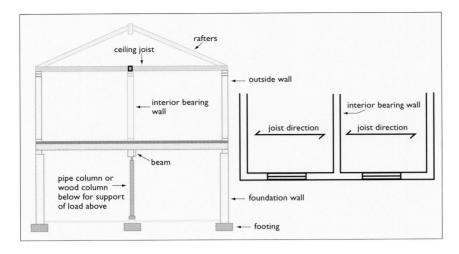

BELOW: Light through the skylight combined with a warm wall colour and polished floorboards are practical in a heavy-traffic area such as this hallway.

LEFT: How to identify a bearing wall.

To determine whether a wall is loadbearing or not, you'll have to do some sleuthing under the floor of the room above or in the attic, to check which way the joists run. If they are parallel to the wall in question, you can be sure it's non-loadbearing. If, however, they're at right-angles to the wall, you can be fairly sure it is bearing a load.

How to find studs

Almost anything you attach to a stud partition will be more secure if you can fasten it to one or more of the studs. How, though, can you locate the studs in the wall without ripping open the plasterboard or plaster?

No one technique works for every situation, but all are based on the same principle – that most of the studs in a wall will be spaced at regular intervals. This means that after you've found one or two, generally you can plot the others with a few measurements.

When looking for studs, begin your search towards the wall's centre, not at the ends, where the spacing might be irregular. Also, ignore the studs on each side of a door or window opening.

There are four common ways of finding that first stud:

1 You can rap along the wall with your knuckles; a solid sound indicates you've found one.

2 If rapping doesn't work, look along the skirting board for signs of nails. They're usually driven in at stud intervals.

3 You can use a special magnetic device that homes in on nails or screws holding the wall surface to the studs.

4 Switch off the electricity at the mains and remove the face plate from a power point. Invariably, these are screwed to studs.

Studs are spaced at 350, 400 or 600 mm centres, so check these distances till you find a second stud.

BELOW: A wall with windows on an upper storey brings in the light and the view.

Solving wall problems

Dealing with damp

Your home may be your castle, but, if it's afflicted with damp, it may feel more like a dank, dripping dungeon. Wet patches on walls and floors are unsightly, unsafe and can peel thousands from the value of the property. Moisture, which could be coming from the ground, through the walls or even from inside the house, is the culprit; you'll have to discover the source before you can tackle the problem.

Rising damp

As the name suggests, rising damp is ground water that is sucked up through the foundations and into the walls of the house. It should be stopped at ground level by the building's damp-proof course (dpc), a waterproof layer, usually of bituminous felt or plastic (or, in old buildings, slate, or sometimes two layers of dense engineering bricks). However, if this is cracked or defective, then the water will get through, leaving brownish 'high tide' marks and whitish deposits on the face of the wall. In the main, these stains occur about a metre above ground level; if they are any higher, they probably are not due to rising damp, but to problems with the roof or flashing around windows or doors. If left unchecked, rising damp will result in bubbling paintwork, mouldering wallpaper and rotten

plasterwork. It's a particularly common problem in older buildings, which typically have poor ventilation and/or inadequate drainage. Some may not even have a dpc at all.

There are several treatments for rising damp, including electro-osmosis, plugging the wall with porous tubes and 'cosmetic' treatments such as applying sealants or render.

However, there are really only two effective remedies: increasing evaporation by improving ventilation and drainage, or replacing the damp-proof course. The latter can be done by inserting a new impervious layer or by injecting a silicone-based liquid to create a chemical barrier against damp. For the best results, both should be done by professionals, although you can hire equipment for the latter.

Penetrating damp

Most noticeable after rain, this type of damp is caused by water pene-trating through the wall. It can result in white powdery deposits on the wall or clearly defined stains that may appear at any level. Penetrating damp can be a particular problem in old homes with solid (single-skin) walls, but even cavity brick walls aren't immune, as problems can arise if a 'bridge' – mortar, broken brick or other debris – allows moisture to cross the gap between the two skins.

Check and repair damage, such as defective brickwork or cracked rendering, visible on the external surface. Look for other sources of moisture, too, such as windowsills with blocked or damaged drip channels, and broken gutters or downpipes. Allow the wall to dry thoroughly, then seal the exterior with a silicone water-repellent treatment. If the wall is porous and regularly exposed to bad weather, consider cladding it with weatherboarding, tiles or rendering.

Clearing cavity 'bridges' is a difficult job and you may be better off seeking professional help. If, however, you're a diehard do-it-yourselfer, you may want to tackle it yourself. You'll have to chop out the joints of two or three bricks closest to the obstruction, lift them out, chip out the offending debris – taking care not to let it fall down inside the cavity – then replace the bricks.

Condensation

Condensation is caused by moisture from within the house. It can leave 'sweaty' patches on walls and steam up windows.

To treat it, you must stop the steam! Always open a window or turn on extractor fans when you're creating water vapour, whether in the kitchen or bathroom. Make sure that your shower is properly enclosed, and run cold water before adding hot when filling the bath (this reduces steam and it's safer, too). Keep bathroom and kitchen doors closed, and cover cooking

---

Stopping damp where it starts

Roof. Inspect regularly – broken tiles may be allowing water through, particularly if damp appears in rooms on the top floor. Check for faulty chimney stacks, and leaking valleys and flashing.

Gutters. Blocked gutters overflow and contribute to damp problems, so clean them out a couple of times a year. Mend cracked gutters by cleaning the inside well with a wire brush, then sealing by covering the crack and its surrounds with waterproof tape. Repair leaking joints by removing the old seal, cleaning with white spirit and fitting a new rubber seal or waterproof tape, applied in overlapping layers.

Downpipes. These can be blocked by birds' nests, leaves and so on, and will back up, causing gutters to overflow. Inspect regularly and clear blockages with a long batten or broom handle. This is relatively easy on single-storey properties; longer, multi-storey downpipes will probably need professional attention. If downpipes are repeatedly blocked (by leaves dropping from an adjacent tree, for example), try fitting a wire cage over the top of the pipe.

Foundations. Clear away any dirt and debris that bridges the damp-proof course.

Air vents. These should also be kept clear of vegetation, dirt and debris to allow sufficient air flow.

Redecorating. Once you've found and fixed the fault, allow walls to dry out, then seal the exterior with a silicone water repellent treatment. Remove any peeling or damaged wallpaper and paint, then seal internal walls before re-papering or painting them.

pots with lids. Use a tumble dryer as little as possible, and avoid gas cylinder and paraffin heaters; slow, steady heaters tend to generate less moisture than those that produce a sudden burst of warm air.

Wet rot

Wet rot results from fungal spores infesting wood that is regularly exposed to moisture. Typically, it strikes ground and basement floors, and unpainted or poorly maintained window and door frames. The affected wood normally feels soft and spongy when wet, crumbly when dry. Tell-tale visual indicators include dark, thin strands of fungus, cracks running along the grain of the wood and flaking paintwork.

Locate the source of the moisture first, take the necessary steps to repair it and allow the surrounds to dry out. Then replace the affected wood completely.

ABOVE: This kitchen has large opening windows that allow steam and cooking odours to escape easily and prevent any build-up of damp. Good ventilation, light and damp-proofing are especially important in wet areas.

Repairs

Knocking out a wall

A little-used small room becomes a household asset when it flows into a bigger space.

If your internal walls are masonry, the actual removal of the wall should be entrusted to a professional builder. Even for a lightweight timber partition, you may feel happier seeking professional assistance.

A steel-reinforced concrete lintel was used to bridge the opening created in the step-by-step sequence shown here. It is the same thickness as one course of bricks. Steel lintels are also available and more suitable for wide openings. In a stud partition, timber would be used.

Consider the advantages of having a wall knocked out and have a go at doing the trimming yourself. You'll be surprised at the immediate improvement it will make.

1 In this old house where the floor joists were actually resting on the ground, subsidence on one side of the wall meant that the two floor levels had to be evened up after the wall was removed. Chock up joist bearers and floorboards to the same level and fill the space left by the wall with boards or sheet flooring material.

2 Use a steel float and sand and cement to render over the new lintel. Hold a piece of timber against the edge to achieve a sharp corner as you proceed.

3 Similarly, fill any gaps in the render at the bottom of the wall that may have resulted with changing floor levels. Remove loose material first.

4 Clean up your archway as much as possible before you begin fitting it out. Remove any rough chunks of masonry and check that the opening is as near to square as can be.

5 Use 19-mm-thick timber to line the arch. Glue and nail the two top joints using three 75-mm-long nails at each corner. Allow the top horizontal to run the full width of the opening to brace the inverted U-shape. Step the verticals in 10 mm increments and use scrap timber to chock behind them, making sure they are perfectly vertical using a spirit level.

6 Drill pairs of 6 mm holes through the verticals at four points down their length. Drill through the timber and well into the masonry. These holes are to take 6 mm dowels, not nails.

7 Hammer 90 mm lengths of 6 mm dowel into the holes and then drive 90 mm nails into the dowels. The timber will expand when the nails are inserted, giving an extra-solid fixing to the lining of the archway.

8 Position the architraves. Choose a moulding that matches the others in your house. Mitre the top horizontal with inside dimensions to match those of the wall opening's span. Pin the architrave in place using 45-mm-long lost-head nails. Do not drive the nails in all the way at first.

5

6

7

8

9

10

9 Now fit the side vertical architraves, checking that the corner joint is as good as possible before you punch the nails below the timber surface using a nail punch. Don't forget, however, that you can always fill the joints before painting.

10 Nail down through the mitres to secure the corner joints entirely. Fill all the nail holes and sand the job before sealing both the timber and the new cement render prior to applying your top coats. You will need a few coats of paint to blend in the new wall render.

RIGHT: The end result, plenty of space and light.

ABOVE: Living and dining flow easily into one another.

LEFT: A soft colour with a moulded coving for interest.

Making openings in plasterboard

Measure carefully and transfer dimensions to the plasterboard's face. For a power point or switch, trace around the mounting box.

Then bore holes at two diagonally-opposed corners, insert the blade of a keyhole saw through each hole in turn and cut along the outlines to remove the section of plasterboard. Protect your floor, as plasterboard dust is difficult to clean up.

Fitting plasterboard around your pipes

Rather than going to the trouble of disconnecting a plumbing fixture, plasterboard to the middle of the studs flanking the pipes.

Next, cut a piece to fit the opening, measure and mark the locations of the pipes, bore holes for them and cut the piece in half through the holes.

Finally, make sure that you check the fit and nail the two pieces to the studs. Cement small pieces in place with joint compound.

Laminating plasterboard

To improve a wall's sound and fire resistance, glue one layer of 12.5 mm or 9.5 mm plasterboard to another, or use this technique to bond a new surface to an existing wall. For either job, you'll need wallboard adhesive and joint compound, plus some 40 mm flat-head nails to tack the top layer until the adhesive sets.

First, find all wall studs and mark their locations on the floor and ceiling. Apply cement to the wall surface according to the manufacturer's instructions, or use dabs of joint compound spaced 200 mm apart.

Fit the panel and then, with a hammer and scrap of timber, go over its surface, firmly tapping to embed it in the adhesive or compound.

Partially drive a few nails through the top layer into each stud to hold panels in place temporarily. Then, after the adhesive has completely set, pull them out. Alternatively, countersink nails and cover the heads with compound when you tape the joints.

Plan to stagger the panel joints so one never falls on top of another. At external corners, laminate layers. At internal corners, nail only the overlapping board of the first layer.

Taping plasterboard

The trickiest part of any plaster-boarding project comes when you finish off the joints and nail heads. For this multi-step process, you'll

BELOW: A dramatic effect is created here by distressed treatment of the wall colours.

need about 15 litres of pre-mixed joint compound and 75 m of paper 'tape' for each 45 sq m of surface. Invest, too, in a pair of 100 mm and 250 mm broad filling knives.

Allow yourself plenty of time to apply the first coat and make sure that the tape goes up smoothly. Starting with the 100 mm knife, apply a full, uniform band of compound to the trough formed by the tapered edges of two adjacent panels. Immediately unroll the tape, using the knife to embed it in the compound. Soak the tape with compound, smoothing out wrinkles. Fill other imperfections at this time, too. Pack in a dab of compound, then level it with the surface.

Allow 24 hours for the 'bedding' coat to dry, apply compound again, feather the edges to form a band 150 mm wide.

When dry, smooth the second coat by lightly sanding or wiping with a damp sponge.

Finally, apply a skim coat with the 250 mm knife or a trowel, spreading the edges to about 300 mm wide. Sand or sponge if needed.

Taping corners

External and internal corners call for slightly different taping techniques. Reinforce the former with strips of lightweight, perforated metal corner bead. Install this by nailing through the plasterboard to the framing at 130 mm intervals.

Apply two or three coats of compound as explained above. Feather it out in a band about 100 mm wide on each face of the wall.

Use joint tape for internal corners, cut it to length first, then crease it vertically down the middle before applying. Spread compound on each wall face, and embed the tape as before, making sure the crease is tight in the corner.

Apply subsequent coats of joint compound with an internal-corner tool, which will spread it on both walls at once. Alternatively, use a filling knife on one wall, let the compound dry, then do the other.

Mending cracks and bubbled tape

You can repair minor cracks simply by filling the voids with compound. But if the joint tape curls up from the plasterboard surface, use a scraper to remove all loose tape. Be careful not to remove any sound tape.

Cut a piece of joint tape to fit. Apply a bed of joint compound to the wall, press the tape in place and apply another coat of compound. Let dry, then add another layer of compound, followed by another if necessary. Feather each coat into the surrounding surface to help conceal the seam.

Patching small holes

Filling nail-sized holes is the easiest plasterboard repair you can make. Use a putty knife to fill the hole with a propriety cellulose filler, allowing it to 'mound' above the surface. When the filler dries, lightly sand away the excess.

Patching medium-sized holes

To mend a medium-sized hole, you must provide a backing to which joint compound can adhere. Fashion this backing from a scrap of perforated hardboard cut slightly larger than the hole, but small enough that it can be manoeuvred through the wall. To hold the scrap firmly against the back side of the wall, run a length of thin wire through a couple of the perforations. Using joint compound, butter around the edge of the backing with a spatula.

Insert the hardboard backing into the hole and centre it behind the opening, using the wire to pull it against the back side of the plasterboard. When dry, the joint compound will help the backing cling to the back of the plasterboard. To hold the backing in place while the compound hardens, bridge the opening with a pencil and twist the ends of the wire around it until the wire is taut. When the compound has dried, snip the wire and remove it.

ABOVE: Panelling to dado height is a classic look.

RIGHT: Rag-rolled walls soften the blue and white colour scheme.

BELOW: A twisted cord attached to the timber border at dado height is an attractive definition between the two wall surfaces.

Now it's simply a matter of filling the recess with joint compound. Because the compound shrinks as it dries, you'll have to apply several coats to achieve a satisfactory result. Let each coat dry before adding the next. Once you've filled in the void completely and can't see any hairline cracks in the compound, sand the patch lightly, using a sanding block to keep the repair flat, and re-texture its surface in order to match its surroundings.

If you don't have any perforated hardboard around the house, try this alternative, which makes use of a scrap of 6 mm or 12 mm plywood. Cut the plywood backing as you would the hardboard. Drill two holes in the centre of the piece to run the wire through. Now follow through with the remaining steps as they are described above.

Patching large holes

After squaring off the area to be repaired so that its edges align with the centres of two studs, cut and remove the damaged plasterboard. Use a keyhole saw to make the horizontal cuts between the studs, and a sharp craft knife guided by a straightedge for the vertical cuts along the stud centres.

Cut out a plasterboard patch to the same size as the hole. Then cut two lengths of 50 x 50 mm timber to serve as backing supports for the top and bottom edges of the patch. Skew-nail these battens in place between the studs, making sure that they're flush with the edges of the studs. (You can make this task easier by first drilling angled starter holes for the nails in the horizontal battens.) Now fit the plasterboard patch into the opening and secure it with 40 mm plasterboard nails, spaced at least 10 mm in from the edges. 'Dimple' each nail head so that it is just below the surface of the plasterboard.

Spread a bedding layer of joint compound around the perimeter of the patch with a 100 mm filling knife held at a 45° angle to the wall. Avoid creating too much of a mound. Immediately centre a length of plasterboard tape over each seam, using your hands to press it into place. Then, with the filling knife, press the tape firmly into the compound, holding one end of the tape secure with your other hand. Follow this with one or more coats of compound, feathering each coat into the surrounding surface and letting it dry thoroughly before applying the next. When the last coat has dried, finish and re-texture the patch.

Finishing and re-texturing the surface

With enough care and patience, you can finish your plasterboard repairs so they'll be all but invisible.

Begin by smoothing the surface of the repair with either 80 or 100 grit sandpaper or a damp sponge. If you use sandpaper and the repair requires a lot of sanding, wear a dust mask to avoid inhaling too much dust. Also be careful not to sand all the way through the compound and into the tape. After sanding the area, wipe the dust off the surface with a cloth.

Most plasterboard surfaces are not glassy smooth. Instead, they have a texture designed to conceal seams, nails and minor defects. You can closely duplicate most textures, each in a different way. (It is a good idea to practise on a piece of scrap plasterboard before attempting to re-texture the actual patch.)

You can approximate an 'orange peel' texture by watering down some pre-mixed joint compound and dabbing it over your repair with a sponge.

If you want to blend a patch into a sand-textured surface, apply some texture paint with a paint roller. To match an existing texture, add a layer of plasterboard compound. Then, using a stiff-bristled brush, replicate the existing pattern. If you're dealing with a travertine finish, apply a layer of compound and let it set up slightly. Then, flick more compound on to the surface, using a paintbrush, and knock off the high spots by lightly trowelling the surface.

Artex-type finishes on ceilings are hard to match. Although you can rent texturing equipment, your best solution may be to call in professional help to identify the type of finish you have and to duplicate it.

Repairing cracks and holes in plaster

Professional plasterers are scarce these days, but, fortunately, with a little practice, you can handle most common plaster repairs yourself.

Choose pre-mixed cellulose filler for small repairs, such as hairline cracks and nail holes. For larger repairs, mix powdered patching plaster with water – it's stronger than cellulose filler and less prone to shrinkage.

Make plaster patching a regular part of your preparatory work whenever you repaint. And be sure to correct any moisture leaks that might be responsible for problems.

1 To prepare hairline cracks for patching, widen them to about 3 mm with a screwdriver, undercutting the edges, then blow out any dust and debris.

A hammer and and cold chisel make short work of removing loose plaster from holes. To ensure a successful repair, work outwards in all directions until you reach sound plaster. Also, knock the plaster from between the laths and undercut the edges, as shown, to help produce a stronger repair.

2 If moisture has rotted the laths behind the loose plaster, cut the plaster back to at least the centres of the studs adjacent to the damaged area. Remove the laths (if using a circular saw, adjust the blade to the proper depth) and

nail up new wood or metal mesh-type laths.

3 To prevent the water in the plaster patching material from being drawn into surrounding surfaces and thereby weakening the patch, moisten the area shortly before making repairs. You can do this with either a spray bottle or a damp sponge.

4 Fill in the hairline cracks by forcing filler into them with a putty knife. Let the filler dry, then apply another layer, if necessary, to bring the repair flush with the surrounding surface.

When dealing with larger repairs, mix a batch of patching plaster according to the manufacturer's instructions. Starting at the edges and using a 150-mm-wide filling knife, work the plaster into the undercuts, then fill in the centre. (Make sure you apply enough pressure to the patching material so that

some of it is forced into the spaces between the laths. This is known as keying, or tying, the plaster to its backing.)

Because patching plaster shrinks as it dries, be prepared to apply two or more coats of material. Let each coat dry completely before applying the next. To achieve the best possible bond between different coats, wet the surface of each preceding coat before laying on more plaster.

5 After the top coat of plaster has had sufficient drying time (at least 24 hours), it will be ready for sanding. Using a medium-grade sandpaper (80 or 100 grit) wrapped around a sanding block, sand the surface with light circular strokes. Direct a portable work light on to the repaired area to help show up slight surface irregularities that you might otherwise overlook.

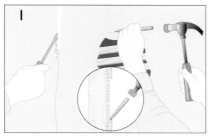

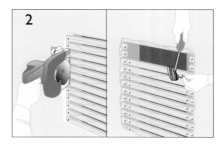

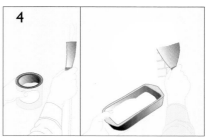

LEFT: Wallpaper is easy to apply and can transform a room.

6 Never try to paint a plaster repair without priming it first. If you do, the surface of the new plaster will absorb paint more readily than the surrounding surface and your patch will continue to show through. Before you begin priming, however, make sure your new plaster has had sufficient time to cure and set up. To be safe, leave the surface for another 24 hours after you have finished sanding.

Installing battens

How flat are your walls? To find out, select a long and straight 100 x 50 mm piece of timber and hold the edge against the surface you want to cover. Move it around, trying out horizontal, vertical and diagonal positions. If you can see hollows under the length of timber, or if it rocks at points, you will need to even up the wall with battens before applying panelling or plasterboard.

Also plan to batten out any bare masonry wall before adding plasterboard. In a basement, you may prefer to build a 100 x 50 mm stud framework instead. This makes more space for pipes, insulation and electrical outlets. Make sure, too, that your basement walls have been properly sealed (tanked) against moisture.

For battening, choose inexpensive 50 x 25 mm or 75 x 25 mm softwood. You'll also need frame fixings (combination screws and wallplugs) and some scraps of plywood or hardboard for shimming (or packing out) the battens.

When putting up battens, install them with 400mm, 450 mm or 600 mm centre-to-centre spacing, depending on the panel width you intend using (normally 900 mm or 1200 mm). Mark the wall with their spacing and transfer the position of the highest point of the wall to the floor and ceiling using a long straightedge and spirit level. Measure out from these points the thickness of the battens and mark a continuous line through these points along the floor and ceiling. This indicates the plane with which the face of the battening will be aligned.

BELOW RIGHT: Cutting an archway into the wall allowed these two rooms to become one large area for entertaining. The glass doors can be closed for everyday living and warmth.

BELOW: Open-plan living is common in many new and renovated houses. Ease of access between kitchen, dining and living areas is practical, and can be achieved simply by knocking out part of a wall.

Fix a continuous horizontal batten along the wall, 25 mm from the floor, drilling through it into the wall and attaching it with frame fixings at a spacing of 600 mm. Where necessary, pack out the batten with plywood or hardboard until it aligns with the floor mark.

Next attach a horizontal batten along the top of the wall, 25 mm down from the ceiling and in line with the ceiling mark. Check also that its face is plumb with the batten along the base of the wall.

Now add the vertical battens between the ceiling and floor battens, making sure they are truly vertical and their faces are flush with the horizontal battens. It is very important that you get this right, as the finished surface can only be as flat and straight as the supporting framework.

Framing a partition

'Roughing in' the studs for a new wall calls for a different style of carpentry than you may be used to. With framing, appearances don't count for much. What does matter is that you keep everything plumb, square and structurally sound.

Start by working out how you are going to tie the new partition into your home's structure. How do the ceiling joists run in relation to your proposed wall? In a basement with an exposed ceiling, that's easy to determine.

If the new wall will cross the joists, simply pinpoint exactly where you want the wall and nail the top plate to the joists at that point. If, however, you want it to run parallel to the joists, you may have to shift the wall's location a few centimetres so you can nail directly to a joist, or install an intermediate joist.

Next, check out the walls you'll be attaching to. Fasten to masonry with expansion bolts. With a hollow wall, you may be lucky enough to find a stud behind it. If not, secure the new wall's end studs with toggle bolts.

After you have decided exactly where everything will be, mark chalk lines for the top and bottom plates. If you're not proficient with a plumb bob, tape your spirit level to a straight 100 x 50 mm length of timber and use it to transfer the position of the bottom plate to the ceiling, or top plate to the floor.

Two different framing techniques are described below. Pre-assembly makes sense for short walls on relatively level floors. Build the entire partition frame flat on the floor, making it 40 mm shorter than the ceiling height, then lift it into place on top of a second bottom plate.

Skew-nailing the studs to the top and bottom plates is the most effective way of assembling the framework in situ, but it takes practice before you can nail the studs without them moving from the vertical.

Pre-assembly

Lay out your new wall with chalk lines, as explained above, then level a 100 x 50 mm piece of timber with plywood or hardboard shims and nail or screw it to the floor.

Measure the height of the ceiling at several points. Tailor your partition to the shortest dimension.

Cut the top and bottom plates, lay them side by side, and mark off stud spacings. Begin 25 mm from one end and mark them at 400 mm or 600 mm centres.

Cut the studs, allowing for the thickness of the plates. Assemble the framework by nailing through the plates into the ends of the studs.

If your new wall will include a doorway, add the trimmers. Cut the bottom plate from the opening after positioning the wall.

You'll probably need help to lift the framework into place. Once it's up, plumb it carefully, then nail the top and bottom plates.

Skew-nailing studs

Installing the top and bottom plates first, then cutting the studs one by one assures a tight-fitting wall without the need for shimming.

You may well encounter problems, though. The first comes when you attach the top plate – a four-handed job that requires you to hold a heavy length of timber against the ceiling, then nail up through it to the joists.

Make this job easier by starting the nails first, then asking a helper to force the plate against the ceiling with another length of timber while you nail.

Expect frustration the first time you try to skew-nail at an angle through a stud into the plates. With each hammer blow, the stud will move a little. To minimise this, cut each stud about 3 mm longer than necessary and tap it into place for a force fit. Next, cut a length of timber to the exact distance between each pair of studs, lay it on the plate and against the adjoining wall or previous stud, then nail so that the block braces the new stud.

With a helper, secure the top and bottom plates and the partition's end studs. Then skew-nail the wall's intermediate studs into place. To skew-nail, drive a nail at a 45° angle through the stud into the plate.

Now drive a second nail from the other side. With practice, if the stud moves, you'll be able to knock it back into its original position.

Until you get the hang of skew nailing, however, use the spacer to brace temporarily each stud against the previous one.

Adding finishes to walls

Choosing and buying ceramic tiles

Made of clay fired in high-temperature kilns, ceramic tiles are relatively brittle. But once you've cemented them to a solid backing and filled the joints with special mortar (grout), you have an exceptionally sturdy wall.

When shopping, you'll discover an enormous range of tile colours, shapes, sizes and textures. Speciality items, especially vivid

ABOVE: A wall in the corner of this room cleverly combines unobtrusive storage for decorative items with the sound system and the television set.

colours, can cost two or three times as much as standard tiles. You should note, too, that wall tiles are thinner and slicker than floor tiles.

For a smooth installation, you'll need two different types of tile. Field tiles (100 mm and 150 mm squares are typical sizes) cover most of the surface; trim tiles round off edges and get around corners. Don't get carried away with a low square-metre price for field tiles until you've checked out what the trim tiles will cost. Sold by the linear metre, these can add quite a bit to the final bill.

Smaller mosaic tiles come in 300 x 300 mm panels bonded to paper or fabric mesh. They go up a little faster, but need more grouting.

Many experts still prefer to set ceramic tiles in cement-based mortar – a tricky process. Fortunately, however, you can choose from a number of pre-mixed adhesives specially developed for amateurs.

Estimating tile needs

To calculate the number of ceramic tiles you'll need for an entire bathroom or other complex installation, draw each wall to scale on graph paper, so that each square is equivalent to a tile. Then count the squares and add about 5 per cent for waste. Or simply calculate the square meterage of the surfaces to be tiled and let your dealer do the arithmetic. You may find that he will give credit on returned tiles.

In a shower, plan to take the tiles to the ceiling. Other bathroom walls usually are tiled to 1200 mm above the floor; kitchen walls to the bottom of wall cabinets.

Estimate trim tiles, such as bullnoses, caps and coves by the linear metre, but order mitred corners, angles and other special items by the piece.

For adhesive, you can choose between all-purpose and waterproof. The former is water-resistant and can be used in kitchens and bathrooms; the latter should be

chosen where tiles will receive regular and substantial soaking, such as shower cubicles.

Wall tiling with a 3 mm bed of adhesive requires 2 kg of adhesive per square metre.

Grout comes in 500 g, 1.5 kg and 5 kg quantities. Usually, 500 g of grout will cover 1 sq m of 150 x 150 x 5 mm tiles with a 3 mm joint, or 300 x 300 x 6 mm tiles with a 5 mm joint. Between 1.5 and 2 kg of grout covers 1 sq m of 150 x 150 mm thicker tiles with a 6 mm joint.

Tools for tile work

Some of the specialised tiling equipment shown below is available from tool hire shops. But since a good job can take a surprising amount of time, plan first to set all the tiles that don't have to be cut, then hire the cutter and nippers you'll need for trimming the edges.

A tile cutter makes quick, accurate, straight cuts. Ask your supplier for a demonstration and expect to ruin a few tiles before you get the hang of it. You can also trim with a glass cutter, but this is slower. Nippers nibble out curved cuts.

Serrated edges on the notched trowel spread adhesive to the right thickness; a smaller notched spreader gets into tight spots.

Tips

- If you have to tile around an existing pipe, cut the tile in two and clip away a semi-circle from each piece using a tile nipper. Leave enough space for the pipe to expand and contract.
- After wiping away excess grout and polishing the tiles, smooth the grouting between the tiles with a length of thin dowel or proprietary tool.
- Remember grout dries quickly, and when hardened it is almost impossible to remove. Never leave anything but a smear on the tiles' surface. Wiping across the tiles diagonally prevents you from dragging the grout out of the joints. Wipe again to even the grout surface.

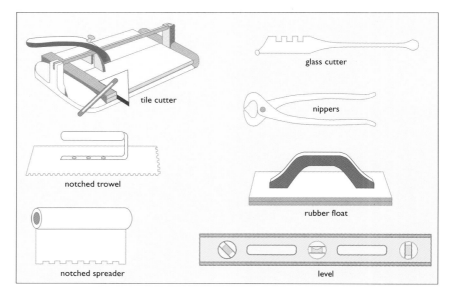

tile cutter

glass cutter

nippers

notched trowel

rubber float

notched spreader

level

BELOW: Large, square tiles finishing at picture rail height are unusual in a kitchen but the result is effective as well as practical.

A rubber float facilitates grouting, but you can also get good results with an ordinary window cleaner's squeegee.

Preparing the walls for tiling

You can apply ceramic tiles to any rendered, fibre cement and some plaster surfaces that are smooth, sound and firm. With existing walls, strip off flexible coverings such as wallpaper and scrape away loose paint. Knock the sheen off glossy finishes with a light sanding.

Don't bother taping and smoothing joints in new plasterboard. Seal it first, though, with a thin coat of adhesive, taking good care to pack any openings where pipes come through.

It is important to pay particular attention to the point where the tiles will meet the top of a bath or a shower tray. Chip away any old material here and leave a 6 mm space.

Now you're ready to begin laying out the job. An installation that starts in the centre of a wall and proceeds towards the ends is best, as it gives you equally-sized cut tiles at each end. If you start at one end of a wall, you may find that you are left with an impossibly narrow gap to tile at the other.

Improvise a layout tool by marking off tile widths, including a 1.5 mm grouting allowance, along a length of timber batten.

Use a plumb line or tape a spirit level to a straight batten and mark a vertical line at the wall's midpoint. Now use your layout tool to mark off tile positions on the wall, working towards each end from the vertical line. If you find that you will be left with very thin cut tiles at each end, shift the tile positions by half a tile's width, then using your layout tool mark off the tile positions again.

Finally, find the wall's lowest point. Mark a horizontal line, one tile's width above it. Begin setting full tiles above this line.

How to tile bathroom walls

Thinking ahead

Before you start, turn off the water supply at the mains and unscrew all taps and shower rose. This will make the job a lot easier.

When you begin tiling, decide on the most obvious point (such as the top of the bath or the basin) that must line up with a tile course. Count the number of tiles downwards to establish a tile position close to the floor. Lay this bottom full course of tiles first — against a timber batten nailed to the wall. Return to the lower course of cut tiles, adjacent to the floor, last (when the ahesive has dried and you can remove the batten without having all the tiles slide down the wall).

Tiling

After you have marked the tile line above the floor and nailed on the batten, spread adhesive with a notched trowel or spreader right up to the drawn line. Work on no more than 1 sq m at a time, otherwise the adhesive may begin to go off before you have positioned all the tiles. Press each tile firmly into place. Insert ready-made tile spacers as you go to ensure even joints.

When the adhesive is dry, remove the spacers, mix the grout and, using diagonal strokes, fill the joints with a squeegee. Remove excess with a damp sponge.

Trimming and cutting

Mark the area of a tile to be cut and gradually nibble out the shape with tile nippers, working inwards. For more awkward cuts use an abrasive coated tilesaw. This is an invaluable tool especially when cutting tiles to fit around taps or pipework.

To cut tiles to width, mark the size, allowing a couple of millimetres grace. Then score along the mark and cut with a tile cutter. Check and adjust the size before fixing.

Timber panelling

Timber panelling has been used as a wall finish for hundreds of years. It's easy to put up and hard to knock around.

1 Remove window and door trims, skirting boards and any fittings. Tap hollow walls to locate studs and mark centres with a pencil. For vertical panelling, apply 42 x 19 mm battens horizontally spaced at around 600 mm centres. Nail the battens to studs or screw them to masonry.

2 Cut the boards 10 mm shorter than wall height: when nailing in place leave 5 mm at top and bottom for expansion. Start with the groove edge to the corner. Check for plumb. Pre-drill all nail holes. Sink the nails with a nail punch and fill the holes. Nail remaining boards through the tongue edge.

3 As you install the boards, tap tongue-and-groove boards together lightly with a hammer, using a piece of scrap planking over the tongue as a tapping surface to protect the wood. Leave a few millimetres of space between planks for expansion. If the boards aren't long enough, join ends together over battens, staggering the joins. Mitre the external room corners or butt them together and cover with trim. Butt all internal room corners and trim the width of the last board to fit.

4 Drill and saw openings in the boards for electrical outlets, light switches and other fittings as the boards go up. You will need an electrician to re-wire power points.

1

2

3

4

5

6

5 After panelling, extend window and door jambs flush with the surface of the panelling with a timber strip of a thickness to match the width of the battens plus panel width. Pre-drill nail holes and use nails that will extend at least 20 mm into the original jamb. The drill bit should be slightly smaller than the nail shank.

6 Apply your finish coats before you replace the trims and cover the holes. Nail the window and door trims in place with the finish nails, making sure the gaps between the jamb extension and panelling are covered up. Replace the original skirting and add a moulding around the ceiling.

ABOVE: Timber panels in this room have been painted to maintain the original character of the old house.

RIGHT: Timber panelled walls in rich natural tones can be overpowering, unless you use a light coloured timber or lime (whiten) the boards.

Ceilings

Combine the framing of a floor with the covering materials used for walls, and you get the anatomy of a typical domestic ceiling.

It begins with the same joists that support the floor above. Next, the builder may level off the joists' bottom edges with battens or, if the timber is even to begin with, plasterboard or plaster lath may be fastened directly to the joists. Finally, the ceiling is finished with plaster, or joint tape and compound.

You'll find several obvious exceptions to this form of construction, though. Sloping top-floor ceilings, for example, usually are attached to the roof framing and, in properly built homes, have insulation above them. You also may encounter lightweight tiles suspended below the joists of an old ceiling. Open-beam ceilings consist of nothing more than the underside of the roof decking above.

Ceiling insulation

Insulation in ceilings places a thick 'blanket' over each room. The cost for an average home is not high and is an investment that could achieve a 30 per cent saving in heating bills.

If you're handy, agile and sure that the wiring in the roof is safe, and the roof is of high enough pitch, you could insulate the ceilings yourself.

Loft insulation is commonly sold as rolls of glassfibre or mineral-fibre blanket material, although loose-fill and rigid sheet insulation is also available. The blanket type is the most convenient to use and is sold in a size to match the common spacing between joists. Measure the floor area of the loft to calculate the amount required.

With a trimming knife (for cutting the material to size), gloves and dust mask, begin packing the insulation lightly between the joists. Leave no spaces. Always keep your weight on the joists and not on the ceiling. A plank will make the job easier. For low-pitched roofs, loose-fill material can be sprayed into place.

Solving ceiling problems

Repairing large holes

Although plaster and plasterboard ceilings resemble walls in many ways, they're more difficult to patch. First of all, you have to tackle the repair from an uncomfortable position. Second, the patch must cling to the ceiling more securely than is necessary with a wall. That's why you may as well forget about trying to re-plaster a broken-out section yourself. Hire a professional, or add a plasterboard patch.

If you choose plasterboard, use ring-shank nails or self-tapping plasterboard screws (these hold better than nails, are easier to drive into ceilings). Protect yourself against dust and debris with goggles, a hard hat and a dust mask.

For a smooth repair, measure the exact thickness of your ceiling, then either buy plasterboard of the same size or purchase thinner material and shim it.

ABOVE: Besides serving the practical purpose of letting in light, skylights can be decorative. Here, a line of fixed skylights in a sloping roof accentuates the upstairs corridor. Fixed skylights are set into a panel of roofing material so that they can be sealed from the weather before they are installed.

BELOW: Anatomy of a ceiling.

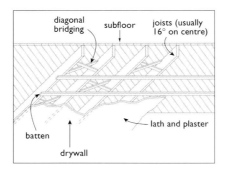

diagonal bridging   subfloor   joists (usually 16° on centre)

batten   drywall   lath and plaster

Plaster ceilings

Small holes and cracks can be filled with cellulose filler, but when the hole is larger, patching is easier. The patching technique works well for repairs when the lath above is in fairly good condition. If the lath is as much of a problem as the ceiling plaster, you'll want to consider redoing the whole thing.

To begin, locate sound plaster around the damaged area, then carefully square off a section and chip it out with a hammer and cold chisel.

Cut a plasterboard patch to size. Butter the edges with joint compound and press into place. Drive nails or screws into the lath above.

Plasterboard ceilings

The technique described above will mend a plasterboard ceiling, too. But because the plasterboard's backing is as regular as its face, you'll obtain an even smoother repair with the technique illustrated here.

Begin by squaring off around the hole, then bore holes at the corners and cut out the section with a keyhole saw. Cut a piece of 8–12-mm-thick plywood that's about 50 mm longer and 50 mm narrower than the opening. Make sure the plywood will clear the joists on each side, then slip it into place, securing it and the plasterboard patch with screws as shown.

Tape a ceiling repair as you would any plasterboard joint. But when you apply the second and third coats of compound, feather them to a greater distance than you would on a wall. To check your progress, shine a strong light on the ceiling, stand back and note where you need to do more work. On ceilings, imperfections in taping don't become obvious until you paint.

Raising a sagging ceiling

Look at the diagram shown here and you'll see that a plaster ceiling is keyed into its lath support

Common ceiling problems		
Problem	Cause	Cure
Cracks	Settlement and vibrations. These conditions bedevel plaster ceilings especially, but also affect the joints of plasterboard.	Try packing them with filler or joint compound.
Popped nails	Improperly nailed plasterboard ceilings pulling away from the joists or battens.	Shore up the ceiling, then drive in plasterboard screws or ring-shank nails.
Peeling tape	Excessive humidity or improper installation.	In high-humidity areas, improve the ventilation, then re-tape.

system. Sometimes, humidity, vibration or age causes several of those keys to break, allowing the ceiling to drop. More rarely, the lath itself begins to pull away from the joists.

If big expanses are sagging, resign yourself to the arduous task of ripping them out and either adding plasterboard or replacing the entire ceiling.

For minor sagging, try anchoring the plaster with screws and washers. Make a T-shaped brace about 12 mm taller than your ceiling's height, then wedge it in place to raise the sag. Space the anchors about 10 mm apart, drilling pilot holes first and gouging out shallow depressions for the washers and screw heads. Where you encounter a joist, drive in several longer screws for extra support.

Replacing a damaged ceiling tile

Completely cut away the damage first so you can get a grip on the tile, then work in a knife and slice the edges free.

Trim a new tile, guiding your cuts with a metal straightedge. Lift the tile into position to check for a snug fit.

Clear away any old adhesive or staples from battens and the other tiles, then apply an even layer of fresh adhesive to them.

Fit one edge first, then press the tile firmly into position and hold it for a few minutes until the adhesive holds the tile in place.

BELOW: Patching a plasterboard ceiling.

BOTTOM: Raising a sagging ceiling.

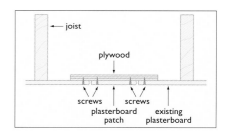

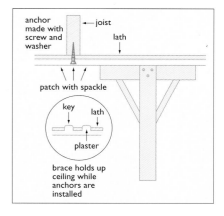

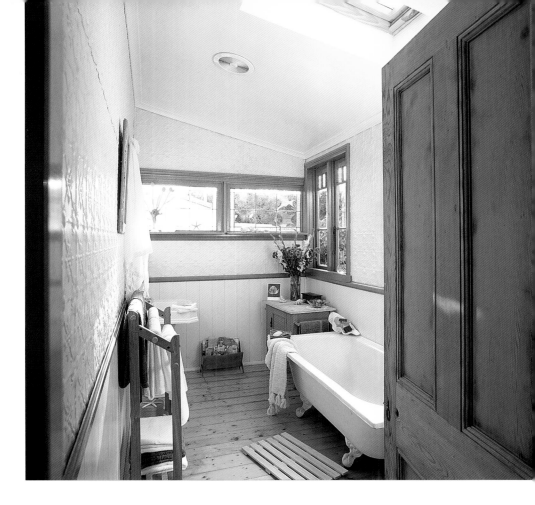

RIGHT: A new ceiling and skylight.

Putting up new ceiling materials

Replacing a ceiling

When a ceiling becomes unsightly, one option is to paint it. If this won't do the trick, you may have to replace it. However, it's not always necessary to pull down the old ceiling. If the plaster is generally sound, you may be able to leave it in place and simply add a new ceiling below it.

If you have enough headroom (minimum 2400 mm floor to ceiling in a bathroom is the general rule, but there are exceptions), you can simply put new battens on the existing ceiling and plasterboard over these. The battens must be screwed to the existing ceiling joists to ensure adequate support for the heavy plasterboard sheets.

To determine whether or not you need battens, stretch level, diagonal strings 12 mm below the old ceiling or joists. If the surface rises or falls by more than 6 mm, batten it with 50 x 25 mm softwood battens. Otherwise, you can nail the plasterboard directly to the existing joists.

If you're going to replace the ceiling in the bathroom, make sure you use plasterboard that incorporates a vapour barrier. Conventional plasterboard and water should never meet.

Plasterboard sheets come in varying sizes, so be sure to measure the dimensions of the ceiling and order so that cutting and waste are kept to a minimum. It's a good idea to give the plasterboard sheets a couple of coats of paint before nailing them to the ceiling. This will reduce the amount of awkward painting required after they are in place.

The hardest part of this project comes when you have to wrestle those big plasterboard panels into place. You'll need help to lift the sheets into position, as well as a couple of ladders and preferably trestles with long planks between them. Fit the battens at right-angles to the run of the joists. Then nail the plasterboard to them, making sure the nails are long enough to penetrate the battens by 25 mm. Keep going until the whole ceiling is covered.

To help when positioning the plasterboard sheets, try donning soft hats and supporting each sheet with your heads while fastening it to the joists or battens. If that proves cumbersome, rig up bracing as shown here. For bigger ceiling jobs, you can rent a jack designed for ceiling work.

If you need to cut the plasterboard, the best way is with a sharp knife. Mark out the section you want to cut and score the surface of one side only. The plasterboard will then snap along this line so you don't have to cut through the whole thickness. Nail on the sheets so that the tapered edges that form recesses for the joint compound face the floor.

Joints are filled in much the same way as those on walls. First, a band of joint compound is applied along the length of the joint. Then joint tape is pressed into the compound using the filling knife. Subsequent bands of filler are applied, each progressively wider than the previous band, the edges being feathered out to produce a smooth transition with the adjacent plasterboard surfaces in order to conceal the joints completely.

When the joint compound has dried, it will need a light sanding to smooth the surface in preparation for final painting.

Choosing and buying ceiling tiles

Compared with installing plasterboard, putting up ceiling tiles or panels is a breeze. Instead of handling awkward, 2400 x 1200 mm sheets, you work with lightweight materials and modular installation techniques tailor-made for do-it-yourselfers. And once your new ceiling is up, just wipe off any fingerprints and forget about it – there's no need to mess around with jointing compound or paint.

Before choosing from the dazzling array of materials available today, ask yourself a couple of questions. First, how's the headroom? If you have space to drop the new surface a minimum of 75 mm, and especially if you want to cover pipes, wiring and ducts, suspend panels from a grid system, as shown on page 58 (see under Installing a suspended ceiling).

If however, a dropped ceiling would cut the room's overall height to less than 2.4 m, you'll have to apply interlocking tiles to the old ceiling or to a network of battens. You can cement or staple tiles directly to a sound, even ceiling; with uneven surfaces or exposed joists, you must put up battens first.

Also ask yourself what you expect the tiles or panels to do. Some, but by no means all, have acoustic properties that help to reduce noise. But don't expect them completely to muffle sound transmission from one room to another.

Finally, calculate your ceiling's area by multiplying the length of the room by its width and use this

BELOW: Plasterboarding a ceiling.

1 To locate hidden joists, drill a hole, insert a bent wire and rotate. Double check the joist's location by tapping with a hammer.

2 Next, measure carefully to find the ceiling's exact centre, then nail strips across the joists, spaced 400 mm apart.

3 Start plasterboarding at the centre and work towards the edges. Use two braces to hold the panels while you drive nails or screws.

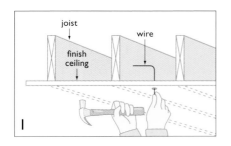

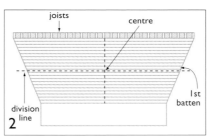

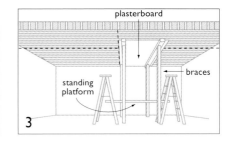

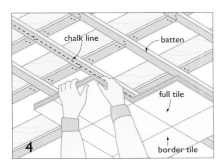

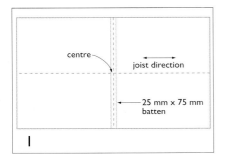

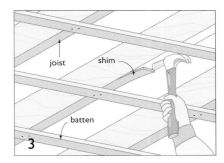

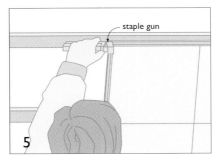

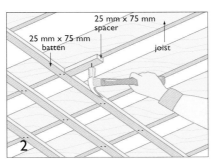

ABOVE: Attaching tiles to battens.

1 Locate the room's exact centre and put up the first batten there. Battens should always run perpendicular to the joists.

2 Space the subsequent strips with centres a tile's width apart, then nail up a spacer wherever two tiles will interlock.

3 Shims level minor irregularities. With a very bumpy ceiling, use the double battens technique shown below.

4 Begin in a corner, cutting the border tiles first. Chalk lines on the battens will help you align the first full tiles.

5 Drive two staples – one on top the other – into each exposed tile corner. The first staple flares the legs of the second.

to determine the number of tiles required. Add several extra tiles to allow for cutting and waste.

Before making a final decision about tiles, shop around and compare the various types available, their characteristics and relative cost.

Attaching tiles to an old ceiling

Make a scale drawing of the room, then lay a tracing-paper grid over it. Move this around until the partial border tiles are equal in width.

With a chalk line, transfer measurements from the grid to the ceiling. Mark starter lines and cut the border tiles to fit.

Begin tiling in a corner. Apply tile adhesive according to the manufacturer's directions or staple as illustrated above.

Attaching tiles to battens

Even up an irregular ceiling or exposed joists with wood battens (shimmed with plywood or hardboard as necessary), spaced to suit the size of your tiles. Some tile companies offer a metal grid system similar to a suspended ceiling, except that all supporting elements are hidden from view. This requires a minimum 50 mm drop from the existing ceiling line.

Concealing obstructions

Heating ducts, wiring, beams and pipes usually need hiding when you finish off a room. If the obstruction is small, you may be able to tuck it against the joists and add battens as shown below.

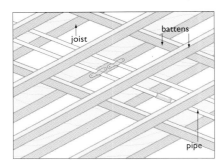

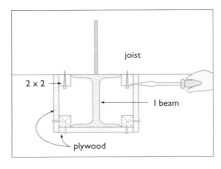

FAR LEFT: Double battens often lower a ceiling line just enough to get below electrical cables and plumbing.

LEFT: To cover a supporting beam, nail up 50 x 50 mm timbers along each side, then build a three-sided plywood box. Attach it as shown.

Chances are, though, you'll need to do some boxing in. If you do, bear in mind that ceilings do only light duty, so you should use lightweight materials – 50 x 25 mm, 75 x 25 mm and 50 x 50 mm for framing, and 12 mm or even 6 mm plywood or hardboard coverings.

Installing a suspended ceiling

Finishing an exposed-joist ceiling isn't the tedious, labour-intensive job it used to be. Today, you can crown any room with a suspended ceiling in a day or so. The secret lies in the components – lightweight steel or aluminium channels that you hang from wires and snap together, forming them into a grid, then flesh out by simply setting the ceiling panels into place within the frames.

Systems differ somewhat, but you'll need to check that:
- The wall angles extend around the room's edges at finished-ceiling height.
- The main tees run at right-angles to the ceiling joists and are suspended from wires. They can be cut to length or spliced together.
- The length of the cross tees will depend on the size of your ceiling panels and the direction in which you want them to run. Clip them to the main tees at each intersection.

The joys of a suspended ceiling installation are that you need to do almost no preparation work; and any ducting, wiring and pipework will be concealed with the minimum of fuss. Just mark the locations of any concealed joists and establish a height for your new ceiling.

BELOW LEFT: Installing a suspended ceiling.

1 Make careful measurements on a scaled layout to plot sizes for the border tiles and locations of lighting panels.

2 Next, determine the height necessary for clearance above the grid, then snap chalk lines along the walls at this level.

3 Attach the wall angles, aligning their bottom edges with the chalk line. If you're fastening to masonry, use screws.

4 To guide you in hanging the main tees, stretch strings across the room at several points. These must be perfectly level.

5 Starting a border tile's distance from the wall, drive screw eyes into every second joist at 1200 mm intervals. Hang and twist wire.

6 Loop the wire through the holes in the main tees, level them, then twist the wire tight. Make minor adjustments with the screw eyes.

7 Install the cross tees now. Cut them to length wherever this is necessary and rest their ends on the main tees.

8 Trim the border panels with a knife and straightedge, set them in place, then fill in the rest of the grid with uncut panels.

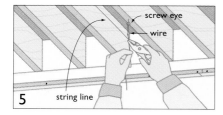

1   lighting panels

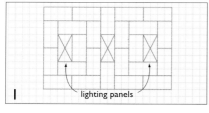

2   joists   chalk line

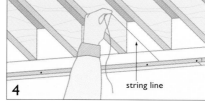

3   wall angle

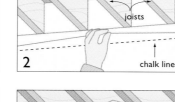

4   string line

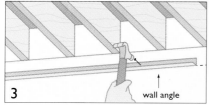

5   string line   screw eye   wire

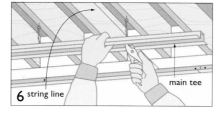

6   string line   main tee

7   cross tee

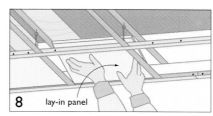

8   lay-in panel

Skylights

The building industry has found many ways of introducing light into our homes. These range from complete conservatory-style rooms of glass in a narrow framework, through custom-made, atrium-style roofing sections, to smaller-scale fixed or opening transparent panels fitted into an existing roof.

No matter how much light you want indoors, it is important to know how to go about it. The diagrams and photographs will give you a good idea of the skylight options available today. Some require relatively inexpensive and small-scale installation work; others involve large-scale, tailored fabrication and design work. Although planning permission may not be required, the work must comply with the building regulations, so consult your local council first.

ABOVE: The new room built on to the back of this house is set at garden level, and the old part of the house looks down on to it. Roofing the addition was a simple matter of adding a single pitch off the back of the house. The inclusion of several skylights has effectively turned the new roof into a grid running between the rectangles of light.

LEFT: Always think about ceiling geometry when you are considering skylights. Long narrow shapes going all the way down to the line of the eaves create the effect of slots of light internally. When all the surfaces are plaster set, the skylight looks even more pristine.

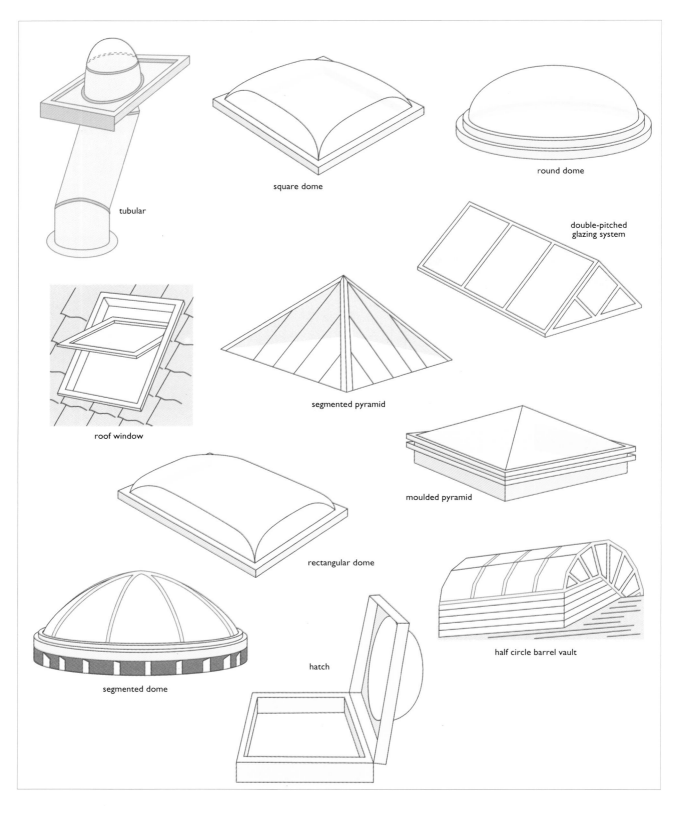

tubular

square dome

round dome

double-pitched
glazing system

roof window

segmented pyramid

moulded pyramid

rectangular dome

half circle barrel vault

segmented dome

hatch

ABOVE: There is a range of options in skylight design. Pictured here are the most commonly used skylights.

RIGHT: A skylight is an excellent way to let light, heat and air into any room.

Installing a skylight

A skylight is a fantastic way to let light and heat into dreary rooms. It is suitable for a roof with a pitch between 15° and 85°. The example shown here is a fixed unit, not to be confused with an opening roof-mounted window.

Putting in a skylight, especially if the shape of the ceiling follows the slope of the roof, is certainly not beyond the capability of the average do-it-yourselfer.

First, decide how large a skylight you require; two smaller windows might be better than a large one. Discuss your needs with several manufacturers or suppliers. When it's delivered, carefully read the installation instructions. Keep in

BELOW: Installing a skylight.

1 Mark the position of the skylight on the ceiling; make sure that one side of it fits alongside the ceiling joist. Drive a stout nail through its centre.
2 Remove the tiles and stack them close by. Cut the battens with a circular saw or a handsaw. Then cut the rafters until they are trimmed. Frame joints must be well nailed – use a minimum of four 75 mm nails in each.

1

2

3

4

5

6

7

8

mind that you're going to put a hole in your roof, which could let in the rain if there is a hold up because you don't know exactly how the unit should be fitted or there's a part missing. Have a small tarpaulin and some ropes to hand, in case.

Drive a thick nail into the ceiling where the skylight is to go. Wearing non-slip shoes, get up on the roof. Walk on the noses of the tiles, locate the area and remove the tiles. The skylight must not interfere with a ceiling hanger or a purlin.

Cut the tiling battens. Mark out the frame size that will hold the skylight, cut the rafters and put in trimmers in accordance with the manufacturer's instructions (see photo 2). Be sure to watch carefully for any wiring.

Cut away the plaster with an old saw. Take the skylight from its box; remove the flashings, trims, etc.

Stand the frame in the recommended position and fix it to the rafters and trimmers using the brackets provided (photo 6). It must be level across the roof at both ends (photo 7).

Fit the bottom flashing, bending it to follow the contours of the tiles.

Fit the side flashings, the top flashing (see photo 10) and so on. Refit the tiles around the skylight. You could use tile cutters or a carborundum wheel fixed in your circular saw for this. (If the latter is used, make sure you wear goggles and long protective clothing.) If you've followed the steps correctly, the room below won't become a swimming pool!

Cut and fix plasterboard so it forms a reveal for the skylight. Cut and fix the metal angles that strengthen the corners.

Plaster the corners. Sand, dry and paint them.

3 Before sawing the hole in the plasterboard, cut deeply into the sheet from underneath with a trimming knife. This will lessen the likelihood of the paper lining tearing.

4 In this instance, an electric cable is running right across the skylight opening. Don't make any attempt to move it yourself! This is definitely a job for an electrician.

5 If you've made the opening the correct size, the brackets of the sides of the skylight should stand on the framing members. Make sure the sarking fits the opening.

9

10

11

12

13

14

6 Read the manufacturer's instructions carefully, then position the skylight and, after double checking it's correct, temporarily fix it to one of the rafters or trimmers.

7 Use a spirit level to check whether or not the skylight is level. If it is not, pack it up on the low side and then, using screws or nails, fasten it securely in place.

8 The flashings are important; they are there to stop leaks developing between the skylight and the roof covering. They must be installed carefully and without damage.

9 When you are fitting the flashings to the roof tiles, a softwood block can be used for beating the metal gently. Do this until it fits the contours of the tiles exactly.

10 When fitting the side and top flashings, proceed slowly. Double check each step. Imagine the volume of water that runs down the roof in a storm — you don't want a drop inside!

11 The final step outside is to replace the tiles. This will involve cutting. Once the job is done, be sure to clear away all the debris that could block the downpipes.

12 Measure the exposed area between the rebate in the skylight and the ceiling and cut the plasterboard to suit. Then nail the plasterboard in place, using plasterboard nails.

13 Metal angles, fixed over corners, strengthen the join and give a straight line to work to when you are plastering. Cut them with a hacksaw and nail them in place.

14 Using a trowel, apply the jointing cement in three separate layers, each one getting wider and wider. Make sure that you feather each of the joints away to nothing.

1

2

3

ABOVE: How to cut plasterboard.

1 Measure and mark the shapes required. Make sure the face side (unmarked) faces outwards. With a sharp utility knife, cut deeply along the line.

2 Turn the board over and, holding one edge in your hand, give the sheet a bang with your fist. This should cause the sheet to break, creating a 'V'.

3 Using the utility knife, cut along the 'V' on the back of the sheet. This will ensure that the paper does not get ripped. Alternatively, use an old saw to cut the sheet.

LEFT: Opening roof windows solve all the ventilation and sunlight problems associated with internal rooms. Particularly in the case of attic conversions like this one, where dormer windows are not an option, an opening skylight turns an old roof cavity into a useful space.

Floors

The choice of floor surface is usually determined by the function of the room. This section provides a practical guide to the types of flooring and how to maintain and repair them.

What's afoot?

When you are deciding on what to use on your floor, remember that this is one of the largest spaces in your room to decorate. It is the area you are least likely to change and, unless you are using paint, the floor covering is likely to be a sizeable investment. Consider how much traffic each room will receive and allocate your funds accordingly. Try to buy the best quality you can.

Choose carefully, because the type of flooring you select will have a great influence on the mood and style of your room.

ABOVE: Place a beautiful, bright rug over the top of wall-to-wall carpet to give a whole new look. The rug's colours and pattern can then be continued in a wonderful array of plump pillows and scatter cushions. This is specially suitable if the carpet is not to your liking or you are in rented premises.

RIGHT: Traditional polished floorboards are easy to maintain and add an air of elegance to the room.

ABOVE: Casual coir matting makes a delightfully natural background for big, comfortable canvas-covered chairs. You can lay it as wall-to-wall carpet or have it finished around the edges and use it as an area rug on timber or tiled floors. If a dressier look is what you're after, a similar design is now available in wool.

LEFT: Quarry tiles can look formal or casual, depending on the roughness or smoothness of their surface and whether they are machine or handmade. Hand-painted feature tiles in this dining alcove act as a decorative space definer.

ABOVE: The regular grid pattern of terracotta quarry tiles in this hallway repeats the clean architectural lines of the building and provides a background for richly patterned Persian rugs.

ABOVE RIGHT: Real marble tiles are beautiful but expensive. If they are beyond your budget, there are many excellent vinyl substitutes, which have the advantage of being softer and warmer underfoot. A classic design looks good even in a small space.

RIGHT: After sanding the floor, you could bleach it and stencil on a diamond pattern or other design with thinned paint. The grain of the timber will show through.

The file on flooring

The ground rules for flooring emphasise both appeal and practicality. The floor finish you choose will have a considerable impact on the rest of your decorating scheme. Appearances aren't everything, though, so it is important to bear in mind that the function of a room will determine the degree of durability you require and in some instances will limit your choice of floor covering. And, because subfloor (and, therefore, building considerations) play their part in the decision making, floors are not solely the domain of the decorator.

Vinyl squares

Subfloor. Any level surface.
DIY. Yes.
Decorative character. Plain, chequerboard or flecked.
Advantages. Cost efficient, serviceable and crisp looking.

Seagrass matting

Subfloor. Any floor surface.
DIY. Yes. Installation instructions included. No underlay necessary.
Decorative character. Casual.
Advantages. Cost efficient. Distinctive natural look. Serviceable.

Inlaid vinyl

Subfloor. Any perfectly level surface.
DIY. Not possible because it requires precision cutting. Executed by specialist layers only.
Decorative character. Dramatic and sharp.
Advantages. Allows the floor to make a graphic statement.

Slate

Subfloor. Timber or concrete with rubberised glue.
DIY. Laying yourself requires comprehensive technical advice.
Decorative character. Rocky, natural and organic in many colours and shapes.
Advantages. Absorbs solar heat. Warmth of feel and appearance. Can be resealed for maintenance.

Marble squares

Subfloor. Timber or concrete with rubberised glue.
DIY. Better to employ a tradesperson.
Decorative character. Cool, crisp, severe, elegant.
Advantages. Prestigious, opulent, classical and natural appearance. Light reflective. Available in a wide range of colours.

Ceramic tiles

Subfloor. Timber or concrete with rubberised glue.
DIY. Yes, but should seek expert advice.
Decorative character. Depending on selection – crisp and contemporary or Mediterranean and traditional.
Advantages. Fully glazed and, therefore, extremely serviceable – ideal for wet areas and where interior and exterior floor surfaces merge.

Cork

Subfloor. Perfectly level surface.
DIY. Possible but not recommended.
Decorative character. Rich, warm and textured.
Advantages. Shiny surface but still soft to walk on.

Terrazzo

Subfloor. Concrete slab for concrete terrazzo. New lightweight epoxy requires 6–10 mm of epoxy and can be laid on timber/particle-board floors.
DIY. Professional laying essential.
Decorative character. Hard, flecked surface that can vary in colour and texture depending on its composition.
Advantages. Ideal for indoors and outdoors. Easy to maintain. Distinctive, fashionable appearance.

Sheet vinyl

Subfloor. Concrete, timber or particle board.
DIY. Possible to lay yourself if subfloor is even.
Decorative character. Fresh. A wide range of finished effects depending on colour and texture.
Advantages. 4 m roll width allows seamless floors. Very easy to clean.

Carpet

Subfloor. Concrete, particle board or timber. Rubber underlay.

DIY. Not recommended.

Decorative character. Soft, plush and luxuriant.

Advantages. Warm in winter, absorbs sound, immediately gives a room a furnished feeling.

Paving bricks

Subfloor. Concrete slab.

DIY. Yes

Decorative character. Rustic.

Advantages. Retain heat. Easy maintenance, especially if you use silicon-dipped, pre-sealed variety. Novelty value for interior application. Good for interior/exterior continuity.

Terracotta tiles

Subfloor. Concrete, timber or particle board with rubberised glue.

DIY. Yes. Especially uneven styles that do not require precision.

Decorative character. Warm, earthy, Mediterranean.

Advantages. Either untreated or with wax surface sealer, terracotta has a soft, natural look and distinctive feel.

Particle board

Subfloor. Floor joists at 450 mm or 600 mm centres.

DIY. Simple to lay yourself.

Decorative character. Warm, textural. Similar to cork.

Advantages. Cost efficient. Can be polished and exposed or laid with a covering of your choice.

Rubber

Subfloor. Any surface that is without irregularities. Subfloor preparations can take the form of self-levelling compounds in the case of concrete slabs or masonite sheets for timber floors.

DIY. Possible to lay yourself using the correct epoxy glue.

Decorative character. Contemporary but can be made to suit different styles of rooms depending on colour.

Advantages. Will last forever. Has distinctive hi-tech appearance. Can be sealed later when required.

Carpet tiles

Subfloor. Any level surface. No underlay required.

DIY. Yes. Instructions supplied.

Decorative character. Bold patterns that can be tailored to room shape and size.

Advantages. Tiles can be replaced and rotated to avoid wear. Appear seamless when well installed.

Floorboards

Subfloor. 100 x 50 mm joists at 400 mm centres or concrete slab.

DIY. You can lay your own floors if you hire floor cramps and seek building instruction. Sanding and polishing can also be a DIY job.

Decorative character. Traditional – ideal for floor rugs.

Advantages. Long life because of ease of maintenance and re-finishing. Cost efficient, especially if renovating where floors are already laid.

Coir matting

Subfloor. Any floor surface.

DIY. Professional laying recommended because of tendency to fray when cut.

Decorative character. Natural, textural.

Advantages. The complete cover of carpet but with a less formal character. Very serviceable.

Parquetry

Subfloor. Concrete, particle board or timber.

DIY. Difficult. Professional laying highly recommended.

Decorative character. Formal, rich and traditional.

Advantages. The most prestigious of timber floor finishes which can be laid in a variety of designs and types of timber.

BELOW: Carpet is an ideal floor covering in a bedroom. Besides being warm in winter, it absorbs sound and feels soft and plush underfoot.

Carpet

Many home owners are confused when it comes to choosing carpet for their house. It's not surprising, given the range of styles, colours, fibres, grades and prices to be considered. But you can make the choice easier by understanding how different types of carpet can suit your needs.

Types of carpet

Carpet comes in several different fibres. The main ones are nylon, wool, wool/synthetic mix and polypropylene. Wool and nylon are both excellent if you buy good quality.

Nylon is the most durable carpet, but it does not retain its appearance as well as wool. Wool is generally regarded as having better stain resistance, but improvements in stain treatments to nylon carpets have meant both fibres are excellent when it comes to cleaning and stain resistance. Nylon carpet isn't as resistant to burns as wool. Generally, nylon carpets have a brighter colour range because they're easy to dye.

Wool carpet will continue to look good longer, cleans well, resists burns and wears well. It is softer than synthetic carpet and also will age more gracefully.

Wool/synthetic-mix carpet was produced originally to reduce the cost of wool carpet and to add durability to it. The mixed carpet is not as soft as pure wool carpet and is only slightly cheaper than wool.

Polypropylene is comparatively inexpensive and has good durability, although not as good as nylon, but is harsh to the touch. It also has a good resistance to soiling.

Grading

The lifespan of any carpet will vary according to fibre, quality and wear and tear. Areas that will wear most quickly include the stairs and turning points in any room or hall. As a result, it's imprortant to assess the traffic areas in your house and use the correct grade of carpet.

Wool and synthetic carpets are both manufactured in grades that are based on the amount of fibre in the carpet. There are four grades – light, medium, heavy-duty and extra-heavy-duty use. You should buy the highest grade you can afford for best durability.

Medium and light carpets are fine for bedrooms, although you may like heavy-duty if you have children. Heavy-duty or extra-heavy-duty are suitable for halls, entrances and stairs. Living areas should have heavy-duty at least.

Underlay

Good underlay will absorb the pressure of furniture and people walking on the carpet, reduce wear, prevent dirt from the floor getting up into your carpet, cushion the carpet from uneven floors and help insulate the room from heat and cold.

Felt underlay is good for sound deadening on wooden floors, but it's not used as much as rubber and foam. Rubber underlay is a waffle-like construction and, together with foam, it is very good for use on concrete floors because it acts as a barrier against moisture. Remember to choose an underlay that is firm rather than soft, otherwise the carpet will stretch.

Maintenance

Carpet will look better longer if it's properly maintained. At the very least, you should vacuum it once a week, moving the vacuum cleaner slowly over the pile to loosen the dirt. This will prevent the dirt from collecting in the base of the carpet pile where it can rub and cut fibres loose.

Don't forget to replace your vacuum cleaner bags when they are half full – if the bag is completely full, the suction will not be as effective. It's also vital to treat stains and spills immediately after they occur. Apply stain removal techniques that are appropriate for your carpet.

With proper care, your carpet won't need major cleaning for many years, but when you do want to clean it completely or revive the fibres, steam cleaning is the best option – however, make sure it's done by a professional. Once every two years should be sufficient.

Texture options

The main methods of making carpets are Tufted, Axminster and Wilton. Tufted is the most common and comes in three main textures – loop pile, cut pile or a combination of both.

Loop pile is made up of loops of yarn of uniform or different length. It wears well and tends to hide footprints effectively. Cut pile is achieved by cutting the tops off the loops so that they will stand upright and form an even surface. The most common cut-pile carpets are plushes and hard-twist piles. Plush carpet has been twisted slightly and heat set, while hard-twist cut pile uses yarn that is highly twisted and set. This type of carpet minimises footmarks, shading and shedding. Cut-and-loop pile is a combination of loop and cut yarn with a sculptured appearance.

The Axminster and Wilton carpet-making processes produce intricately patterned and multi-coloured carpets of a more traditional style.

LEFT: Carpet is practical and warm in a sunroom.

RIGHT: A decorative rug under the dining table reduces noise and defines the area.

Dos and don'ts of cleaning rugs

- Rugs will last a lot longer if they are cleaned and moved regularly.
- Vacuum your rug regularly or use a flat-faced carpet beater to clean it.
- Deal with spills and stains as quickly as possible. Use warm water and a light detergent. Most importantly, do not use harsh chemicals.
- Use a proprietary rug-cleaning product to clean your rugs regularly – do not let dirt build up.
- Do not immerse your rug in water or hang it up to dry.
- Valuable rugs will need periodic cleaning by a professional cleaner.

Rugs

How to install a rug underlay

Underlay prevents your rug from slipping underfoot and will keep it perfectly even on the floor. There are several varieties to choose from (for a timber floor, polyester underlay is the most effective).

Most rug suppliers will provide underlay when you buy your rug for a minimal extra charge. Here's how to install it:

1 Roll out your rug into the exact position you want it.
2 Carefully roll it up again, ensuring it does not move out of line.
3 Apply underlay to the floor surface and ensure it is held firmly.
4 Align the rolled edge of the rug to the edge of the underlay. Then unroll the rug and press down to ensure the rug adheres to the underlay.
5 Use scissors to trim off any excess underlay.

Laying new floor materials

Choosing and buying wood flooring

Wood flooring comes in strips and blocks. Strip flooring, which is by far the most common, typically measures from 50 to 150 mm wide, but has a smaller cover size due to its interlocking tongues and grooves. Most block (or parquet) flooring consists of strips that have been glued together into squares of rectangles.

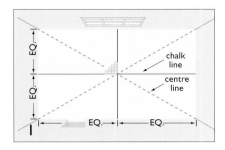

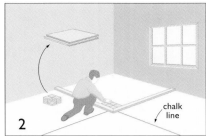

LEFT: Laying a parquet floor.

1 Plan the installation by squaring off the room with chalk lines.

2 Lay a pair of 50 x 25 mm battens along the chalk lines and you'll get off to a square start. Tongued-and-grooved edges keep later courses true.

You can purchase all these types of flooring finished or unfinished. Pre-finished flooring costs more and you must install it with extreme care so you don't mar the surface; unfinished flooring, on the other hand, must be sanded to smooth minor surface irregularities.

Flooring grades vary somewhat, depending on the kind of wood. Before you lay flooring, let the wood acclimatise to the conditions at your house. Have it delivered at least 72 hours in advance and spread it out in the room where it's to be laid.

Laying a parquet floor

One reason for the popularity of parquet flooring is that it's fairly easy to install, but it is not easy to do well. On concrete, it's best to put down a layer of polyethylene film, sleepers positioned at 450 mm centres and a subfloor of boards or panels before laying the flooring.

Using a power nailer

Almost all wood flooring interlocks in tongue-and-groove fashion. To fasten it to your old floor or sub-floor, blind nail at a 45–50° angle through the tongue along the length of each board, then set the nail so that the groove of the next board will fit over the tongue of the one you've just nailed.

A power nailer, available from tool hire shops, speeds the job and saves your back. Clips of special nails load much like staples into a stapler. Using a heavy flooring hammer, simply strike the machine's piston drive mechanism to set each nail. With one of these tools, you can lay several hundred square metres of flooring in a day.

Laying wood flooring over concrete

Strip-and-plank flooring can be cemented directly to concrete, but it is a job for a specialist. If you don't want to build a subfloor, lay a polyethylene vapour barrier, fasten down 100 x 50 mm 'joists', then nail flooring to the joists. First, be sure the concrete is properly sealed against moisture.

BELOW LEFT: Laying wood flooring over concrete.

1 Attach joists to the floor every 450 mm. Secure them with adhesive or masonry nails.

2 Lay the flooring, cutting the strips or planks so joints are centred over joists – a must for sound floor construction.

BELOW: A power nailer.

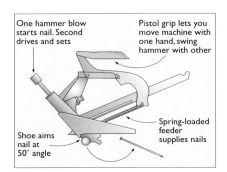

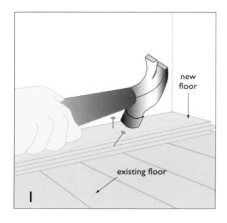

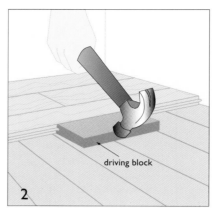

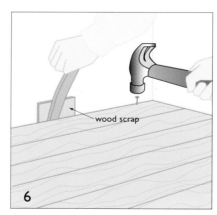

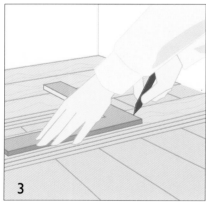

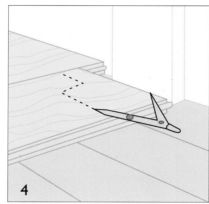

LEFT: Laying strip-and-plank flooring.

1 Place the groove of the first board 10 mm away from the walls. Blind nail through the tongue at 300 – 400 mm intervals.

2 To keep the courses parallel, tap boards together before nailing. Protect the tongues from damage by using a wood scrap.

3 Measure carefully before cutting the last piece in each course, and don't cut off the tongue or groove you'll need at one end.

4 To fit around irregularities, scribe a piece that's longer than you need with a compass, or use a contour gauge.

5 For scribed cuts, use a coping or jigsaw. If the board is the last one in the course, make the cut-out first, then cut to length.

6 Pull the last few courses tight with a crow bar, protecting the wall with a wood scrap. You'll need to face nail the last course.

If the floor is cold, you should lay rigid foam insulation between the joists.

Laying strip-and-plank flooring

Always lay strip-and-plank flooring at right-angles to the run of existing floorboards. But if you're nailing directly to sheets of plywood or chipboard, the direction of the finished floor should be at right-angles to the joists.

Start by sweeping the old floor, setting protruding nails and removing skirting boards. Level bad dips by pulling up the old flooring, nailing shims to the joists and re-nailing the boards. You can smooth minor irregularities by laying heavy building paper before you begin. Since wood expands and shrinks with humidity changes, leave a 10 mm gap between the floor and walls. This can be concealed with beading pinned to the skirting.

ABOVE: Top off the sanded floor with a decorative rug.

Do-it-yourself floor sanding

If you have a boarded floor, no matter how old, with a few days to spare, the right equipment and these tips you can have a beautiful polished floor. Although sanding floors yourself is not as easy as you might think, if you are careful and work methodically, you can produce a very professional finish.

Once your floors have been sanded and polished, they will be easy to maintain – all you need to do is mop them over with warm water mixed with a little methylated spirit to bring up the shine.

I   Remove carpet. Pull up the old carpet and make sure you remove all the underfelt, battens and staples.

If you are painting at the same time, it's a good idea to do the painting first as it's much easier to touch up the skirting board with paint than it is to fix up a paint-splattered floor.

I

3a

2   Punch nails. Remove any nails that protrude above the level of the boards and punch down the rest. Be systematic when punching down the nails, and follow the rows. This way you are less likely to miss some of the nails along the way.

3   Fix problems.

3a
This floor had a strip of painted plywood filling a space where a wall had been knocked out.

3b
The plywood was removed and small struts were wedged across the space, held in place with screws drilled into the brick foundations.

3c
New planks were measured, cut to fit exactly across the

2

3b

3c

space and nailed to the timber struts.

When patching floorboards, search your timber yard for the same type of timber as the old planks. Although the colour will probably differ because of age, at least the grain will be the same.

4

5

6

7

8

9

4   First sanding. The first sanding is done with a large-barrel sanding machine, using a coarse grade of sandpaper. It will remove most of the top layers of dirt, paint and even shellac. Do not be too fussy about this first stage, as it is mainly done to level the floor.

Working diagonally from one corner of the room to the opposite corner, start each run by holding the sanding drum off the floor until the sander is at full speed. Then repeat, working to and from the remaining corners to form a criss-cross grid and overlapping each run by 50 per cent. Never leave the sander stationary with the drum running as it will damage the floor.

5   Fill nail holes. Using a good-quality wood filler to match the timber of the floor, move along the rows of nails, leaving the filler a little proud as you go.

Make sure you choose a filler that is of the right consistency; not too dry and not too oily, as excessive oil will bleed into the wood and leave a stain. This will make any nail holes more obvious.

6   Edging. Using the small sander, go carefully around the edges of your room. You can do this twice – once with a coarse sandpaper and then with a fine one.

It is important that you don't press down too hard on the sander – guide it instead, using a circular motion. As there are several types of edging machine,

make enquiries when you hire your machine to make sure you end up with the sander that suits you best.

7   Corners. Using a hand scraper remove the final layers that the sanding machine is unable to reach. Make sure you take particular care to get right into the corners of your room.

Check that your scraper is very sharp to ensure that you get a smooth finish. And try to go with the grain of the wood, rather than against it.

8   Second sanding. Change to a finer grade of sandpaper and go over the entire floor once more. Always work along the grain of the timber with this second sanding and never across it.

10a

10b

This sanding is very important, as it will give you a good idea of how your finished floor will look. It is important carefully to go over sections that are marked, and if all else fails, you can gently use the scraper on areas where the boards have worn below the level of the surrounding floor.

9   Fine sanding. It is worthwhile employing a professional for this final stage.

After the fine sanding is finished, use a heavy-duty vacuum cleaner to make sure the floor is clear of all dust debris. Don't forget to clean the skirting boards as you go. Any dust left behind will spoil the finished job.

Rather than change to a finer sandpaper for this final sand, simply re-use any sheets that are left over from the last sand. As the tooth of the paper will have worn down, the effect will be more of a buff than a sand.

10 First coat.

10a
First go carefully around the hard-to-get edges and corners with a paintbrush to ensure an even coat.

Line a rectangular mop bucket with a heavy-duty plastic bag and then pour in your sealer. To pour any excess back into the can, simply lift the bag from the bucket and snip the corner off the bag to form a spout.

10b
Using a lambswool applicator and working quickly, spread on the sealer evenly along the grain of the timber.

11 Final coat. Repeat as for the first coat and then leave it to cure for at least 48 hours before moving the furniture back into place.

11

ABOVE: This striking floorcloth design is easily created with painted geometric patterns and simple flowers.

Other wood floor repairs

Here's how to restore the natural good looks of a wood floor – from smoothing away annoying scratches to replacing whole sections of damaged boards.

In both cases, success depends on how well you match your repair to the surrounding floor. So be sure to exercise due care when removing the damaged flooring and when selecting stains and replacement boards. When purchasing new wood flooring, take a sample of what you have now so you can match it exactly.

Hiding scratches

1 To hide minor imperfections on waxed or varnished floors, first try rubbing the scratched areas with a rag moistened with stain that approximates the stain on your floor.

    For surface cuts that don't 'disappear' when you treat the surface with stains, use steel wool and a solvent such as cleaning fluid. You must realise, however, that if you apply solvent, you'll need to rinse, then refinish, the treated area.

2 You can lift off most food stains and heel and caster marks by buffing the surface with the grain, using fine steel wool that has been moistened with mineral turps. This technique works especially well for oil-finished wood floors. With acrylic finishes, you'll also need to refinish the area you've abraided.

Replacing damaged wood flooring

1 To remove a damaged, tongued-and-grooved floorboard, make several cuts down the centre of the board with a circular saw. Adjust the cutting depth to the thickness of the flooring (usually 18–22mm) so you won't damage the supports below. Work from the centre towards the ends to avoid over-cutting.

Tips

- If your floors are slippery, there are several products available that will anchor rugs to the floor. Most carpet retailers will be able to advise you as to which will best suit your needs.
- The best way to look after your floor is with warm water and methylated spirit. For extra protection, glue small pieces of felt to the bottoms of furniture, especially chairs which are moved often, and ask your friends to leave their stilettos by the front door.

Restoring wood floors

Warped floors may require work to the joists beneath or a simple application of weight (bricks on a sheet of scrap plywood works well) followed by careful nailing to hold the boards down tightly against the joists.

Many old wood floors require finishing – something that can pose a major restoration challenge. The obvious, but expensive and disruptive, solution is to have them professionally sanded and refinished. A quicker and less costly option is to remove darkened, wax and varnish deposits with steel wool pads dipped in denatured alcohol.

If the varnish is spattered with latex wall or trim paint, first spread some lanolin-based hand cleaner on the spots and let them set for 10 minutes. Then scrape off all the paint with a putty knife. Pigmented wood putty should be matched to the floor and applied to nail holes and small cracks. This won't work for large cracks or gouges; you'll have to cut out the timber and replace it. Then sand and refinish.

That done, make sure the work area is well ventilated and that any nearby flames, sparks or heat sources are extinguished or removed. Then pour alcohol on to a 1 sq m area of the floor. Let it work for 3–5 minutes. Scour it with steel wool and wipe with a clean rag. The wood grain will shine through beautifully.

Comparing resilient floorings	
Material	Properties
Sheet vinyl	Solid vinyl. Several grades are available. Must be laid by a professional. Vulnerable to burns, but quite durable otherwise.
Cushioned	Several grades of this material available, from sheet vinyl moderately durable to very durable. Resistant to abrasion and discolouration. Durability ranges from that of commercial vinyl tile to cheaper imports, which are approximately half as durable. Vulnerable to burns. This product usually contains a vinyl foam layer.
Roto sheet vinyl	Design is printed on a cellulose-felt or mineral-fibre backing, then coated with a thin film of vinyl. Easy to lay loose or with tape. Mineral-backed grade can be used from basement to bedroom. Cellulose-backed is less durable than other types listed. Vulnerable to burns and tears. This product usually contains a vinyl foam layer.
Solid vinyl tile	Basically the same composition and characteristics as sheet vinyl. Vulnerable to cigarette burns.
Comercial vinyl tile	The most popular of today's tiles. It ranks just a notch below solid vinyl tile in durability. Good resistance to burns, impact, scuffing, dents, oil and grease. Easy to install, especially if you choose adhesive-backed versions.
Asphalt tile	A pioneer among resilient floor coverings. Durable, but difficult to maintain, grease will soften it, poor recovery from indentation. Brittle composition makes it difficult to cut.

Now chisel out the board, starting with the kerfed mid-section and finishing with the sides. Be careful not to damage the groove of the adjacent board.

2 When you're dealing with more than one damaged board, you should begin by outlining the perimeter of the area to be replaced using a framing square. Go only as far as the edges of the nearest sound boards.

Now, with your circular saw adjusted to the proper cutting depth, cut along the ends of your outline (across the boards, not along their length). Again, cut from the centre to the edges. Then make a series of cuts only the length of the damaged area, as described for a single board.

3 To remove the boards, wedge or drive a crow bar between a couple of the lengthwise cuts, then work it back and forth until you're able to lift one of the boards. Continue prying boards loose one by one.

If you're replacing a damaged area of parquet flooring, dispense with sawing and simply nibble away at individual blocks,

using a hammer and wood chisel. Be careful not to cause any damage to adjacent blocks.

4 Secure replacement boards by nailing through their tongues at about a 50° angle. To fit the last board, you'll have to chisel off the bottom of its groove. Apply adhesive to the subfloor, tongue and half-groove of the board, then tap it into place.

Glue parquet tiles with wood-tile floor adhesive.

Choosing and buying resilient flooring

Resilient flooring, so-called because it's softer underfoot than anything but carpeting, includes tiles and sheet materials. Tiles have been a popular do-it-yourself item since World War II, although they've changed quite considerably since that time in size (from 225 to 300 mm), appearance (from dull, streaked greens and beiges to vivid colours and patterns) and composition (from asphalt to varying blends of vinyl).

Sheet materials have been around a while, too, but because

they come in bulky rolls up to 3.6 m wide, installation is best left to a flooring contractor. An exception to this is cushioned vinyl. Whether you choose to install tiles or sheet vinyl depends to some extent upon the use your new floor will receive.

Cushioned vinyl is soft underfoot, has a minimum of dirt-catching seams and does a decent sound-proofing job. Tiles, on the other hand, are less expensive, easier to install and more resistant to dents from items such as chair legs and pointed heels. For more comparisons, see the chart above.

Consider also whether you want a smooth or textured surface on your resilient floor. Smooth tiles and sheet materials can be mopped easily, show dirt more readily and inevitably collect a few scuffs and dents that won't come out.

Before you buy the flooring, be sure you're clear about the manufacturer's installation recommendations. Most of today's resilent floorings can be installed on any subfloor. A few, though, shouldn't be laid on concrete in contact with soil. Most shouldn't be applied over an existing resilient floor, either.

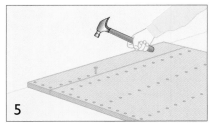

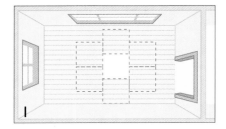

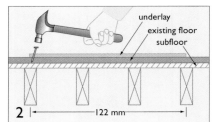

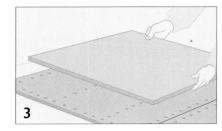

If an old wood floor is in good condition and has a subfloor underneath, you can successfully lay resilient materials directly over it. Otherwise, you'll have to put down an underlay first.

Since all but a few of today's tiles are 300 x 300 mm sq, determining how many you'll need requires only simple calculations. Estimating the amount of sheet flooring needed is trickier, especially if there's a pattern involved and you have to form a seam somewhere. It's best to make an accurate plan of the room on graph paper and take it to the flooring supplier for him to calculate your needs.

Preparing old floors for resilient flooring

Installing underlay

You must smooth badly worn wood floors with underlay before you install resilient tiles or sheet materials. But make sure that the material you choose is suitable for use as underlay (6 mm or thicker hardboard or plywood will work well). Hardboard is available in standard 1200 x 2400 mm panels, but a variety of smaller sheets are also available and easier to work with. It is a good idea to acclimatise the sheets to the room. Do this by standing them on edge in the room for a couple of days.

To secure the underlay, you'll need lots of ring-shank flooring nails. Drive one in every 150 mm across the face of each panel and every 75 mm at the edges. Stagger the panels and space them about 1 mm apart.

Laying building paper

A layer of building paper will quieten wood floors, and smooth out minor irregularities in both wood and resilient floors. Cut the paper in strips that will stretch from wall to wall. Lay it at right-angles across old floorboards, or in any direction across underlay.

Choosing and buying hard-surface flooring

Hard-surface floor materials — ceramic, mosaic, slate and quarry tiles — come in myriad sizes, shapes and colours. They're easy to maintain once laid, but some can be difficult to install.

ABOVE: Laying hardboard underlay.

1 Begin at the approximate centre of the room and arrange the panels so you'll never have four corners converging at one point.

2 Tap with a hammer to locate a floor joist, then centre one edge of the first panel over it and nail through the subfloor.

3 At edges, slide a full sheet against the wall, overlapping it with previously nailed panels and squaring it up with them.

4 Next, using a scrap piece of underlay as a guide, draw a line along the entire length of the border piece. Cut along the line.

5 Lay the piece into place. Don't worry if it doesn't fit exactly — the skirting will cover irregularities. Nail the border in place.

BELOW: Laying building paper.

1 Apply adhesive with a serrated trowel and unroll the paper. Butt edges of adjacent strips; don't overlap.

2 Smooth out bubbles with a flooring roller, which you can obtain from a tool hire shop, or

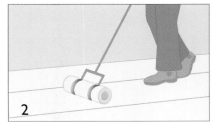

Comparing hard-surface tiles		
Material	Description	Installation
Glazed ceramic tile	Sizes range from 19 x 19 mm to over 300 x 300 mm and thickness varies from 7 to 13 mm. The 300 x 300 mm is a popular size. Wide selection of colours, glazes, patterns and shapes.	Moderately easy
Ceramic mosaic tile	Available in 19, 25, 30 and 50 mm squares and various-sized rectangles, these are mounted to sheets of paper or mesh. Very popular with do-it-yourselfers.	Easy
Quarry and paver tile.	Made from natural clays in large sizes, 150–200 mm squares and 100 x 200 mm rectangles and are normally 13 mm thick. They also come in hexagons. Earthen colours in reds, browns and buffs, also available in a variety of irregular shapes suitable for both indoor and outdoor use.	Fairly difficult
Special-purpose tile	Usually larger than 125 mm, with sizes up to 450 mm sq, 10 mm thick. Widest selection of colours, glazes, patterns, designs and shapes.	Difficult

Bear in mind that floor tiles are heavier than wall tiles, and those with mirror-like glazes will be slippery when wet.

Preparing your floor for hard-surface flooring

Because hard-surface materials are brittle and inflexible, they can only be laid over a surface that's absolutely smooth and rigid.

Over wood floors, you must lay down an 8–10 mm fibre cement underlay to prevent movement that could crack the grout. Install as explained on page 80.

Concrete also makes an excellent tile base. But check the floor carefully with a straightedge to locate any low spots, fill them with a self-levelling floor screed. Clean the floor thoroughly to ensure a good bond between flooring and base. A special dry-set mortar does a good job of bonding tiles to concrete, but don't use it over underlay.

Lay out the job so you'll have full tiles at the doorway, by working from the doorway to the opposite end of the room. Snap a chalk line from the doorway to the opposite wall. This line must be at right-angles to the face of the door.

Now dry-lay a row of tiles along the line, beginning at the door. If the tiles aren't self-spacing, use scraps of thin wood or cardboard to space them evenly. Nail a guide board to the floor at right-angles to the chalk line, at the point of the last full tile. Dry-lay along the board.

Adjust this row to obtain cut tiles that are an even width at each end. Snap a second line, parallel to the first, from the point where the border tiles begin. Start laying from here.

ABOVE: Natural coir used as a rug tones in with the polished timber and furniture in this elegant living room.

1

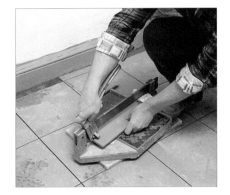

5

9

Tiling you can do

Here are step-by-step instructions for tiling your floors – a major job to take slowly and surely to its successful completion.

ABOVE: The finished tiling with its elegant grey squares makes a wonderful background for the old furniture. Maintenance is easy too — a simple mop-over is all that's needed to restore the tiles to perfection.

1 Cut and lay chicken wire over the floor surface and fix the mesh down with clout-head nails. The mesh provides a reinforcement bed for the mortar.

2 Mix mortar thoroughly in the proportion 3 parts sand to 1 part cement. Mix to a moist, spreadable consistency (not runny) and spread over a workable section of floor.

3 Where tiles finish at doorways, fix aluminium angle edging to contain them and take mortar over them.

4 Spread out the mortar with a long timber straightedge, making sure that the mesh is well covered.

5 Use a float to smooth the surface of the mortar and

check that it is even using a spirit level.

6 Sprinkle the immediate area to be tiled with a little dry cement to provide a 'key' for the tiles.

7 At this stage, stand on a board in order to distribute your weight evenly. Start laying tiles from the doorway.

2

3

4

6

7

8

10

11

12

8 Tiles should have approximately 5 mm of space left between them. You can use a slim batten as a spacer between the tile being laid and the previous one. Remove the batten as you go. Tamp down gently on the tile with a wooden block or hammer end to bed the tile firmly.

9 If you need to trim tiles to fit you can hire tools to help score and cut them.

10 Fit 'fill-in' tiles and tamp down as before.

11 When the tiles are laid, mix the grouting in proportion 1 part sand to 1 part cement, adding enough water to make it of a fairly loose consistency. Work the grouting over the tiles until all the spaces are filled, finishing the process with a rubber squeegee to remove any excess grouting.

12 Wipe off residue with a damp sponge or cloth, rinsing it regularly.

Step-by-step slate floors

Slate is available in a wide range of colours and textures to suit almost any area of the house.

1 Cover the floor to be tiled with hessian. Spread with slate membrane, which will penetrate it. Leave overnight.
2 Sprinkle the floor with dry slate adhesive powder (you can stand on this), then mix adhesive as directed on the packet.
3 Spread the mixture with a notched trowel (10 mm) to key the surface of a manageable area.
4 Butter the back of a tile with an even layer of slate adhesive.
5 Position the tile accurately into the keyed surface.
6 Tap down to expel air and bed the tile firmly. Leave for a day.
7 Spread grouting, mixed as directed, over the floor in sections. Work in with squeegee. Scrape off excess.
8 Sponge off the surface before surplus grouting sets on tiles, changing water frequently.
9 Give the floor surface a final clean with steel wool if necessary.
10 Coat with slate sealer, resealing traffic areas yearly if required.

Laying mosaic tiles

Sold in 300 x 300 mm sheets (faced with paper or backed by non-removable mesh), mosaics go down much faster than individual tiles. And you don't have to worry about equalising borders. Square-up the room with guide boards and begin laying from a corner. Use spacers between sheets so that the gaps will be the same.

Align the edges of the sheets carefully against the guide boards, lay in place and twist slightly. Peel back the paper to check that the tiles line up.

After you've laid several sheets, tap them into the adhesive by pounding a piece of plywood on top of the sheet of tiles. Wipe off excess adhesive.

Mark sheets for border cuts on the underside. Cut sheets between tiles by snipping the paper with a sharp knife or scissors.

Cut tiles themselves by nibbling them with tile nippers. To make a hole, cut a tile in half and nibble notches in each side.

After the adhesive sets, soak the paper facing thoroughly with warm water and, starting in a corner, carefully peel it off.

A squeegee simplifies grouting floor tiles. Pack grout into each joint, then scrape off the excess.

Cutting a ceramic tile

Whether you are tiling floors, walls or bench tops, you will find the correct way to cut a tile is a useful skill to have mastered. Tiles are very brittle and, if scored, will crack along that line of weakness. There are many specialist tools for the job, but here we show you a simple method.

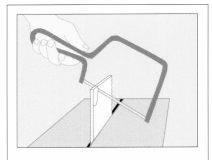

Tip

- When you are cutting a curve on a tile, make a template of the shape you want then mark the tile with a felt pen. Hold the tile vertically in a vice while cutting with a rod saw.

BELOW: Cutting a ceramic tile.

1 To make a straight cut on a tile, use a try square and the scribing edge of a tile cutter to score the face of the tile.

2 On a flat, smooth surface, position the scored line on the tile over a thin piece of dowel and apply gentle pressure with your hands.

3 If the cut is close to the edge of the tile, 'nibble' the waste away with a pair of pincers after scoring.

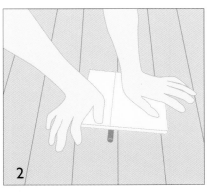

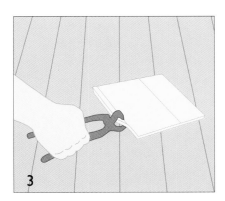

Hard-surface and resilient floor repairs

Hard-surface floors require little maintenance. But occasionally you'll need to remove stains and patch or replace a damaged tile. Repairing resilient floors is not difficult, provided you can obtain matching tiles or sheet materials, although the older and more worn the goods, the harder it will be to make the repair unobtrusive.

Removing common stains

Regardless of the type of stain you need to remove from your hard-surface floor, the sooner you do it the better. Always wear rubber gloves when working with harsh chemicals and never use flammable solvents around an open flame.

The chart below lists cures for common stains on ceramic and quarry tiles, slate and brick, as well as on grout and concrete. For stains of an unknown nature, consult a flooring supplier for advice.

Filling cracks and voids in concrete

Prepare the damaged area by chipping away and brushing out all loose concrete. Then use a hammer and cold chisel to undercut its edges to 'lock in' the patch.

Now fill the void with latex or epoxy patching material, packing it in with a taping knife or a rectangular trowel. Check the manufacxturer's instructions on whether to dampen or otherwise treat the area before filling.

Replacing resilient tiles

Begin by covering the damaged tile with a damp cloth. Now run a warm iron back and forth across the damaged tile to soften both the tile and the underlying adhesive. (Also use this technique when you simply need to dab more adhesive under a good tile whose corner has curled.)

If you don't have an iron handy, a propane torch works just as well. With this, however, take care that you do not scorch any of the surrounding tiles.

Score the perimeter of the tile with a knife and straightedge. Then, using a stiff-bladed putty knife, pry up the softened tile. If this doesn't do the job, use a hammer and chisel, working outwards from the tile's centre.

Scrape away the old tile adhesive and apply new adhesive with a notched trowel.

Before laying the replacement tile, warm it slightly under a damp cloth and iron to make it more flexible. Then align one edge with an adjoining tile and press (don't slide) it into position.

Immediately clean up any excess adhesive and weigh down the new tile with a heavy object.

Patching sheet materials

Repairing a damaged area in sheet flooring is essentially like replacing a damaged floor tile: you lay in a 'tile patch' that you've cut from a piece of matching sheet material.

Treating common hard-surface flooring stains		
Material	Stain	Treatment
Ceramic tile	Soap film	Scrub with vinegar, rinse.
	Grease	Keep wet 1 hour with a 1:4 lye-water solution, then rinse and dry.
	Gum, tar, wax	Scrape off solids, treat remainder with a rag soaked in methylated spirit; dry.
	Inks, dyes	Keep stain wet with household bleach. Warm water rinse and dry.
	Food stains	Scrub with trisodium-phosphate solution (or bleach); rinse and dry.
	Paint	Soften and remove with acetone.
Brick pavers,	Efflorescence	Scrub with a 1:15 (for light bricks) or 1:10 (for dark concrete, grout bricks) solution of muriatic acid and water. Let stand, then rinse. (Don't apply acids to coloured concrete or grout.)
	Grease	Absorb what you can with sawdust and powdered cement, dissolve remaining with de-greaser. Lighten with bleach.
	Paint	For wet paint, use the appropriate solvent. For dried paint, use a remover.
	Rust	Scrub with bleach, let stand, then rinse.
	Soot	Scrub with scouring powder, then rinse.
Slate or quarry		Blot all spills at once and scrub with detergent. Spills that penetrate these porous materials become permanent stains. To prevent stains, apply a sealer.

But unlike working with tiles, patching sheet materials demands a bit more attention to correctly sizing the patch and carefully matching its pattern to that of the existing floor.

Start by positioning the patch material over the damaged area, taking care to align it so the pattern matches the flooring exactly. Secure the patch to the floor with masking tape.

Cut through the new material and the damaged flooring, using a sharp knife guided by a straight-edge. Make sure your cuts remain outside the damaged area. Cutting along pattern lines will help to conceal the patch.

Remove the old flooring just as if it was a tile.

Before you apply new adhesive for your patch, trial-fit the patch into the cleaned out opening. You may need lightly to sand the patch's edges for a perfect fit. Finish by placing a weight on the patch and leaving it to 'set' for 24 hours.

LEFT: What was once a grim, grey inner-city courtyard has taken on a new lease of life with a simple painted geometric pattern in earthy terracotta tones, which contrast sharply with the design highlight of blues and golds.

Stairs

The addition of an extra storey means the inclusion of a staircase. It also means additional storage underneath, although in a limited space you may opt for a spiral staircase.

Anatomy of a staircase

A staircase has many parts, all of them interlocked with sophisticated joinery that usually is concealed from view.

The basics are simple enough: a pair of stringers slopes from one level to the next. The composite illustration here shows both 'open-' and 'closed-stringer' staircases.

The stringers support a series of steps called treads. A very simple staircase, such as you might have to a basement or a deck, consists of little more than stringers and treads. Complications begin when risers are added to fill the gaps between treads.

Finally, there's the balustrade, consisting of the handrail, balusters and a newel post, which provides the safety of the staircase.

Stair edging can help to protect carpeted and hardwood tread fronts from excessive wear.

You can treat most of the ills that afflict staircases with patience and a few hand tools, as shown on the following pages.

Solving stair problems

Silencing stair squeaks

Every house has at least one: a floorboard or stair tread that groans and creaks every time it's stepped on.

ABOVE: Narrow vertical windows afford natural light on to the small staircase.

BELOW: A drop-down ladder is the ideal form of access to the attic.

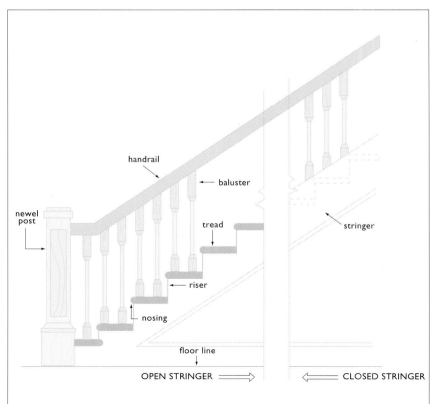

handrail

baluster

newel post

tread

stringer

riser

nosing

floor line

OPEN STRINGER ⟹

⟸ CLOSED STRINGER

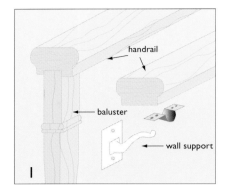

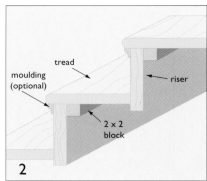

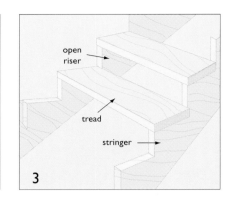

When you consider the weight and traffic borne by floors and stairs, it's not surprising that they occasionally develop problems needing attention. Most staircase squeaks are caused by a tread rubbing against the top or bottom of a riser or stringer.

Whether the wood stress causing the problem is in the flooring or the stairs, silencing these annoying squeaks is mainly a matter of locating them, then securing boards or stair components that have become loose and are rubbing against each other. If you're lucky, you'll have access to these trouble spots from below. If not, there are ways to tackle them from above.

Silencing stairs from above

To fasten down the front edge of a tread, drive spiral-shanked flooring nails at an angle into pre-drilled holes. (It's useful to have a helper stand on the tread as you nail.)

ABOVE: Anatomy of a staircase.

1 Some balusters fit into holes in the handrail and treads. Others are skew nailed and glued. Brackets support wall-mounted rails.

2 Treads and risers may be butt-jointed or connected with tongues and grooves. Glued wood blocks underneath provide additional reinforcement.

3 Treads on open-riser staircases usually are nailed to the stringers. Note that this staircase also has open stringers.

LEFT: A good design for your builder to tackle is this simple and stylish staircase, made from natural wood, with a painted white finish. The uncomplicated lines give it both a sophisticated and country feel, making it suitable for either style.

RIGHT: What a breakthrough this is, in more ways than one. A short-cut stairway to an upper floor is achieved with maximum effect and minimum use of space with a spiral staircase; in this case a curve is the shortest distance between two points.

BELOW: Never overlook the excellent storage space that can be created under the stairs. Choose the storage system you need, then finish with doors and trims to match the staircase.

Next, set the nails and conceal the holes with wood filler.

To eliminate squeaks at the back edge of a tread, drive one or more wedges of scrap wood (coated with glue) into the gap between the tread and the riser. Later, trim away the protruding wood.

Silencing stairs from below

Squeaky stair treads that have parted company with their risers will respsond well to treatments carried out from underneath.

Drill pilot holes through small blocks of 50 x 50 mm timber for the screws that will attach them to both the tread and the riser. Then coat the contacting surfaces of the blocks with wood glue and drive the screws into the tread and riser.

Tightening rails and balusters

Wobbly handrails call for some detective work. Are the rails working loose from the balusters, or are the balusters parting company with the treads? You can cure either problem as soon as you determine which one you are dealing with. If the rail is pulling away from a newel post, adapt these techniques.

Loose newel posts require an expert's help.

Drill at an angle through the baluster and into the rail or tread, then drive in a long wood screw to tighten up the joint.

Or work glue into the loose joint and drive nails through the railing's side. First drill pilot holes for the nails.

If the entire railing is loose, add blocking to its underside. Carefully cut angles for a snug fit, and then glue and nail.

Some good cases for stairs

A staircase should add a very special touch to your living area, as well as taking you from one level of the house to another.

Whether you're creating a room in your attic or adding another floor, you'll need a staircase. Building a staircase requires special knowledge – and you'll need a specialist contractor or a staircase company.

Alternatively, you can consider using prefabricated stairs that are now available. And don't forget the space under the stairs – it can make great storage.

Doors and Windows

Doors and windows are such essential and functional parts of the house, providing entry, light and a view of the outdoors, that we seldom notice them or think about their style.

Choosing the right type is not always easy. Interior doors are available in a wide variety of styles and finishes from a number of sources, but most home renovators generally find something that suits their needs and their budget in the manufacturer's or retailer's showroom. There are also many outlets that specialise in recycled doors and windows, which are especially useful to those wanting to match a period style. If budget is not a major consideration, a good joiner can even tailor-make doors to suit the house.

Some windows, both wooden and aluminium-framed, are available pre-glazed and ready to fit, although these too can be specially made.

The style of doors and windows should match the house. Good maintenance is most important to ensure efficient opening and closing as well as security. This chapter shows you some of the variety of doors and windows available and how to build, maintain and repair them.

Casement windows are great for catching breezes because they act in the same way as sails, directing moving air inside. Notice that half the windows open from the left and half from the right. The small panes at the top of these windows provide added interest.

Doors

Whether they are heavy-duty exterior types or decorative interior versions, doors can be both stylish and functional. These attributes are best achieved if the doors are in harmony with the overall style of the house.

Doors galore

The range is quite bewildering. Doors now have all sorts of different functions. There are front and back doors, French and sliding doors, internal and external doors, with or without any number of glazing and panelling designs. And then there are solid and hollow, timber or otherwise, security or not. Here are some ideas to help make you door wise.

TOP: Glazed doors fill the entire end wall.

ABOVE: Overhead internal fanlights permit filtered light into the adjoining room.

RIGHT: Panelled and bi-folding doors provide interior efficiency with large-scale openings and small swing.

Door talk

- Most standard doors are 2000 mm or 2030 mm high and 600–900 mm wide.
- Solid timber doors can easily be cut down, but hollow internal doors can be cut down only a little.
- Plain, hollow internal doors are made with a light timber frame covered with fine sheeting and filled with cardboard or chipboard. These are unlikely to hold coat-hook screws.
- Your front door should be in the style of your house. Beware of a hollow door using timber moulding to masquerade as a solid one.
- Aluminium doors are an option, but only if they match the style of your house.

Double doors

Interior double doors are not a new idea, but they have particular relevance these days. Many of our houses feature spacious, open-plan interiors, but we also need to be able to close off rooms from the rest of the house for efficient heating. Double doors give a wider-than-standard passage from one room to another, but have the advantage of keeping the two rooms completely separate when necessary.

ABOVE: These glazed doors allow a visual link between the entry hall and the main drawing room.

LEFT: Throwing the doors open achieves an entrance on the grand scale, making the sitting area a natural extension of the hallway.

Folding doors

The idea of being able to throw the house open to the outdoors is very appealing. Traditionally, this is achieved with one or more pairs of French doors, but sometimes they just do not create a wide enough opening. By using folding doors, part of the wall, or even the whole wall can literally be folded away to merge the interior and exterior.

With a system of rollers and tracks at the top of the doors, and guide channels and pivots at the bottom, you can hinge as many doors together as you like. Each door should be no wider than 900 mm and weigh no more than 60 kg. Depending on where you position the hardware, the doors can be made to swing into the room or outwards on to your patio or a deck.

Installing doors such as these is a job for the experts and, until recently, they have been used only in commercial applications. For quotes, you could try contacting shop-fitting companies listed in the Yellow Pages telephone directory. Alternatively, you could try a local window and door installer, or a joinery company. Provided they know where to obtain the hardware with the correct specifications, there should not be too many problems.

TOP: This opening only measures 2300 mm but it is more than enough to make the terrace seem like a generous extension of the kitchen and breakfast room.

FAR LEFT: When opened wide, the doors protrude outwards on to the terrace. You can choose to have them opening into the room or even half each way.

ABOVE LEFT AND LEFT: The hardware is the key – rollers and tracks at the top and pivots and channels at the bottom. The right hinges are also important.

French doors

Replacing an existing window with a set of French doors will not only transform a room, flooding it with additional light, but also provide a tangible link with the garden or patio outside, allowing you to enjoy the balmy days of summer when the doors can be opened wide. It's not a task to be undertaken lightly, however, because it could have severe structural implications for your home and will require applying for approval under the Building Regulations.

French doors are usually purchased complete with frames and come in a range of standard sizes; those used here are 1685 mm wide by 2100 mm high, measured at the wall opening (including door frame). If you want the doors and frame tailored to fit a non-standard-size opening, expect to pay extra.

In this case, the standard door size was used and the opening adapted to fit the doors.

The first job is to check for any power points or switches close to the proposed opening. This may indicate that there is wiring running through the portion of the wall that is to be cut, in which case an electrician will be needed to re-route the wiring.

Next, the old window frame should be removed. Finding the screws that hold the frame in the opening is likely to be extremely difficult, as they will be covered by layers of paint and possibly filler or dowels. If the frame is not required in one piece, the top, sides and sill can be sawn through and the frame removed piecemeal.

If the opening for the new French doors is not to be higher or wider than the existing opening,

ABOVE: Before.

LEFT: After — additional space and light.

ABOVE: Glass doors in a wall of glass allow you to enjoy the aspect beyond.

RIGHT: French doors mean easy access from the outdoor living area.

the masonry below can be chopped out. If, however, the width or height is to be changed, the masonry above will need supporting with stout lengths of timber and adjustable props. A new concrete or steel lintel will also be needed to span the top of the opening and support the masonry above.

With a cavity wall, it is necessary to close off the cavity at each side of the opening by adding a return to the outer leaf. This is done by removing the cut bricks from the outer leaf to leave a 'toothed' edge. New bricks can then be laid in these cut-outs to span the cavity, and cut bricks used to infill between them. To prevent damp penetration, a length of dpc material must be inserted between the inner leaf and the return of the outer leaf. Similarly, steps must be taken to ensure that the dpc at the foot of the wall is not damaged while making the opening or fitting the new frame.

Wooden wedges and packing pieces may be necessary to square up the frame in the opening. Then it can be secured by driving frame fixings through the frame and into the surrounding walls.

Gaps around the frame on the outside should be sealed with a silicone mastic, while inside the plasterwork can be made good up to the frame. Or an architrave fitted if the surroundings permit. Paint or stain both doors and frame before hanging the doors.

A variety of locks is available. All should come with fitting instructions and a template showing where to cut and drill. Mortise locks are best, as they are stronger than surface-mounted types. In addition, bolts should be fitted top and bottom to shoot into the frame head and sill.

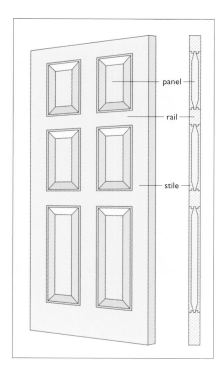

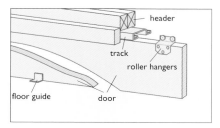

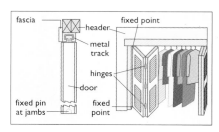

Door construction

Anatomy of a panel door

Almost every modern door has a framework of vertical stiles and horizontal rails. This construction helps counteract the wood's tendency to shrink, swell and warp with changes in humidity.

With a panelled door, you can see the framing. Spaces between frame members can be filled with wood, louvred slats or glass.

Anatomy of a flush door

Flush doors hide their framing beneath two or three layers of veneer. Alternating each layer's direction minimises warping.

A solid-core flush door has a dense centre of hardwood blocks or particle board; a hollow-core door uses lighter material, such as corrugated cardboard.

Anatomy of a sliding door

Sliding doors come in pairs. Panelled or flush, solid- or hollow-core, they roll along an overhead track and are guided by metal or nylon angles screwed to the floor.

Anatomy of a folding door

Folding doors – sometimes call bi-folding – are hinged together. One pivots on fixed pins; the other slides along track fixed at the top and the base of the door opening.

FAR LEFT: Anatomy of a panel door.

ABOVE LEFT: Anatomy of a sliding door.

ABOVE: Anatomy of a folding door.

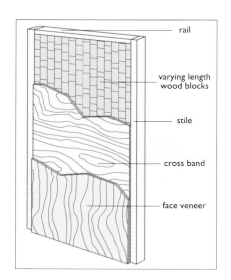

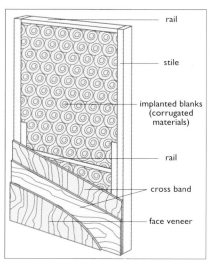

LEFT: Anatomy of a flush door.

as it should, and that the latch engaged the striker plate correctly. As time passes, however, a house settles; both the jamb and the door expand and contract at different rates. Also, the door is opened and closed countless times. These factors (and others) can eventually cause problems such as binding doors and loose hinges.

Repairing hinged doors

When a hinged door gives you trouble, don't be too quick to take it down and begin planing its edges. Many difficulties call more for analysis than for work – and they're better dealt with by making minor adjustments while the door is in place.

Almost all problems result from one or more of these causes: improperly aligned or loose hinges, an improperly aligned striker plate, warping of the door itself, or a frame that's out of square.

If a door sticks or refuses to fit into its frame, close it as best you can and sight carefully around its perimeter. Look for an uneven gap along the hinge jamb, which means the hinges need attention. If the door seems too big for its frame – or out of square – mark the tight spots, then sand or plane them.

Freeing a binding door

If your door is binding near the top or bottom of the latch edge, first make sure that the hinge leaves on the door and jamb aren't loose. You may be able to solve the problem by shimming out one of the hinges. Shim the top hinge to cure binding near the bottom, and shim the bottom hinge for binding near the top.

To shim out a hinge, open the door and insert a wedge beneath the latch edge for support. Then remove the screws that hold the hinge to the door jamb. Trim a piece of thin cardboard to fit the rectangular recess on the door jamb, and insert the shim between the jamb and the hinge flap.

ABOVE: Internal French doors leading to a glassed-in verandah maintain an atmosphere of light and warmth.

Solving door problems

A sticking door can be extremely irritating, but usually you need spend only a few minutes with a screwdriver, some sandpaper or a plane to get it swinging freely again. Finding where it binds can be the trickiest part of the job.

When your house was built, care would have been taken to ensure that doors were plumb and square in their openings. Once the jambs had been set and the door knob-and-latch set had been installed, a check would have been made to see that each door opened and closed

If shimming takes care of the binding on the latch edge, but causes the door to bind at the top or bottom, pinpoint the trouble spot while opening and closing the door. Scribe a line along the door's face to indicate where you want to remove wood. If this is along the top edge, partially open the door, drive a wedge under its latch edge and use a block plane to remove the high spot. Work from the end towards the centre to avoid splintering the end grain.

If the high spot is on the door's bottom edge, or along the hinge edge, release the door from its frame by unscrewing the hinge flaps from the edge of the door.

Anchor the door in a freestanding work vice, holding it firm by wedging one end in a corner or by straddling it. Then plane down the high spots. If these are on the hinge edge, work a jack plane in the direction of the grain, holding it at a slight angle to the door. If you're planing end grain on the door's bottom edge, use a block plane and shave from the ends to the centre.

Curing striker problems

When a door won't latch, or if it rattles when it's latched, examine the striker plate attached to the jamb. A minor adjustment here will probably solve the problem for you.

First, take a close look at what happens when the door closes. Is the latch engaging the striker? If it isn't, determine if the latch is too far from the striker or if it's hitting the striker but missing the hole. Often, scratches on the plate will give you a good idea of exactly how far it's out of alignment.

A door that doesn't fit snugly against the stop moulding will almost certainly rattle. To silence it, you must either move the striker plate or reposition the stop.

If the striker plate is off by only a few millimetres or so, enlarge the opening with a file. You may need to chisel away some wood, too.

Accommodate a larger disparity by relocating the striker plate. You will, in addition, need to extend the mortise.

Use thick cardboard or thin wood to shim out a striker that's too far away to engage the latch. Resetting hinges can cause this.

What to do about warping

For latch-side door warpage, pry off the stop, close the door and trace the line of its inside edge on the frame. Re-nail the stop on this line.

For a hinge-edge warp, add another hinge to the centre of the door. Force the door into line before screwing down.

You may be able to straighten a warped door by taking it off and weighting it down. To prevent new doors from warping, seal all edges and surfaces.

BELOW: These floor-to-ceiling windows in a dining alcove have the effect of French doors. The top of the window follows the line of the ceiling, and the warm, natural timber is continued around the room by the picture rail.

RIGHT: Glass above with
timber panel below is a perfect
combination for a back door.
With the top open and the bottom
closed, air and light are admitted
while children and pets can
be confined easily.

Lubricating stiff latches

Turn the handle to retract the latch, then puff powdered graphite into the works. Lubricate the collars of knob shafts on each side, too.

Lubricate a thumb-operated latch lever by puffing graphite into the latch body. Never use oil – it will clog the mechanism.

Latch assemblies are not terribly expensive, so if you find that lubricating won't free one, replace it.

Repairing sliding doors

Compared with hinged doors, sliding doors hardly ever malfunction, and when they do, a few turns of a screwdriver will usually put them right again. The maintenance required for sliding doors is practically nil, as well, since almost all of them roll on self-lubricating nylon wheels.

If a sliding door sticks or jumps its track, it probably has alignment problems. Check that the door hasn't warped. You may be able to compensate for minor warping by shifting the guides slightly; otherwise, you should replace the door.

A few sliding doors – most notably the glass versions – roll on wheels along a bottom track. You should adjust and maintain these as you would a sliding window (see page 127).

To remove a sliding door, lift it and tilt slightly. With some designs, the wheels will lift off at any point along the top track. With others, you can only free the door when its wheels are adjacent to a 'key' opening. This arrangement prevents track jumping. The plates holding sliding doors in position can work loose and slip out of alignment. If this happens, re-align them and tighten the screws.

Fix or replace floor guides that are broken, bent or out of line. The doors should clear the floor by at least 1 cm.

Repairing folding doors

Use a spanner to raise or lower folding doors. A screw and slot on the lower pivot bracket help you to set them plumb, too. Don't lubricate the top assembly glides, as most of them are self-lubricating.

Installing new doors

Hanging a door

Replacing a door or hanging a new one in an existing opening makes a satisfying carpentry project, provided you keep everything square, measure and cut carefully, and visually check your work at every step.

Doors come in a range of standard heights, usually 2000 mm, 2030 mm and occasionally 2170 mm, while widths range from 600 mm to 900 mm. If you have to alter the size of a door, allow 3 mm for clearance at the top and sides, and 10 mm at least at the bottom – more if it must clear carpeting. Never cut more than 20 mm from either end.

Once you've hung a door, install stop mouldings on the jamb so the door can't swing against its hinges. To mark for stops, just close the door and draw the lines of the door's edges on the frame.

Check to see whether the frame is square, measure its height on both sides, then trim the door to fit. See above for clearances.

Now measure the frame's width, checking it at several points. If you have to plane the door, work towards the centre of each edge.

Unless the frame already has stops, you'll need help to prop the door in its opening. Square it up with shims at all edges.

Measure for hinge locations and mark them with pencil on the door. Solid-core doors should have three hinges. Position the upper hinge no less than 150 mm from the top and the lower hinge at least 230 mm from the floor.

When cutting a recess for a hinge flap, begin by scoring around the edges with a chisel. Take care you don't cut deeper than the thickness of the hinge flap.

Next, make a series of parallel cuts across the grain. Work from the side to knock out chips, then lay in the hinge flap. Ensure that it lies flush in the recess.

Screw the hinges to the door, set the door in place, mark around the hinges on the jamb and cut recesses for the flap. Finally, screw the hinges to the jamb.

Cutting in a doorway

If you've done little or no basic framing work, opening up an internal stud wall for a new doorway provides a great introduction. Just be sure to measure carefully and keep everything plumb and square.

Choose a location that won't involve having to move any plumbing. You may encounter wiring, in which case you must call for an electrician to relocate it.

Size the opening to match your new door and frame. Most require about 6 mm clearance all around.

BELOW: Solid doors are not always suitable in the interior of a house. In this hallway, a doorway was cut in and glass doors were installed so that light and warmth would still be retained in the sunroom.

BELOW: A whole wall of French doors in this extension means there is plenty of natural light and the owner has the ability to adjust the temperature inside by opening one or several of them at a time.

Choosing the right tools will make the job much easier. Use a hammer and chisel to break open a plaster wall. Cut wood lath with a saw; use snips on metal lath. A jigsaw or keyhole saw makes short work of cutting plasterboard.

Note that these instructions apply only to interior walls that are not load bearing.

Begin by marking stud locations. Open up the wall to the ceiling and nearest stud on each side of the new opening.

Before removing studs from the opening, measure down the appropriate distance from the ceiling. Make cuts along this line.

Build a header by skew-nailing a length of 100 x 50 mm timber between the studs on each side.

To save timber, locate one side of the opening against an existing stud. Then cut and fit door-height studs for each side of the opening. These add support for the header and make the doorway much more rigid.

Cut the bottom plate last. You may need a chisel and hammer to pry it out. Patch the floor if needed.

Making an opening in an internal masonry wall is somewhat more complex, because it is likely to be load bearing, and even if it isn't, steps must be taken to support the masonry above, as the door frame won't be strong enough. This means it will be necessary to add a concrete or steel lintel.

The first job is to cut a couple of small holes through the wall above the proposed opening and push

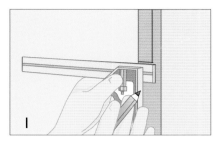
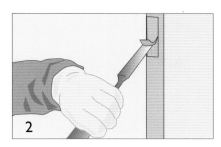
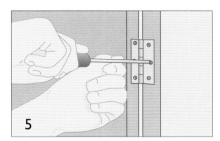
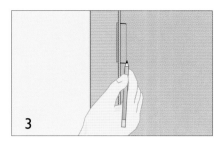
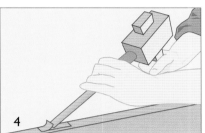
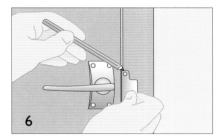

ABOVE: Hanging a door.

1 Mark the hinge positions on the door frame. Use a combination square to obtain the correct width of the hinge plate recess.

2 Drive the chisel blade into the wood at right angles to the surface to outline the hinge plate recess. Then pare out the waste wood, using the chisel bevelled edge down. Smooth the recess with the chisel held bevel edge up.

3 Wedge the door into the opening and transfer the hinge positions to the door.

4 Stand the door on edge and fix it securely. Outline and cut hinge plate recesses. Drill pilot holes for the screws and attach hinges.

5 Wedge door in place so that hinge plates fit in the recesses in the frame. Fit each hinge to the frame with one screw. Check the door closes and fit remaining screws.

6 Mark the position of the striker plate on the door frame. Cut its

stout lengths of timber through. These should be supported on each side of the wall by adjustable props. The props and timber will bear the weight of the wall above, allowing a slot to be cut above the proposed opening for the lintel, which should be mortared in place.

When the mortar has hardened, the props can be removed and the holes bricked up. The opening below the lintel can be chopped out. Keep the edges as neat as possible to reduce the amount of making good. If the floor is timber, remove masonry to below floor level and add a bridging section between the floors on each side of the wall.

Once the opening has been completed, the new frame can be screwed in place, the plasterwork made good and the door hung.

Closing up a doorway

Pry off skirtings on each side of the door, then slip a hacksaw blade between the frame and studs, or masonry, to cut the nails. Remove the frame in one piece.

Nail 100 x 50 mm timbers to the top, sides and bottom of the opening, then skew-nail a stud in the centre. Finish with plaster or plasterboard and replace the skirting.

Choosing and buying hinges

Most full-sized doors hang on butt hinges. Besides standard butts, there are special-purpose butts that close themselves, carry heavy loads on ball bearings, and even lift a door in mid-swing to clear carpeting.

If you're replacing a butt hinge, replace its mate, too. Before buying the new hinges, measure the old hinges, noting first their height, then their width when open. With some types, you may also need to know whether yours is a right- or left-hand door. A hinge's 'hand' refers to the side of the door it is installed on. To check this, stand opposite the door's swing.

Most hinges require recesses to be cut in both jamb and door edge for their flaps. These make the neatest installation.

For a half-mortise hinge, you cut a recess only in the jamb. You can fasten the hinge to the door with bolts for extra strength.

Surface-mounted hinges require no recesses at all. This arrangement works only on doors that are flush with their casings.

In general, both half-mortise and surface-mounted hinges are more likely to be found in use on outbuildings.

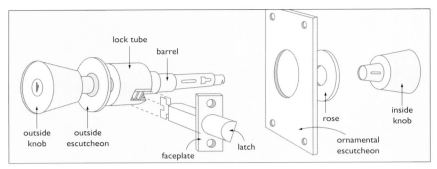

lock tube
barrel
outside knob
outside escutcheon
faceplate
latch
rose
ornamental escutcheon
inside knob

Installing a knob set

Interior knob-and-latch sets differ surprisingly little in overall design, although you can choose from a vast array of different styles and levels of quality. Some modern doors have a cylinder-type knob-and-latch, or a slight variation called the tubular lock. However, most will be found with the conventional mortise-type latch.

An older, defective knob and latch can easily be replaced with a new unit. Large-sized escutcheons will hide holes left by a separate knob-and-keyhole arrangement.

Measure the door's thickness before buying a knob set. Some units may fit a range of thicknesses; others only one.

If you're installing a knob set in a new door, you may need spade bits of various sizes to bore the necessary holes. Most companies provide fairly complete instructions, plus a template for locating the holes.

Be warned, too, that a cylinder set provides little protection for exterior doors or other points of entry to your home. These should be fitted with mortise dead locks.

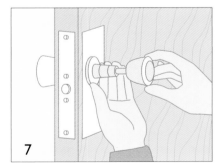

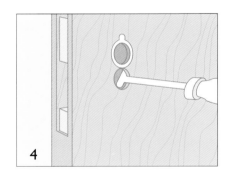

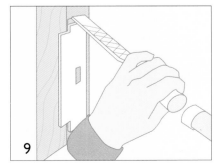

1 To remove an old mortise latch, take off the knobs, unscrew and pull out the latch assembly, and dismantle any trim pieces.

2 You'll probably need to rework the mortise to accommodate the new unit. Make adjustments with a file or chisel.

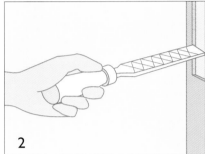

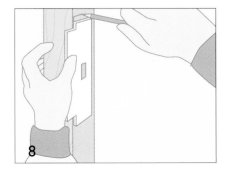

3 Now carefully position the new latch assembly as shown and mark where you must bore a hole through the door.

4 To avoid splintering, bore halfway through from one side, half from the other. Keep the bit perpendicular to the door's surface.

5 Slip in the latch assembly and fasten it with screws top and bottom. On new doors, locate knob sets 900 mm from the floor.

6 Install the escutcheons, then slip on the outside knob assembly. Most catches can be set for left- or right-hand operation.

7 Complete the door work by securing the rose, then the inside knob. Before tightening, make sure the latch works freely.

8 Now close the door, carefully locate the strike plate, then open and mark its position on the jamb with a sharp pencil.

9 You'll probably need to enlarge the original mortise both top and bottom.

Improving existing doors

Weather-stripping doors

A poorly weather-stripped exterior door can leak up to twice as much air as a window in the same condition. Couple this with the fact that most doors are used far more often than windows, and you can see why their seals merit a careful inspection every so often. First, check any existing weather stripping to see if it is crimped, flattened or missing altogether. You might be able to adjust spring metal – a commonly used door weather-stripping material – by bending it lightly. Other types probably will have to be replaced.

Next, feel along the threshold. Draughts here mean you need to add some form of barrier to stop air flow. And how about the door itself? A warped door or a frame that is out of square will give air a chance to get through even the tightest weather stripping.

Finally, check out any interior doors that open to an attic, garage, basement or similar unheated space. Builders often don't bother to seal these at all, but they can lead to substantial heat losses and draughts. Worse yet, some cut costs by installing hollow-core doors at these points. If that's the case in your house, you might save on heating bills and make the house more comfortable by investing in the far greater thermal efficiency of a solid- or foam-core door.

There are many types of seal you can use on doors. Some are more effective and durable than others:

- Foam tape installs easily. Just cut strips to length, peel off the backing and press in place on the inside of the door stops.

- Tack rolled vinyl stripping to the stops' faces. Align so that the bulbous edge projects a bit.

- Nail spring-metal strips to the jamb inside the stop. With this type, be sure to fit carefully around the latch and any locks.

- Interlocking metal channels form a good seal, but are tricky to align. You must nail them to both the door and the stops.

- Metal 'J-strips' look and seal best, but they're most difficult to install because you must rout a channel in the door.

- Use special insulated moulding to seal the gap between double doors. Nail it to the face of the door that's usually closed.

French doors filter light and allow the air to flow through the house. Here they provide direct access from the dining room to the garden.

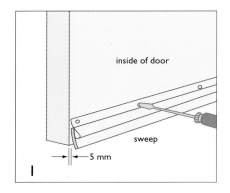

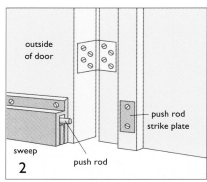

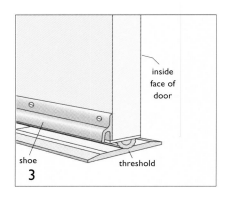

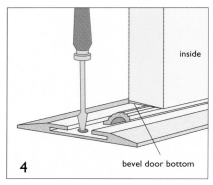

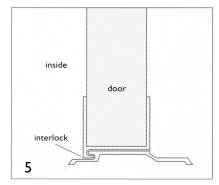

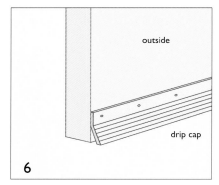

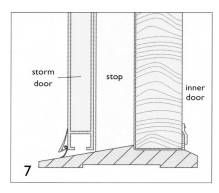

Sealing underneath doors

A door's bottom edge poses two special weather-stripping problems. First, the sill, or threshold, across the bottom of the frame has to withstand lots of traffic and may become worn. Second, any seal you attach to the door itself must be able to clear any carpeting or unevenness on the floor within the arc the door traverses.

The devices shown here solve these difficulties with varying degrees of effectiveness. If your door has a badly worn sill, consider replacing it with one of these or with a wooden version.

1 A sweep works fairly well if the floor is relatively even. You simply attach it so the sweep seals against the threshold.

2 An automatic sweep uses a spring action to hoist itself up as you open the door, then drops down again when you close it.

3 A shoe on the door's lower edge makes a durable seal. To install one, you'll have to remove the door and possibly plane it, too.

4 A bulb threshold works like a non-moving shoe. Bevel the door bottom. You'll need to replace the bulb periodically.

5 Interlocking thresholds make the tightest seal. Installing one calls for some tricky carpentry work and fitting, though.

6 If your door lets water into the house, nail a metal drip cap to its outside face. Stop air with a bulb threshold.

7 Don't forget to check weather stripping under storm doors, too. You can buy replacement rubber or plastic sweeps for these types of doors.

8 To weather-strip the bottom edge of a roll-up or swing-up garage door, you can purchase a special gasket.

Restoring a door

Many a dim room can be brightened up by replacing the wooden panels of a panelled door with glass, allowing light to spill through. It's a great idea for a poorly-lit hallway, but is also an excellent lighting trick to play anywhere in the house. If privacy is required, use frosted or patterned glass instead of completely transparent panels.

LEFT: Solid timber doors with inset glass panels look equally attractive as front entrance doors or internal doors. Doors such as the one shown here can often be bought for a reasonable price from architectural salvage companies. They can be transformed by stripping and staining or repainting.

BELOW: Restoring a door.

1 Carefully lever beading off so the timber is not damaged.

2 Pull out nails with pincers.

3 Drill a hole at each inner corner of the beading line. Use a jigsaw to remove the rectangle formed by the holes. (The beading on the other side of the door remains.)

4 Clean the rebate.

5 Apply putty to the rebate.

1

2

3

4

5

6

7

8

9

6 Press in the pre-cut glass panel, with the smooth side facing you if the glass is rippled or etched.

7 Secure the glass with pins.

8 Apply a little putty to the beading you have removed.

9 Secure with skew nails, punch in, fill and sand. Finish the door as desired.

BELOW LEFT: The timber on this door has been stripped and sanded. Coloured glass was used as a border with a transparent panel in the centre to provide a clear view to the next room.

Tips

Painting doors and windows

- When painting windows, work from the inside out, start with the glazing bars and progress to the sashes, casing, lintel and sill. Use an angled cutting-in brush for narrow sections of the frame. If your hand is unsteady, use a paint shield or apply masking tape around the edges of the panes.

- As with windows, paint doors from the inside out and start with any recessed panels. Mini-rollers and foam pads speed painting of narrow portions of the door. For tight spots, use an angled cutting-in brush.

Fitting a new external door frame

A common problem with external door frames is rot. You may be able to repair a rotten door frame if the rot has not travelled too far. Using a saw, make a 45° cut well above the rotted wood. Lever the rotted piece away from the wall. Size the new wood using the old piece as a template. Seal the new wood and the newly cut end of the frame with a preservative. Fix the new piece into place with countersunk screws and wall plugs. If the rot has weakened the timber, you may have to replace the frame.

Removing the old frame

To remove a doorframe, chop away any mortar or sealant around the edge of the frame to open up a gap between the frame and wall. Then insert a hacksaw blade and cut through each fixing you encounter.

At this stage, you could lever and/or drive the frame out of the opening in one piece. If it is stuck, however, cut through the jambs, and head and lever it out in pieces. You may find that the head projects beyond the frame at each end, the resulting 'horns' being mortared into the brickwork, and these may need chopping free.

Fitting the new frame

Assemble the new frame, skew-nailing or screwing the jambs to the sill. Add a length of dpc material to the underside of the sill to protect it from rising damp. Then offer up the frame to the opening, propping it in place and checking that it is upright in both planes. The frame can be fixed in place by the same means as the old one, that is, nailed to wooden wedges, attached to brackets mortared into the brickwork or secured with frame fixings. Seal with a flexible mastic or mortar. Then make good any damaged plasterwork inside.

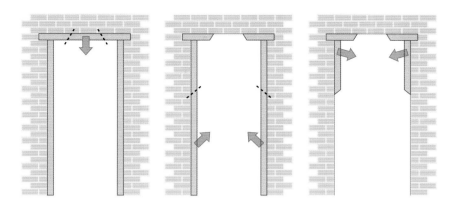

ABOVE: Removing an old door frame.

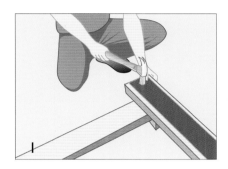

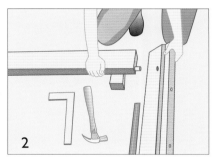

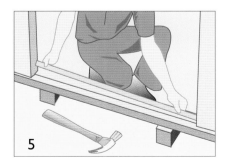

ABOVE: Installing a door frame

1 Nail dpc material to the underside of the sill, painting the nail heads with bituminous emulsion to protect them from rust.

2 Assemble the sill to the jambs of the frame and skew-nail or screw them together.

3 Lift the frame into the opeining, setting it in the correct position. Wedge it in place, making sure that it is upright using a spirit level and that the sill is the correct height.

4 Drill through frame into the wall and secure it with frame fixings.

5 Apply a bead of mastic to the groove in the sill and press the metal weather bar into it firmly.

How to keep your home secure

Nearly four out of five household burglaries occur in broad daylight. It would seem that most robbers like to work the same hours you do.

Insurance companies warn that only about a quarter of the houses broken into have adequate security at the point of entry. Fortunately, you can make your home safer by upgrading the security on your doors, and there is a wide range of devices to choose from.

Patio doors

A broom handle or dowel laid in the bottom track of a patio door is an effective security device if the door cannot be lifted out of the frame.

A patio door pin is simply a chrome pin that keeps two doors together when placed in a hole drilled through the frames.

Anti-lift plates can be fitted in the head track of the frame to prevent lifting. They also can be used on sliding windows.

Patio door bolts are 10-mm-thick bolts that lock the stile to the frame at the head and/or floor.

The handle fitted to your sliding door should operate anti-lift pins to prevent the door from being lifted off its track. It should also be capable of being deadlocked from inside and out for double security. If it doesn't have these features, consider replacing the door.

Timber doors

The door chain, that old favourite, is now available in a keyed version. Also available is a door guard, a bit like a hasp and staple.

Interlocking deadlocks feature a clutching action that interlocks with the striker. They are available with single or double cylinders.

Deadbolts are very secure bolts that can't be opened without a key

ABOVE: A selection of locks and sensor lights for doors and windows.

FAR LEFT: For complete security this keypad provides access by PIN number only.

LEFT: Brass deadlock suitable for domestic doors.

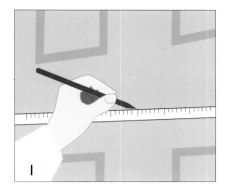

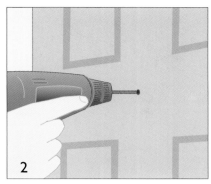

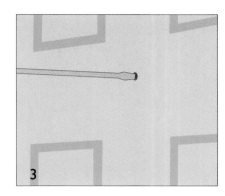

and are difficult to wrench off or cut. They have the advantage that the bolt itself enters the frame. They can be placed a third of the way up the door to provide extra strength against it being kicked in.

The double-cylinder deadlock locks inside and out, and easily covers marks left by previous night latches. Combined with a door frame strengthener, it gives greater protection against intruders kicking in the door.

The digital lock, a variation of the deadlock, is opened by tapping in your own entry code, which is easy to remember if you use your bank PIN.

There are locks available for internal doors, but the consensus is that once intruders have gained access, they won't be inhibited about making noise and will simply smash doors down.

Fitting a security door viewer

The lens in a door viewer allows you to see what is happening outside the door over quite a wide angle. It is easy enough to fit to any door, whether solid or hollow, from 32 to 51 mm thick.

Fitting a safety chain

A safety chain on a timber front or back door allows you to open the door marginally to see who's calling, but won't afford an opening sufficient for anyone to enter. It also doubles the security of a lock

and makes you feel a great deal more comfortable about being home alone.

Use a hefty safety chain, preferably one made from stainless steel. The screws supplied with it must be stout and at least 38 mm long (50 mm is better).

Position the safety chain close to the lock on a hollow-core door (so that you'll have something solid to screw to) and mark the screw holes. With solid timber doors, the height is up to you. The fitting with the chain mounts to the frame's jamb.

Pre-drill each screw hole to suit the shank size, and no deeper than the shank's length. Then continue the hole with a twist drill that matches the average diameter of the core of the screw around which the thread is formed. Drill to a depth slightly greater than the length of the screw.

Select a screwdriver that fits the head of the screw. It should be slightly narrower than the head diameter and fit tightly across the width. Excess movement when tightening the screw could cause the screwdriver to turn out of the screw head and damage the slot.

Drive in all the screws until they are tight. Slip on the chain. The chain should be long enough to reach between the two fittings, allowing the door to open a few centimetres so that you can see a caller without allowing the person the opportunity to enter.

ABOVE: Fitting a security door viewer.

1 With a tape measure and pencil, mark the centre of the door at a comfortable eye level.

2 Drill a 3 mm hole and then, using it as a guide, drill from both sides of the door with a 13 mm drill bit.

3 Screw the two halves of the viewer in from both sides of the door. When choosing the viewer, make sure you select one with as wide an angle of vision as possible.

Tip

- French doors look attractive, but securing them satisfactorily can be a problem. Installing heavy-duty barrel bolts top and bottom, plus a quality rebate lock, will help provide you with good protection.

Windows

Because we use windows to allow natural light inside the house and provide a view of the outdoors, we seldom notice them. But occasionally, when an errant ball finds its way through a glass pane, when a sash absolutely refuses to budge, or when a wooden frame begins to rot, windows make their presence known. This chapter has been written for those occasions.

ABOVE: If a pitched ceiling is a part of your renovation, this window treatment may give you some ideas. Sliding sashes, capped by a fixed semi-circular window, French doors and vertical, dado-height panelling create a very attractive room.

You should realise, however, that with proper maintenance you can do a great deal to prevent some window problems. To keep windowsills from rotting, for example, make sure they always have a protective coat of paint.

Check windows regularly. To keep sliding sashes working, occasionally clean the channels they ride in. You will be amazed at how smoothly you can make hinged and pivoting windows operate with a periodic squeeze of powdered graphite or a drop of penetrating oil in and around their mechanisms.

On the following pages, you'll find the solutions to a host of window problems, including balky sashes, broken panes, damaged sills and many others. No longer will you have to go to the expense of employing a repairer or, worse, ignore the repair completely.

The link between house and garden

Windows give your house its own personality. But as well as making an impact on the interior and exterior, windows themselves can possess personality. When small, they can imply secrecy, intimacy and protection. Conversely, they are extroverted, welcoming and all-embracing when large. Medium-sized, they are just right. If a window is less than perfectly proportioned, its decorative (and frequently functional) treatment can create an illusion that will solve the proportion problem, and promote the window from being a mere donor of light and fresh air to a focus for beauty. Additions and alterations to windows can make an incredible difference to a room and invariably to the whole house.

A window can also grow out into the garden if it is given sides, a base

and a sloping roof and pushed beyond the wall to create a miniature 'conservatory' or 'glasshouse'. This type of window is known as an oriel window, and it is a wonderful way of adding extra light and an unprecedented feeling of space to a dark, small room.

Window types

Anatomy of a sliding-sash window

Often, there's more to a window than meets the eye. That's especially the case with the sliding-sash type shown on the next page. Its secrets include heavy sash weights concealed behind the frame's jambs. Connected via a rope-and-pulley system, the weights provide counterbalances that not only make the sashes easier to open, but also hold them in any vertical position you choose.

ABOVE: This charming little bathroom window, allows an extra-wide tiled sill. The hardwood frame stands up to moisture and is very suitable for bathrooms.

LEFT: Conservatory-style windows can transform as well as extend your living area. If the addition is to house plants, use a floor surface that is appropriate to the use.

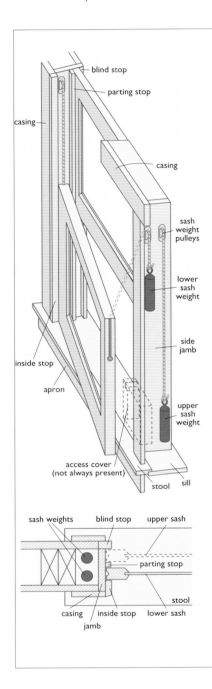

to rest behind a flat stool; its outer counterpart, the sill, slopes so water can run off. Trim – called casing at the sides and top, and an apron below – covers any gaps between the frame and wall.

Anatomy of a casement window

Casement windows open and close outwards, the sash being hinged to the frame at one side or the other. Construction is very similar to a door and frame. The sash may contain a single pane of glass or several smaller panes held by glazing bars. A simple pivoting catch is fitted to the sash, while at the bottom a peg and stay allow the sash to be held open at a number of positions and lock the window closed. In some cases, a small, top-hinged sash, or vent, is fitted above the main sash and secured with a peg and stay.

Anatomy of a sliding window

In some cases, you may come across horizontal sliding sashes. There may be one fixed and one sliding sash or two sliding sashes, which run on continuous tracks.

ABOVE: Consider two tall vertical windows instead of one large horizontal one to add a classic elegance to your rooms. These are double-hung, powder-coated aluminium with fixed glazing bars.

FAR LEFT: Anatomy of a double-hung window.

LEFT: Anatomy of a sliding window.

BELOW: Anatomy of a casement window.

A series of stops fitted to the jambs form channels in which the sashes slide. Check the top view and note that although the outside blind stop is more or less permanently affixed, the parting stop and inside stop can be pried loose if you want to remove the sashes.

Modern sliding-sash windows do away with the weight-and-pulley and use spring lift devices. In some cases, the lower, inner sash comes

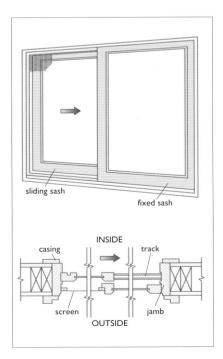

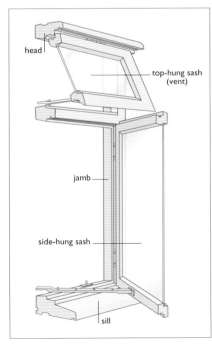

Anatomy of a pivot window

Constructed in similar fashion to a casement window, the pivot window has its sash mounted on a pair of special pivoting hinges, which allow the sash to be turned beyond 90° for easy cleaning. A limiting stay can be fitted to this type of window to prevent it from being opened beyond a certain point.

Anatomy of a louvre window

Louvre windows let in lots of air, the operating mechanism pivoting a series of glass slats for maximum flow control. The frames consist of short metal channels at each end of the slats. Those glass-to-glass joints tend to leak air, so usually you will find louvres only in areas that normally are not heated.

BELOW: Use windows as a decorative and practical room divider.

RIGHT: Custom-built windows can be any shape or size. This renovation made the most of the pitched roof with a sturdy sculptural window system.

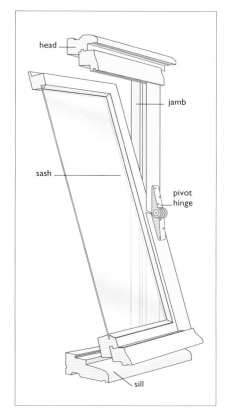

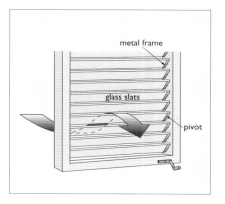

ABOVE: Anatomy of a louvre window.

LEFT: Anatomy of a pivot window.

Improving natural light

There are both major and minor ways of improving the flow of natural light into your house. If you need to make major changes, chances are your house is an old one. Old houses are definitely the worst offenders when it comes to dark rooms.

It's not that people once disliked light and built houses in such a way as to block it out – although you could be excused for thinking so. It's just that old-fashioned small windows have been replaced as a result of a revolution in the making of glass, frames and other window-related technology.

Major renovations

A common, major renovation is to install floor-to-ceiling sliding glass patio doors in place of narrow, heavily-framed French doors, allowing in masses of light, and giving the effect of bringing the garden or patio 'inside' as well.

A more radical major renovation might be to replace an entire wall or part of one with glass bricks, either clear or frosted, depending on privacy requirements.

Removing unnecessary dividing walls also qualifies as a major change. The fewer the walls and doors, the more light can flow through the whole house.

Tips

- Before you begin renovating or extending, collect lots of pictures and ideas for windows from magazines and brochures. Eventually, the style that you really like will become apparent.
- If the existing windows in your home are tall and narrow, your new windows should be also.

BELOW: A new bay window in traditional style.

Inspirational windows

Window design can set the tone of your home. Today you can choose from a very wide range of single- and double-glazed units in wood, aluminium and plastic. These duplicate many early styles of window, including leaded lights, as well as providing modern designs, so you should have no trouble in matching the architecture of your home. If you're planning a renovation, the ideas pictured here may inspire you to create an interesting arrangement to suit your natural lighting needs. If you don't want to use stock windows, you can have a local joiner make something unique.

ABOVE: Floor to ceiling glass provides a dramatic glimpse of the outside.

RIGHT: Painted timber venetian blinds filter the light.

ABOVE: The mirror's position gives the illusion of space and reflected light plays on these classic windows.

LEFT: A fixed pane in a cosy corner beside a door.

ABOVE RIGHT: Wraparound windows can easily stop at normal windowsill height.

BELOW RIGHT: The absence of a corner window mullion and floor-to-ceiling glass give the wraparound window an unobstructed outlook.

Corner windows

Windows that wrap around corners are a design feature that regularly comes back into fashion. Now, however, they've returned with a stylish refinement.

By placing verticals or posts approximately 300 mm on each side of the corner, overhead lintels can be cantilevered without needing support where they meet at the corner. This means that the two panes of glass can meet with only a silicon seam to waterproof the join.

Because we are used to seeing the corners of our houses boxed in, the effect of them seeming to be supported by glass alone is both very stylish and eye-catching.

This type of design detail was originally seen in commercial architecture only. However, there is no reason why it could not be adapted to a domestic situation. Obviously, careful planning would be required, and an architect would need to draw up the plans and specify the materials for the job, which should be entrusted to a builder.

ABOVE: In the form of a large glass gable, this 'dormer' is lined beneath the roof's collar ties. Vertical blinds are one of the few ways of furnishing triangular window shapes.

ABOVE RIGHT: The space under this dormer was designed to take a double bed. The sill height coincides with the low, unusable section of the roof cavity and lines up with the low vertical walls.

BELOW RIGHT: The traditional proportions of the single dormer in this attic bedroom project outwards from the main roof, starting close to the ridge. The alcove provides a head-clearance area on the low sloping side of the room.

Tip

• Plan a gabled dormer to have the same pitch as the roof of the house; this ensures that it doesn't look like an afterthought.

Dormer windows

The word 'dormer' traditionally refers to a small roof shape, with a vertical window, which projects out from the main roof pitch to allow light into an attic room.

Until recently, dormers were most commonly seen on period-style buildings, but now they can be found in contemporary architectural designs. The dormer is seen as an attractive device that is also practical, as it turns a roof cavity into a usable space.

The modern-day popularity of the dormer has led to variations on its original format. Today's dormers can sit back from the facade of your house or be a continuation of it; they can spread across an entire roof or be scaled down to become an incidental roofing shape. In a bungalow, you could use them to channel light into ground-floor rooms. The photographs here will give you some idea of construction technique, but note that many builders claim that adding a dormer is one of the most difficult building tasks. So you should seek expert help before you attempt to turn your dormer dreams into reality.

Shutters

Louvred shutters are common in hot parts of the world. They allow the heat of the sun to be shut out, while permitting some light to enter a room and the windows and doors to be opened for fresh air. They provide privacy, too. In cooler regions, they make unusual, decorative features.

You can adapt ready-made louvre doors – designed for wardrobes – to make shutters. Alternatively, you can make your own.

ABOVE RIGHT: Custom-made solid shutters.

FAR RIGHT: Shutters become an integral part of the wall.

RIGHT: Two part bi-fold shutters give plenty of options.

BELOW: Floor-to-ceiling shutters allow both light and privacy.

ABOVE: Window locks provide essential security on windows not covered by external bars. A keyed security lock for a window can be combined with the closing mechanism to make it unobtrusive.

RIGHT: Use a keyed sash lock or security lock to secure ground floor sash windows such as this.

Tips

- Save window cleaning for a dull day. Bright sunlight will dry the windows too quickly, leaving smears on the glass.
- Polish with a pad of newspaper, the printers' ink will buff and prevent a smeared surface.

Fitting an architrave to a window

Varying the profile of an architrave and adding detail at each top corner will enable you to dictate a room's mood and period.

Architraves are simply timber mouldings. Try to find a moulding that matches the original at your local timber yard.

1 Measure the height and width of the window to determine the inside measurement of the pieces of architrave and where they should be cut.
2 Cut the mitred joints on the architrave, sawing on the waste side of the pencilled lines.
3 Nail the architrave to the window frame at the top, bottom and centre, but don't drive the nails home until all pieces are in position and their alignment has been checked.

4 Drive nails home and add extra nails at 300 mm spacings. Punch the nail heads below the surface of the timber, fill, sand and finish.

Window locks

The extensive use of glass in our homes makes it relatively easy for burglars to smash or cut their way in. However, you can make it difficult for them to remove your belongings if you install deadlocks on external doors and keyed locks on all the windows. Unless the burglars can locate the keys, they can't open anything and are forced to clamber out through a window edged with broken glass.

Putting locks on timber windows is relatively easy; it may even reduce your insurance premiums and, better still, may considerably reduce the likelihood of burglary.

Purchase locks that need a single master key. Keep the key in a secure, secret spot. Locks featuring one-way screws are the best to install; a one-way screw can be driven in, but can't be unscrewed.

Installing a window lock

Make sure the type and number of locks you select will suit your windows. If you're unsure, ask at your hardware or DIY store.

Window locks

More than 50 per cent of break-ins are through windows, so that makes them your number-one weak point. Listed below are window types and the locks that will suit them.

Sliding-sash windows

- keyed sash lock;
- keyed security bolt, with various-sized bolts to suit either timber or aluminium windows.

Both locks can be easily installed and have optional one-way screws to prevent removal.

Casement windows

- keyed security bolt;
- window bolt.

Again, one-way screws are recommended.

Sliding windows

- keyed security bolt;
- sliding-window push lock.

The sliding window push lock is slimmer, as it is intended for aluminium windows. It also prevents the window from being lifted out of its tracks and can be locked in a partly open position to allow ventilation.

Pivot windows

- keyed security bolt;
- window bolt.

Most bolts that can be fitted to a standard casement window will work on a pivot window.

There are more sophisticated options to these standard types, among them simple push-button locks, and locks that operate by turning a knob. In both cases, a key is required to release the lock. For windows that are opened only occasionally, there are screw-down types that require a special key to tighten and release them. By fitting the same type of lock to as many different windows as possible, you will reduce the number of keys required.

BELOW: Installing a window lock.

1 Carefully read the instructions supplied with your chosen lock. Place the fitting in its recommended position and accurately mark around the screw holes with a sharp pencil or, alternatively, use a punch.

2 Using the correct-sized drills, pre-drill the holes, first for the screws and then for the locking bar. Drive the nail 3–4 mm into the centre of each screw position before drilling; this will help keep drill holes in the correct place. Drill the hole for the locking bar with a drill bit of a largish diameter, which will be easier to turn with an electric drill.

3 Screw the fittings on with the 'one-way' screws and test. Continue until all the windows are lockable.

1

2

3

Solving window problems

When a window binds or refuses to budge, don't try to force it – you risk damaging the sash, the frame or both. Instead, take a look around the sash's perimeter, both inside and out. Chances are, you'll find that paint has sealed the window shut or that a stop moulding has warped. Both difficulties usually respond to the gentle techniques described below.

With sliding-sash windows, the culprit also could be a faulty spring lift or a broken sash cord. Having to replace these involves dismantling the window, which is not as difficult as it sounds.

BELOW: Freeing a balky sash.

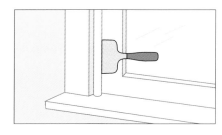

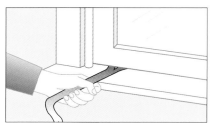

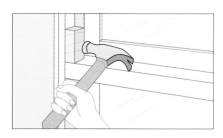

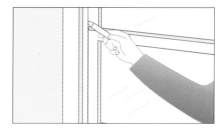

Repairing sliding-sash windows

Freeing a balky sash

To break a paint seal, tap a broad-bladed scraper between the sash and window stop, then work it back and forth. Alternatively, try prying from outside with a wide-bladed tool such as a crowbar. Work right around the window's perimeter until the sash pops free.

If a sash is binding between its stops, you can often separate them slightly by tapping along their length with a wooden block.

Tips

- Don't paint sash cords. It makes them brittle and prone to jam and snap. Parting and stop beads are quite common mouldings and should be readily available from good timber suppliers and some DIY stores.
- Check the conditions of the pulleys. They can rust and damage the cords. They are easy to replace.
- Be careful not to mix up the weights. They are fitted to suit specific sashes.

Once you get the window moving again, lightly sand its jambs, then lubricate by rubbing with a candle or a bar of soap.

Replacing sash cords

Working from inside the window, first remove the stop (or staff) bead that holds the inner sash in place. Use a craft knife to break the paint seal with the frame, then use a chisel to prise it loose. It should bow enough to pop the ends out of the mitre joints. If not, push it back in place and pull the nails out (bowing the bead will have made them show through the paint). It should now come out quite easily. It is often possible to remove the inner sash after removing the stop bead on one side. If not, take out the other, then carefully lift out the sash.

If one sash cord is broken, it's wise to assume they're all worn and replace them all at the same time. If only the knot at the counterweight has come undone and there are no obvious signs of wear, it is probably safe to deal just with the problem at hand. After removing the inner sash, disconnect the sash cord (mark where the end of the cord comes to on the sash and pull out the nails). If any counterweights are still attached, tack the end of the cord to the main window frame so they don't drop down inside.

Right at the bottom of the frame is the weight pocket cover. Remove enough of the parting bead (often this is not nailed) to expose the cover and open it up

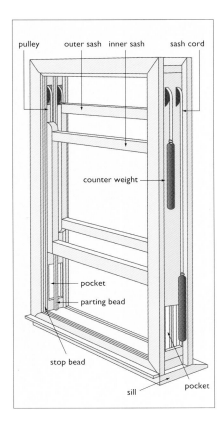

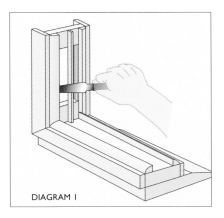

DIAGRAM 1

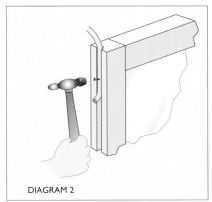

DIAGRAM 2

bottom, the cord is too short. Make any necessary adjustment, then tap in a couple of more nails.

Replace the pocket cover, the outer sash if it was removed, the parting beads and the inner sash. When replacing the stop bead, you should try to use the same nails and holes to ensure a neat fit. Add a couple of extra nails to keep them tight. The repaired sash should slide up and down easily.

ABOVE: Replacing sash cords.

BELOW: This sash window-cum-door glides up to allow access to the enclosed verandah beyond.

(see diagram 1, above right). It will be screwed or nailed in place. The weights and broken cords can now be reached, and cords retied or replaced. Measure the old cords (if broken, join the bits together) and make the new cords the same length (add a little extra for possible adjustment later). Use a piece of string with a small weight attached (a mouse), such as a bent nail, to feed the new cord over the pulley and down the weight passage. Thread the cord through the top of the weight and tie into a double knot.

Attach the other end of the cord to the sash, lining it up with the mark, and fix it with a single clout nail (see diagram 2, above right). Make sure the nail is further down from the top of the sash than the distance from the top of the frame to the centre of the pulley. Try the sash in the frame when both cords are attached. If the weight hits the bottom when the sash is at the top, the fixing nail is too high up the sash. If the sash doesn't reach the

Adjusting spring lifts

Tube-type lifting devices include a spring-driven twist rod or spring that helps lift the sash and hold it in place. Before tampering with one of these, first check that the window hasn't been painted shut. But if the device doesn't seem to be working at all, it's probably broken and needs to be replaced.

Get a good grip on the tube before you remove the screw that is holding it to the jamb. Otherwise, the spring will unwind in a hurry.

If the window sails up and down too easily, hang on to the screw and then let the spring turn for a couple of revolutions.

If the window is hard to move, tighten the spring by turning it clockwise. You may need to adjust both lifts.

Replacing spring lifts

Begin by removing the inner stop from one side of the window. This should make enough room to remove the sash.

Next, remove the screw that secures the tube, allow the spring to unwind, then pull out the sash. You may need to pry it a little.

Remove the twist rod/tube unit and replace it with a new one. Then re-install the sash and adjust the tension as described.

Repairing casement windows

Casement windows may stick because the frame has become loose or because the timber has

swollen from the damp or from a build-up of paint. Take out the sash – it's only a matter of removing a few screws. Lay the window on a flat surface. Fit two sash cramps, being careful not to overtighten them and crack the glass, and square the frame. Screw through the side of the frame to tighten up the joints, countersinking the screws and plugging the holes with dowels. If the wood is at all suspect, it may be necessary to fit metal angle plates at the corners instead.

Before refitting, sand the window back to the bare timber and repaint. Be cautious of old lead paint. Wear a dust mask and carefully vacuum any dust for disposal in sealed bags.

When putty is not protected by paint, it tends to crack and fall out. Carefully hack out any suspect putty and replace it, using a putty knife. Ask the hardware store for the putty or glazing compound to suit your frame type.

To replace glass, measure the opening, allowing 3 mm for clearance and lay your new glass in a 3-mm-deep bed of putty. Secure the pane with small nails or triangu-

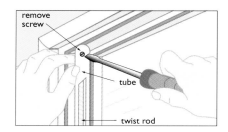

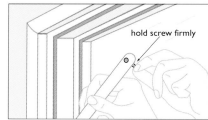

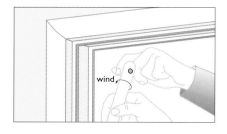

ABOVE: Adjusting spring lifts.

BELOW: Replacing spring lifts.

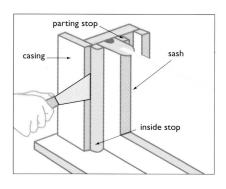

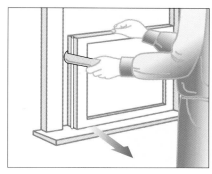

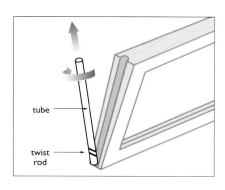

lar glazing sprigs) at 200 mm centres, then apply more putty to the depth of the rebate. Smooth off the surface, dipping the putty knife in water to stop it sticking to the putty. Clean surplus putty off the glass with white spirit.

Heavy accumulations of paint, grease or dirt cause most casement window difficulties. If you have one that's malfunctioning, open it wide and check all sash and frame edges. Usually, a few minutes with a wire brush, scraper or some sandpaper will remove the problem. If not, partially close the sash and check its fit. Wooden sashes sometimes suffer from the same warping, swelling and out-of-square problems that can bedevil doors.

Finally, examine the unit's mechanical components. You'll probably need only a screwdriver and the right lubricant to set things right.

Bent, sagging or loose hinges will throw a sash out of alignment. Replace, shim or tighten them up. Tighten loose latch screws. If a handle won't pull its sash snug, shim under it or – with lipped windows – add weather-stripping.

If a wooden sash has warped, try counter-warping it by inserting wood strips between it and the frame. Leave them in place for a couple of weeks.

Servicing operators

Some casement windows are fitted with operator mechanisms, most of which consist of a sliding or scissor-arm that may or may not be driven by a geared cranking device.

If a sash isn't opening and closing smoothly, check its arm first. Look to see if loose screws, bent metal stays, rust and caked grease or paint are interfering with the action. Next, turn your attention to the cranking system. You may have to remove it for servicing.

A sill-mounted sliding-shoe device traps dirt. Unscrew the channel, clean it and the sill, then lubricate both with candle wax.

To keep the crank assemblies turning freely, apply a few drops of light oil.

To dismantle an operator, first disconnect its arm from the sash, then remove the screws that hold it to the frame.

If the gears are encrusted with old grease, soak the unit in a solvent, then repack it with a multi-purpose lubricant.

Sometimes you can free jammed gears with a coat-hanger. If they're stripped or badly worn, replace the entire assembly.

Repairing sliding windows

To keep sliding windows moving smoothly, clear any paint or debris from their tracks and lubricate with candle wax or silicone lubricant. When a slider jams, binds or jumps loose, you will usually find that something's lodged in the lower track or that the track itself is bent.

If everything seems clear and straight, lift out the sash and check its grooved edges. Clean and wax these, too, if necessary.

Bigger windows and sliding glass doors roll on sets of nylon wheels, which are self-lubricating and rarely need attention. If a wheel has been damaged, remove the assembly and replace it.

To remove a sliding sash for repair, unlock and partially open the window, then lift it and flip its lower edge towards you.

To straighten a bent track, cut a wooden block that just fits in the channel, then carefully tap the soft metal against it.

'Catch-and-dog' window latches sometimes get bent out of shape. Adjust them so that the dog's 'hind leg' hits against the catch.

Repairing pivot windows

Pivot windows operate much like casements and require the same type of repair procedures.

ABOVE: Ensure window frames are well-maintained with regular painting.

BELOW: Repairing sliding windows.

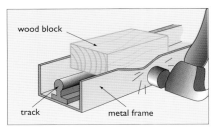

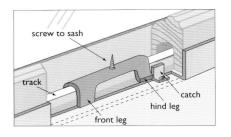

Keep latches, hinges and any other mechanisms moving freely. If you neglect an arm assembly on a projecting type that's too stiff, it could pull screws loose, or even force sash joints apart. Clean off any rust with steel wool, and lubricate with graphite; never use oil – it attracts dust.

To remove a pivot sash, open it up as far as you can, then disconnect any stay or operating arm.

Now tilt the sash to a horizontal position, get a helper to support it and unscrew its hinges. Lift the window free from its frame, taking care not to damage the latter.

Repairing louvre windows

Louvre windows resemble venetian blinds, except that instead of cords and tapes, their mechanisms depend on a series of pivots, gears and levers that may be partly or entirely concealed within the jambs. This makes louvre windows relatively difficult to repair; often you have to dismantle the entire window to get at its vertical arms. If your unit jams, try freeing it with graphite or another non-oil lubricant.

Simple tab-like clips hold the glass louvre slats in place. To remove one, just bend open the tab and slide out the pane. Note that replacement panes should have their edges rounded off.

Don't force a balky operating mechanism. Instead, lubricate all pivot points, then work the handle back and forth.

Getting balky operator mechanisms operating again

Start by opening the window far enough to disengage the arm from the track in which the arm slides. Clean both the track and the portion of the arm that connects to the track with a rag soaked in alcohol or cleaning liquid. Lubricate with a light grease or petroleum jelly.

Next, squeeze penetrating oil into all pivot points and work the

parts back and forth until things loosen up. Wipe off any excess oil. The final step is to remove the operator itself – if possible – and coat the mechanism with a liberal amount of light grease. Replace the operator mechanism and test the window movement to determine if your effort has paid off.

If it hasn't, the only solution may be to replace the operating mechanism, if this is possible (contact the manufacturer to check). However, if it is not removable, or you can't find the manufacturer, you may be faced with no other solution than to remove the entire window and replace it with a new one.

Snugging up a sash

After lots of use, many windows, particularly wooden-framed types can become warped and will no longer close tightly, letting in draughts. You can remedy this problem by installing extra weather-stripping or shimming.

Replacing broken windows

Expect to pay dearly if a repairer comes to your house to replace a broken pane of glass, which is a good reason to do the job yourself. The techniques for repairing wood- and metal-framed sashes differ considerably, but neither is difficult. Be sure to wear thick leather gloves when you work with glass panes.

Reglazing wood-framed windows

1   Start by removing any loose shards of broken glass, then use an old wood chisel to hack out the putty or glazing compound that holds the pane in place. (You may be able to soften the compound with a propane torch.) Remove the old glazing sprigs or nails that held the pane in place.

2   Determine the size of the replacement pane needed by

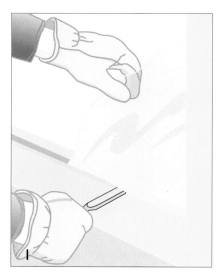

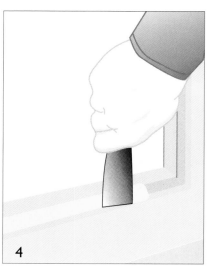

ABOVE: Reglazing wood-framed windows.

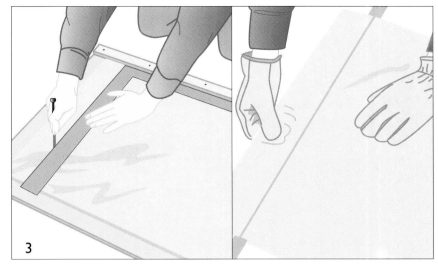

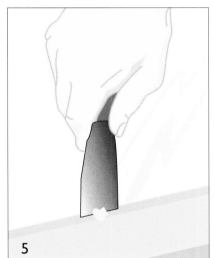

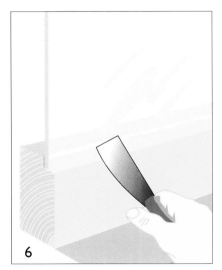

measuring the opening. Subtract 3 mm from each dimension.

3 Have a glass supplier cut your new pane to size, or cut your own by making a single score along each cut line with a glass cutter guided by a steel framing square. Then place a matchstick under each end of the scored line and press down to snap off the scrap piece. Trim any rough edges by nipping the glass with pliers.

4 Prime the rebated area of the frame with linseed oil, wait 20 minutes, then apply a 2 mm bed of putty or glazing compound.

5 Position the glass pane, insert matchsticks around the edge to centre the glass, and then press into the putty or glazing compound. Install two metal glazing sprigs or small nails per side, driving them in carefully by sliding the hammer head against the glass.

6 To complete, roll some putty or glazing compound into a 6 mm 'rope' and press it around the edges of the glass rebate.

7 Bevel the putty or compound with a putty knife held at a 30–40° angle. Allow a week for it to dry, then paint around the new pane, overlap the paint on to the glass by 2 mm for a tight weather seal.

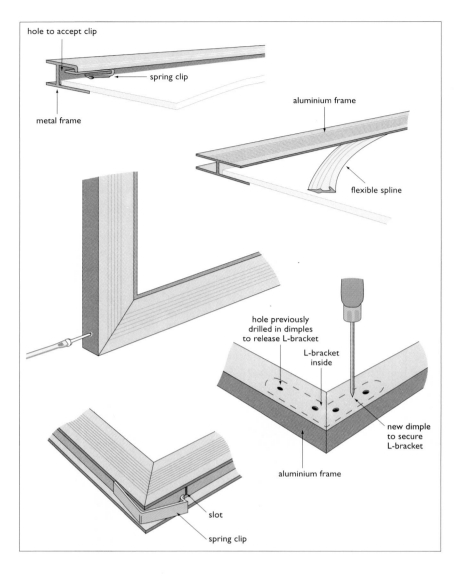

hole to accept clip

spring clip

metal frame

aluminium frame

flexible spline

hole previously drilled in dimples to release L-bracket

L-bracket inside

new dimple to secure L-bracket

aluminium frame

slot

spring clip

ABOVE: Reglazing metal-framed windows.

Reglazing metal-framed windows

Metal sashes come in a variety of configurations. Some are of one-piece construction in which glass is held in place by removable metal clips (augmented by glazing compound) or a flexible gasket (also known as a spline). Other sashes have frames that must be dismantled for reglazing. With the exception of some of the one-piece spring-clip types, you should remove all metal sashes from their frames when working on them.

Like wooden sashes, one-piece steel sashes make use of glazing compound to hold glass in place.

But underneath it, metal spring clips take the place of glazing sprigs. One-piece aluminium frames use a vinyl or rubber gasket, which you can pry out with a screwdriver and re-install with a putty knife.

In the 'knock-down' category, many sashes are held together by screws at their corners. Once these have been removed, you simply pull the frame members away from the glass. Then re-assemble them around the new pane. Some pin-type aluminium frames have internal L-brackets 'dimpled' in place at their corners. To release them, drill out the dimples. To reassemble, make new dimples with an awl to hold the L-bracket in place.

Repairing rotten frames and sills

Although today hardwood window frames are quite popular, softwood remains the most common material. While this has a very long life if properly treated initially and subsequently, it is vulnerable to rot if water is able to get through cracked and flaking paint finishes or old shrunken putty sealing glass panes. The most vulnerable parts of the frame are the bottom rails of sashes, the feet of the stiles and jambs and the sill.

To protect against rot, paint or varnish frames regularly, and rake out and replace putty or sealant when it shows signs of ageing.

Checking for rot

You should examine all window frames every year, looking for signs of rot and dealing with any problems as soon as you find them. When rot attacks the wood, it becomes soft and crumbly; you'll easily be able to push the blade of a knife into it, and even your fingernail. In some cases, you may not be aware of it until you push your finger into it if the paint film itself doesn't appear damaged.

Tiny amounts of rot that are unlikely to have weakened the frame can be scraped or cut out, and the damage made good with a special filler, which will protect the surrounding wood against rot. But this may only be a short-term fix.

Larger areas of rot will weaken the frame, and the only solution is to cut them out and replace the damaged portion of the frame.

Replacing a damaged rail

To replace a rotten rail in a sash, remove the sash from the frame and take out the glass, putting it somewhere safe. The frame will be held together by mortise-and-tenon joints, and the easiest way to remove the rail is to saw down between the stile and the end of the rail from each face of the frame and at each end. Then knock out the tenons and their wedges. You may have to use a drill and chisel to achieve this.

Good timber suppliers will offer a range of timber profiles for things like window frames and if you're lucky you'll be able to find one that matches the section of the damaged rail. Otherwise, you will have to make it yourself or have it machined. Since you won't be able to fit the rail in the same manner as originally without completely knocking the frame apart, extend the mortise to the foot of each stile with a saw. Then cut a tenon on each end of the new rail to fit.

Apply waterproof wood glue to the tenons and tap the rail into place. To strengthen each joint, drill two staggered 6 mm dowel holes through the inner face of each stile and each tenon, but not into the outer portion of the stile. Tap the dowels into place, cutting and planing their ends flush with the frame when the glue has dried.

Repairing a rotten sill

The sill is a major component of the window frame, and any significant damage that it suffers from rot could seriously weaken it, requiring a new sill. However, minor damage can generally be cut out and either repaired with filler, which is specially designed to combat rot or replaced with a fresh piece of wood.

If the sill needs replacing, you may have quite a job on your hands, depending on the style of window and how it is fitted in the opening. In some cases, the entire frame will need removing before a sill can be fitted.

Obviously, the sashes should be removed, along with all the fixed glass. Break away the mortar joints around the sill, using a hammer and cold chisel, then saw down through the sill adjacent to each jamb. Remove the centre portion of the sill and chisel the remaining pieces from around the tenons of the jambs. Then cut the tenons off flush with the bottom of the jambs, unless the jambs themselves are rotten, in which case the rotten portions must be cut off, too.

Cut the new sill to length and slide it under the ends of the jambs, aligning it carefully. Skew-nail or screw through the jambs into the sill. Make sure you treat the new sill and the bottoms of the jambs with preservative, and apply a bead of silicone mastic along the bottom of the sill to provide a waterproof seal where it meets the brickwork of the wall.

Make good the mortar joints around the sill, or seal with silicone mastic, then fill the nail or screw heads and paint the frame before replacing the glass and sashes.

RIGHT: Repairing a rotten sill

1. Saw out rotten piece.

2. Clean up with a chisel.

3. Mark and cut new piece.

4. Screw new piece in place

5. Plane to shape, fill and paint.

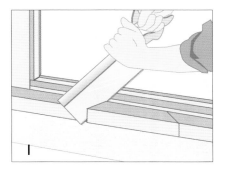

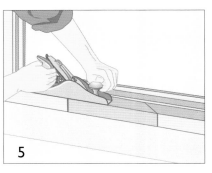

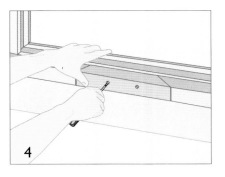

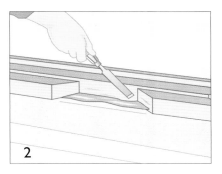

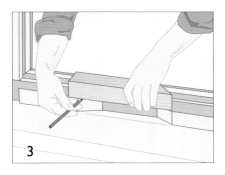

RIGHT: The oriel window provides more space as well as light.

BELOW: Replacing a concrete sill

1. Remove loose material, drill holes for reinforcing rods and mortar them into place.

2. Construct wooden formwork around the sill, tamping it down to remove air.

3. Finish off with a steel float for a smooth surface. Protect with polythene and leave for seven days before removing formwork.

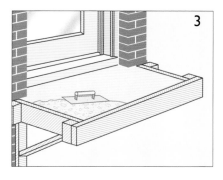

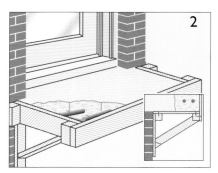

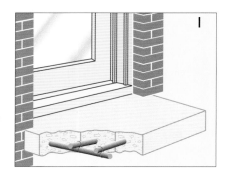

jambs themselves are rotten, in which case the rotten portions must be cut off, too.

Cut the new sill to length and slide it under the ends of the jambs, aligning it carefully. Skewnail or screw through the jambs into the sill. Make sure you treat the new sill and the bottoms of the jambs with preservative, and apply a bead of silicone mastic along the bottom of the sill to provide a waterproof seal where it meets the brickwork of the wall.

Make good the mortar joints around the sill, or seal with silicone mastic, then fill the nail or screw heads and paint the frame before replacing the glass and sashes.

Repairing a concrete or stone sill

Older houses may have stone or concrete sills below the wooden sills of windows, which will be set back in their openings. Over the years, these may become damaged by the weather or subsidence.

Minor cracking and erosion can be dealt with by filling with quick-setting waterproof cement or exterior filler. Serious damage or missing pieces can only be repaired by building a wooden former around the sill, adding steel reinforcing rods if necessary and casting a new section in concrete.

Do-it-yourself oriel window

Unless you're a very experienced do-it-yourselfer, this project may be rather ambitious. You can, however, use it to inspire your builder to be adventurous. An oriel window will give any room an extra dimension, as well as being a cosy suntrap and a way of bringing the outdoors into your home.

Before you begin, decide whether you will fit your oriel structure with tailor-made windows

The large front window is fixed glass. This could be a ready-made sash or simply a sheet of glass sandwiched between lengths of beading fixed to the main frame.

Where the sloping glass that forms the roof meets the horizontal framing, it should be allowed to overhang by about 50 mm.

Be sure to use a silicon-based sealer on all joints, especially those where the glass and timber meet. It is also vital to fix flashing at the junction of the wall and the roof to provide protection against rain. Lead or zinc flashing will need to be set into the brickwork, and

shaped to fit snugly against the roof, providing a weatherproof seal.

This kind of window design is marvellous when a room suffers from a deficiency of natural light. If a window opens into a light well where an extension would be out of the question, an oriel window can expand greatly the area of glass, and its deep shelf/sill makes the perfect stage for a pretty array of plants. To make the most of the available light, paint the wood in white gloss and house your pots in pale containers. Alternatively, you could opt for a varnished finish, as in our picture.

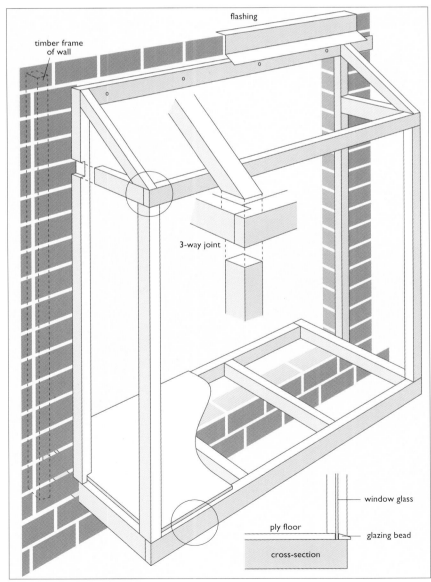

ABOVE: An oriel window is ideal in a kitchen. Besides letting in plenty of natural light and providing a view, it creates additional worktop space that is ideal for herbs or delicate indoor plants.

LEFT: Installing an oriel window in a wooden-framed wall.

Wet Areas

Whatever your lifestyle, good design and planning of the kitchen, bathroom and utility room (the work areas) can make the tasks performed in these rooms easier and even pleasurable. The kitchen is often the most important room in the house, while the bathroom's 'look' is now considered as important as that of the living areas.

Whether starting from scratch or improving an existing kitchen, bathroom or utility room, there is a variety of options available to the home renovator. Very often, the kitchen is a gathering place as well as a work station. An open-plan kitchen close to dining and living areas ensures the cook does not have to work in isolation, away from social or family activity. Utility rooms with plenty of worktop space for folding and ironing clothes may allow an additional work area for sewing. In smaller, older houses, it may be possible to create a utility area within the bathroom, or even hide one in an alcove or cupboard in the kitchen.

If you are not limited by space, your first step is to decide what you want – a large kitchen/diner, a bathroom with bath, double hand basins and marble finishes, a utility room-cum-workroom – or something less grandiose.

If you intend to redesign your existing layout and move services such as plumbing, electricity or gas, the undertaking is considerable. As with any renovation, you need to be aware of the legal restrictions. Creating an extra bathroom, for example, may sound great, but it could be a luxury you either cannot afford or will not be allowed. In all these rooms, the cost of the fittings often determines the final plan and, as with any renovation, it's all in the planning.

Today's kitchens are multi-functional and are usually the centre of household activity. A well-planned kitchen that allows room for children to do homework or visitors to sit without interrupting the cook makes a pleasant and efficient work space adjacent to the dining area.

Kitchens

The methods employed in planning a new kitchen are similar to those used in planning a good meal. Who will be using it? How many people are to be catered for? Do any of them have special requirements? What ingredients are required? Do they go together? Finally, and most importantly, how much will it cost?

Begin by making a wish list of the equipment you would like. If you cannot afford it all at once, be sure to allow some space in your design for the future installation of these extras. Other important factors to take into account are the location and type of kitchen required. Is it to be open-plan with a lot of passing traffic? Do you want to eat in it? If not, how accessible is it to the dining area? How much storage do you need?

If your cooking caters for a number of people, a walk-in pantry is a good idea; if you live alone and eat out often, a large pantry may be a waste of space. Remember, also,

kitchens receive a great deal of hard use, so choose work surfaces that are resilient and will mellow. The kitchen is a work area and should be practical and easy to use, so the positioning of hob, refrigerator and work surface should be in a logical order. Safety aspects are also a prime consideration, especially if there are young children in the house. Try to position gas burners or electric elements and equipment out of their reach.

A dream kitchen may not be achievable, but simply redesigning existing space, or even just freshening the paint, can work wonders.

ABOVE: When planning, consider the cook's view.

RIGHT: Appliances such as the dishwasher should be within easy reach of the sink.

Planning

It's not how a kitchen looks, but how it cooks that matters; thousands of pounds worth of marble will do nothing to improve a bad design. After all, it's not only the quality of the ingredients that gives a good result, it's how you put them together. So before you start trying out taps and dallying over door handles, decide on the overall kitchen design by making a plan.

Templates are included here to simplify the process.

Work flow and the work triangle

The best way to conserve your energy in the kitchen is to create an efficient work-flow plan. Look at the sequence in which regular tasks are done, as this will dictate the practical basic positioning of appliances and storage space. In its most simple form, this flow takes the shape of a 'work triangle' between the fridge (and pantry), the cooker and the sink. In larger kitchens, it's easier to look at these items as part of the preparation centre, the cooking centre and the cleaning-up centre.

These three kitchen elements form a triangle that plots the most frequent journeys the cook will make. As a general rule, the total distance around the work triangle should be no more than 700 mm.

Because the kitchen is a work area, it should be planned to make the tasks as easy to perform as possible. If the kitchen will allow it, the sink and cooker should be positioned along the same wall, with at least a 600-mm-long stretch of worktop on each side of them. The location of the refrigerator needs to be as close as possible to the sink and cooker.

TOP: Easy to maintain surfaces are the most practical in a kitchen.

ABOVE: In a large kitchen an efficient work flow plan will conserve your energy.

LEFT: An island unit is ideal for extra storage.

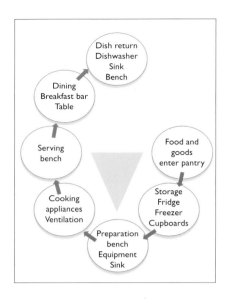

Shown on these pages are some of the most common kitchen layouts to illustrate how the work triangle fits into each of them.

Kitchen shapes

The kitchen shape you use will depend on the space you have available. Consider the traffic flows, the minimum space you need between worktops, and the wall space for tall storage. The U-shaped plan is usually the most efficient, as it excludes traffic movement through the kitchen, although ultimately it doesn't matter what shape the kitchen is as long as it follows the work flow shown here.

Shallow U-shape

Where one end of a much larger room is turned over to food preparation, the shallow U-shape is the most likely configuration for a kitchen. The addition of an island worktop will help to separate the kitchen off from the rest of the room. In this instance, the work triangle takes in the extremities of the plan.

The hob and refrigerator are opposite one another, with the sink placed centrally. The result is an expansive kitchen that is exposed to the rest of the room. This helps to create a mood that is warm, generous and welcoming.

Deep U-shape

This is perhaps the most popular kitchen layout. It occurs automatically where the kitchen is a smallish, self-contained room. The deep U-shape combines the parallel-worktop advantage of the galley with the bonus of a third side to achieve maximum efficiency.

Especially were the space is very compact, this layout makes for multi-directional kitchen activity, allowing the cook to reach out equally in all directions from the central space.

Similarly, the three sides of the work triangle are more likely to be equal. Ideally, a tall refrigerator should be placed at the end of one of the arms of the U so that it allows as much continuous worktop space as possible.

ABOVE: Work flow plan.

BELOW: Standard kitchen shapes.

BELOW RIGHT: Shallow U-shape.

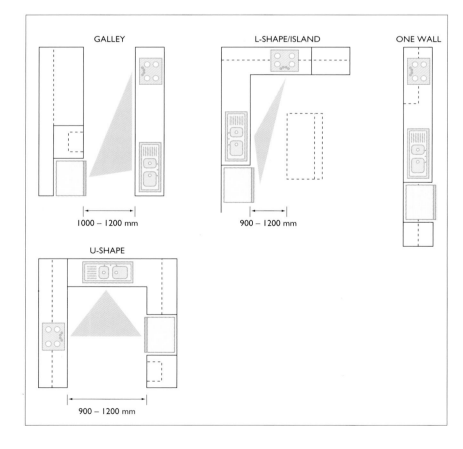

ABOVE: Before.

RIGHT: After – The deep U-shape is ideal in a small space.

BELOW: L-shape.

L-shape

Where obstacles such as doors, windows or even narrow room widths get in the way, your kitchen will not be able to spread along three walls. Where two walls are the limit, the L-shape is the best option. Without the addition of an island or extra worktop, your kitchen clutter will always be on show, and this is the major drawback with this type of plan. On the other hand, the open L creates a generous and accessible feeling.

There will never be human traffic problems because there is a total lack of restriction on floor space. And because the layout is triangular in shape anyway, the work triangle is easily accommodated. The open space allows other rooms to spill into the kitchen area.

Galley

Where the available space is long and narrow with parallel worktops, a galley is created automatically. It is important to remember that one metre is the absolute minimum workable space between the two worktops. In the kitchen shown on the following page, the galley was prevented from becoming a U by the existence of a doorway at the end of the space. The sink and cooker are situated adjacent to one another, with as much worktop space as possible between them.

An under-worktop refrigerator and freezer have been placed opposite, maximising the amount of usable worktop space.

In this case, much has been made of the limited available space, which was made more problematic

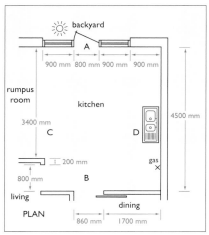

by circulation demands. What is essentially a thoroughfare has been carefully handled to become a thoroughly workable kitchen.

The fact that this is the smallest and most awkward of the four kitchen examples makes its success all the more impressive.

Making a plan

To verify what you'll need, consider such aspects as how much cooking you do (a large family will need plenty of storage and workspace); the type of cooking (convenience-food chefs should make sure the freezer and the microwave are easy to get to – gourmets will need more specialised appliances and more storage); and whether you want to keep an eye on the kids while cooking. Collect brochures (with dimensions and installation specifications) detailing the appliances you intend to buy. Gather together the items you'll need and you are ready to draw up a plan.

Start by drawing up a rough sketch of the floorplan and each

wall, then measure each dimension and mark it on the drawing. Show positions of fixed objects such as doors, windows, fireplaces, plumbing and gas connections, as well as the less tangible items, such as traffic flows, sun direction and views. Measure the appliances and fittings that you already have and intend to re-use.

Using the dimensions from your rough sketches, draw the plan properly to scale on graph paper. Use a scale of 1:20 (1 cm on the plan represents 20 cm in real life). Once you have done this, pencil in a line representing 600 mm or 700 mm around the perimeter walls, allowing for traffic routes and door arcs. If you prefer wider worktops, you can adjust that later. Mark in the plumbing, as this will influence where you put the sink (it's cheaper to keep it close to the original position). Turn to the templates and choose examples that match your appliances. If the sizes are different, draw your own templates to the same scale. Do the

ABOVE LEFT: Galley shape.

TOP: A kitchen and living area plan.

ABOVE: Elevations for the plan.

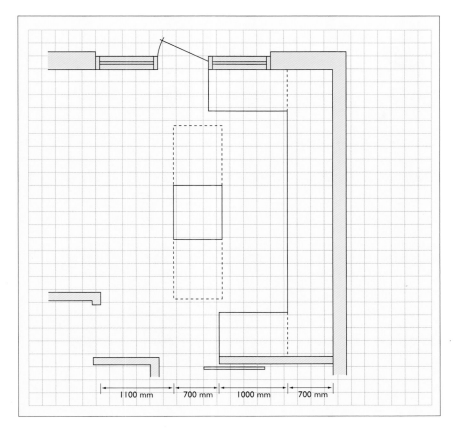

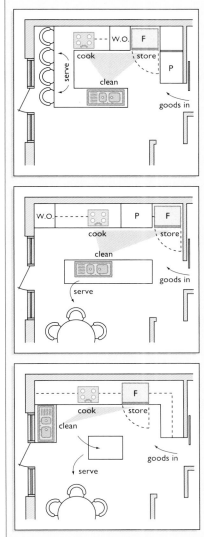

ABOVE: Photocopy and pencil in the best areas for benches.

RIGHT: Move the templates around and trace off some different options.

BELOW: Elevation B.

same for furniture modules if you are buying a prefabricated kitchen.

Draw the wall elevations as well (two are often enough) and pencil in the best areas for worktops.

Move the shapes around the worktop area until everything fits well together and the work will proceed in a smooth flow. Position the main appliances (allowing clearance for door opening) and the sink before you site cupboards and drawers. Trace the different arrangements so that you have something to compare. Draw in the work triangle and direction of the work flow: the most efficient design will stand out as being the simplest.

Draw up an overall plan before you start pondering the details.

Choose the plan that works the best and paste the templates into position. Pencil in drawers and doors. Use a dotted line to show wall-mounted cupboards and

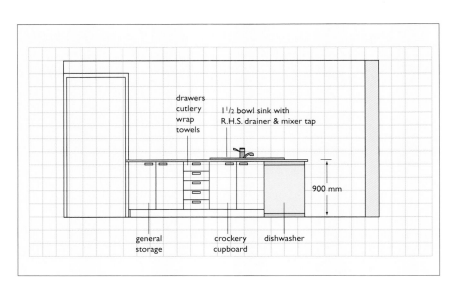

Kitchen design tips

Minimum worktop lengths:

- for safety – 300 mm on both sides of hobs;
- for preparation – at least 1200–1800 mm;
- for unloading – 450 mm for fridges, high-level ovens and pantries;
- for serving – 300 mm for two plates, 600 mm for four plates.

Storage

Working out where to put storage is easy; fitting it in is usually the hard part. The main thing to remember is that all food, utensils and appliances should be stored where they will be used. Consider accessibility (visual and physical), location (near use) and flexibility (allow for future changes).

Ventilation

The best option is a powerful cooker hood with readily accessible filters for cleaning. It should exhaust through the wall into the open air.

Lighting

Adequate natural, general and task lighting over the main work areas will help prevent eye strain and save you from slicing your fingers when chopping food.

Safety

- Do provide worktop space on both sides of the oven/hob, and separate work areas from storage and eating areas.
- Do install a smoke alarm; they are straightforward and cheap to put in. Also keep a small fire extinguisher and fire blanket handy.
- Don't place an oven/hob near a doorway (allow at least 300 mm), in a corner or under a window.
- Don't store hazardous cleaning chemicals and sharp implements where they will be within reach of small children.

under-worktop shelves. Mark important dimensions and notes on the drawing. The finished drawing should show everything in place (you can mark all the power points, lighting and wall and floor finishes on the drawings, too) and, if you like, you can trace or photocopy the result to try out different colour

BELOW: Elevation D.

BOTTOM: The finished plan for Elevation B.

RIGHT: A coat of paint may be all that's required to update your kitchen.

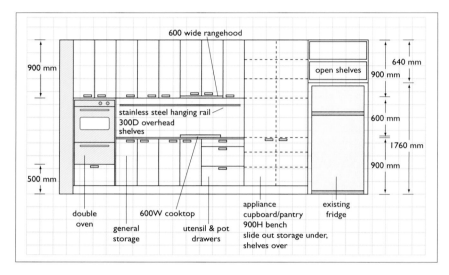

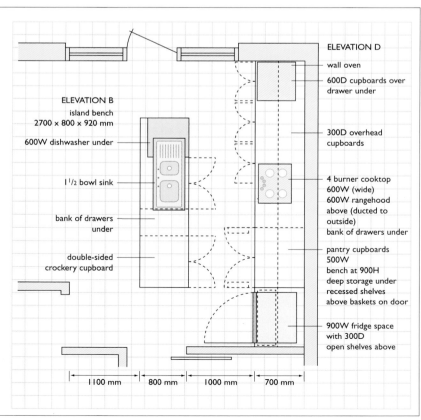

CENTRE LEFT: Fridge elevations and dimensions.

BELOW LEFT: Elevations for standard appliances.

BELOW: Sink elevations and dimensions.

BOTTOM: Oven elevations and dimensions.

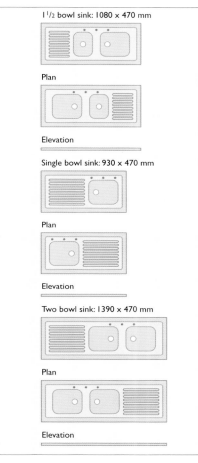

1¹/₂ bowl sink: 1080 x 470 mm

Plan

Elevation

Single bowl sink: 930 x 470 mm

Plan

Elevation

Two bowl sink: 1390 x 470 mm

Plan

Elevation

Compact fridge:
850 mmH, 545 mmW,
600 mmD

Plan

Elevation

Family-size fridge:
1700 mmH, 790 mmW,
670 mmD

Plan

Elevation

Large fridge:
1740 mmH, 910 mmW,
730 mmD

Plan

Elevation

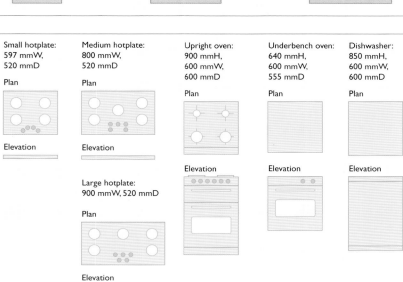

Small hotplate:
597 mmW,
520 mmD

Plan

Elevation

Medium hotplate:
800 mmW,
520 mmD

Plan

Elevation

Large hotplate:
900 mmW, 520 mmD

Plan

Elevation

Upright oven:
900 mmH,
600 mmW,
600 mmD

Plan

Elevation

Underbench oven:
640 mmH,
600 mmW,
555 mmD

Plan

Elevation

Dishwasher:
850 mmH,
600 mmW,
600 mmD

Plan

Elevation

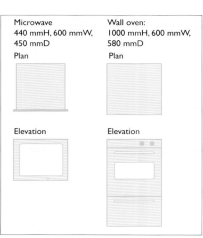

Microwave
440 mmH, 600 mmW,
450 mmD

Plan

Elevation

Wall oven:
1000 mmH, 600 mmW,
580 mmD

Plan

Elevation

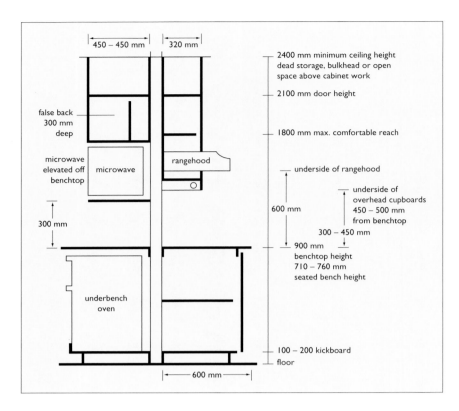

ABOVE: Average kitchen component dimensions.

FAR RIGHT: Floorplan for the tailored kitchen.

combinations. If you are still a little unsure of your plan, you can consult a kitchen designer, but obviously this will cost money. And don't forget to check with your local council to see if any of the work is subject to Building Regulations approval.

The right height

The recommended heights and depths shown above were arrived at through a study of what works best in the average domestic kitchen, for the average cook. If you are considerably taller or shorter, or disabled, alter them to suit your needs, but remember that this may affect the resale value of your house.

Choosing and buying kitchen cabinets

Quality control and a broad range of styling options make today's mass-produced cabinets competitive with all but the most costly of tailor-made units. You can order standard cabinets, then assemble and finish them; purchase units that require only finishing; or select pre-finished versions ready for installation. You should also keep in mind that most manufacturers offer several lines, each constructed of slightly different materials and priced accordingly.

Judge construction by taking a close look at how joints are fitted and the way in which interiors and backs have been finished. Check out the hardware, too. Quality cabinets have doors that swing freely and latch securely, and drawers that roll on metal runners.

Measuring for new cabinets

Standardised dimensions and modular designs greatly simplify the job of tailoring cabinets to suit your kitchen. Just measure the space available, order a series of units that comes close to fitting it, then make up the difference with fillers between cabinets or at ends of runs.

First, carefully plot your kitchen on graph paper, making both floor-plan and elevation drawings. For base cabinets, measure at worktop height as well as along skirting boards and note any variations. Be sure that you make allowance for features such as door openings, power points, window casings, pipes, appliance sizes and any other items that could cause an unpleasant surprise.

Comparing cabinet materials	
Cabinet material	**Features**
Particle board	The better units are faced with wood or plastic veneers, but some lacquered and photographically-produced finishes work well, too.
Hardboard	May be used for backs and sides on wooden frames.
Hardwood	May be veneered plywood with hardwood frames. Sturdy construction, easy-care finishes. Doors can be of solid hardwood.

Now fill in the layout you want, using the following information as a guide. Height measurements shown accommodate the reach of an average-height person and are accepted as standards throughout the kitchen and appliance industries.

Base cabinets typically measure 900 mm high by 600 or 450 mm deep. Wall cabinets may be anything from 450 to 900 mm high and 300 mm deep.

Manufacturers offer plenty of choices when it comes to cabinet widths. You can purchase them from 225 to 1200 mm wide.

Fillers fit between units, letting you adjust a run of cabinets to the space available. Cut them to the width you need.

Installing kitchen cabinets

Achieving a built-in look with prefabricated cabinets might seem to call for some complex carpentry, but not so. Examine a unit and you'll see that the manufacturer has done most of the work, providing you with perfectly square modules that you can lock together with screws or dowels.

Assembly consists of carefully levelling and plumbing each cabinet, then fastening it to the wall and to its neighbours.

Level the base cabinets. You'll probably need to use shims to accomplish this. Use screw sizes specified by the manufacturer; drive the screws through the frame, not the thinner back and side panels. And never install cabinets with nails – they don't have the holding power of screws, and they might split the wood.

If a skirting board, door or window architrave gets in the way, remove it and trim to fit after the cabinets are in place.

Cap off base cabinets with a worktop from a kitchen or building supplier. Most will cut one to size and may even make a cut-out for the sink if you supply a pattern. (Measure carefully, though – mistakes are costly.)

You can also make your own worktop by facing exterior-grade plywood with plastic laminate.

Install the worktop by screwing angle brackets to the underside and to the cabinet frames.

Finish off the job by fitting mouldings to cover any gaps that occur between the cabinets and the wall or floor.

To hang wall cabinets, first build a portable support that you can stand on the worktop. Next, rest a unit on the support, shim behind to plumb the cabinet, then screw through the frame into the wall.

With a hollow stud partition, begin the installation by marking the locations of the studs. Set a cabinet into place, then level it by tapping shims underneath. Level from front to back and from side to side.

Now drill pilot holes and drive screws into the studs. In some cases, if the cabinets don't align with the stud spacing, you may need to screw a horizontal batten to the studs first, then screw the cabinets to this. On a masonry wall, simply drill and plug the wall.

Once you have levelled and secured the unit, carefully chisel away any shims that protrude.

Sometimes a thin shim between cabinets will compensate for minor irregularities. The face edges must butt tightly, however.

Fasten units together with screws according to the instructions.

The tailor-made kitchen

If you are disinclined or unable to build your own kitchen, consulting a kitchen designer/supplier will help you achieve your dream.

Illustrated below is the type of plan you will be given by a kitchen designer/supplier. It includes the sizes of the standard kitchen components as well as the positions of all the appliances and fittings.

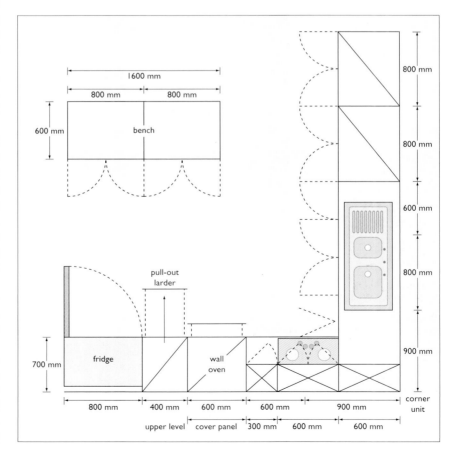

LEFT: The old kitchen table gives this kitchen individuality.

Although the standard worktop height is 900 mm, you can always raise it by building your cabinets on top of shallow plinths. Naturally, in the case of prefabricated kitchen components, this will be more difficult and, therefore, more expensive. Some prefabricated types, however, have adjustable legs on to which the kickplates clip.

Unless you are happy with plain white splashbacks, you should go to a tile shop that offers a large range and choose just the ones you want. Some kitchen installers will provide their own tilers, but with others you will have to organise that part of the job yourself.

Similarly, kitchen companies are likely to offer a limited range of tap fittings as well as sinks. You will almost certainly be able to find something from this range that you are happy with. Otherwise, you will have to specify what you want and ask the company to organise it.

Know what you want

Study as many home magazines and kitchen design catalogues as you can, and keep a folder of pictures, products and ideas that appeal to you.

Consider how you use your kitchen at the moment. What are the things you like most about it and what annoys you? For example, you might have one of those corner cupboards where it is difficult to reach right to the back.

Take along a measured plan of your kitchen space, noting the location of electrical, gas and water services, and windows and doors.

You should draw a rough plan of how you would like your kitchen to be. Show it to your kitchen designer. It will be a good starting point.

Work out a plan with your supplier/designer

Be sure to discuss the range of kitchen options offered by your supplier/designer. You should be able to study a whole list, or catalogue, of standard fittings – everything from cutlery trays and sliding towel rails to pull-out, divided rubbish bins and vacuum-hose holders.

Work out how standard-sized cabinets or units will best fit into your kitchen space. Base cabinets will come in their own range of standard sizes, as will wall-mounted units and cabinets for housing ovens and refrigerators.

Your kitchen design must be the most space- and cost-efficient combination of all these components.

Investigate finishing options

Even if you have set your heart on plain white doors, there can be several different grades, from the cheapest of laminates to reproduction woodgrains.

When it comes to worktops, you can be as extravagant or thrifty as you like. If you choose a plastic-laminate top, run through the edging options your manufacturer has to offer. Many are post-formed, that is, they have a rounded front edge.

Think about the type of door and drawer handles you want. For such small items, they have a great impact on the style and degree of quality of your kitchen project.

Arrive at an overall price and start the manufacturing process

With companies that offer prefabricated kitchen components, the price of what you want is easily calculated. If you are having a kitchen built, however, you will have to obtain a quote and a time framework. Most tailored kitchen manufacturers take several weeks to deliver the goods. This will be set out in a contract. (Take your time in signing any kitchen agreement. The company should offer you a 'cooling off' period after you have signed.) You will have to pay a deposit. Both materials and workmanship should have guarantees.

You should be able to arrange for the installer to take away your old kitchen cabinets, or you can remove them yourself. You will have to establish this when you sign the contract. Remember, the more you do yourself, the less you will have to pay.

Having your kitchen installed

If you have already stripped out the old cabinets, you will have the opportunity to repair the walls and paint them, allowing the new units to slot into a clean environment.

Installing your kitchen cupboards should only take about a day, but the trimming up and finishing will occur in short bursts over the ensuing week. Make sure you are around during this time, because it may be possible to make minor adjustments. For example, worktops are cut on site to fit the room shape. If you are on hand, you might be able to revise the arrangement of the units.

Both the electrician and plumber will have to finish their work after the cabinets are in place.

Don't remove any protective plastic coatings from appliances or fittings until all the work has been done. In particular, protect them while tiling, flooring and painting is being carried out.

Make sure you fill any gaps where your cupboards and fittings abut the walls, floor and ceiling. Where the problem is very obvious, you will have to use wooden beading, otherwise filler will do the job.

Make sure you're completely happy with everything before you pay the balance of the bill.

Installing a kitchen yourself

When the time comes to put in a new kitchen, you can choose from several options. You can employ a builder to do it all, have a kitchen supplier make the fixtures and do the installation yourself, or do the

BELOW: Beautiful natural timber worktops set off tongued-and-grooved cabinet doors, which have been colour-washed in purple.

ABOVE: Pre-fabricated cabinets can easily be given a distinctive look with a painted finish.

BELOW: Pull out bins are tidy and save floor space.

whole job yourself. A good option, if you are handy, is to combine a little of each.

Kitchen designers can advise you on layouts that ensure your kitchen is efficient. You won't be able to lay in the services yourself, unless you are very familiar with working with pipes and cables, or you are a qualified plumber or electrician. You can and should, however, select the locations, quantities and types of service fitting you require. Choose a sink and taps that suit you, and have them put where you want them. Decide how many power points are required for your appliances and have them installed where they suit you. Since you will be using them, you should know best what you need.

When it comes to kitchen cabinets, there are various possibilities, too. Again, there are companies that will do it all: carcasses, worktops, doors and drawers. You could buy prefabricated units to a basic design that you assemble yourself. The latter is probably the cheapest option if you have time. As doors, drawer fronts and worktops generally dictate the overall appearance of the kitchen, you can truly tailor it by building these yourself to your own design.

Take the time to look at the different types of hardware and fittings that are available for kitchens. They can make the difference between a kitchen that is easy to work in and a nightmare. Self-closing, adjustable hinges, slide-away worktops and slide-out storage racks are just a few innovations to consider. Be prepared to spend a bit more to get the best – it will be worth it in the long run.

Demolition

Before pulling the old kitchen to pieces, get the appropriate tradespeople to disconnect the services. Try not to disturb too much of the surrounding finishes, such as plaster, so there's less to repair later.

Splashbacks

Tiles look great and are easy to keep clean. Fix them with tile adhesive directly to the wall between the worktop and any high-level cabinets. You can finish exposed ends with edging tiles or wooden beading. Where your tiles sit on the worktop, replace the grouted joint with silicon so that it doesn't crack.

Carcasses

Ensure that the carcasses are constructed from moisture-resistant chipboard and that all edges are sealed with either ironed-on or glued-on laminate strips. Make sure they are seated on a good base, which is level and securely fixed to the floor. Screw through the sides of the carcasses to join them together, but don't fix them to the wall if they are already fixed to the kitchen floor.

Doors and drawers

A variety of off-the-shelf doors is available, offering laminate and natural timber finishes. If you want

Tips

- Rubbish disposal has progressed beyond the days of a freestanding bin in the corner. Check out what is available from the specialists.
- Your new kitchen probably won't suit your existing lighting. Work this out early, otherwise you will be cutting holes in new finishes to take the altered wiring runs.
- Colours of fixtures, walls, doors worktops and so on all need to complement each other. Get out the colour cards and stain samples early. Don't be talked into a colour or stain that you haven't actually seen demonstrated and matched.

ABOVE: Timber for floors and worktops are a practical choice for a country cottage.

ABOVE RIGHT: An exterior door from the kitchen is useful in providing ready access to the garden or utilities.

CENTRE: This kitchen has well defined work areas even though the space is small.

CENTRE RIGHT: A large bay-window addition incorporates a dining space into the kitchen area.

RIGHT: A wall was demolished between the kitchen and dining room making one usable and inviting space.

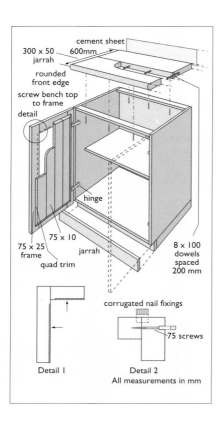

cement sheet
300 × 50
jarrah 600mm
rounded
front edge
screw bench top
to frame
detail
hinge
75 × 10
75 × 25   jarrah
frame
quad trim
8 × 100
dowels
spaced
200 mm

corrugated nail fixings

75 screws

Detail I

Detail 2
All measurements in mm

to make your own, simply construct a frame, then glue and pin tongued-and-grooved pine boards to the back. Leave enough space from the side of the frame for the hinges and trim the edges with beading. Round off the edges of the frame with a router or a sander. Alternative fronts can be fixed directly to ready-made drawer carcasses. Use a piece of pine and stain it to your taste. You can buy drawer packages where the sides and ends can be cut to make drawers of any size.

Worktops

Two lengths of 300 x 50 mm parana pine have been used here, joined with dowels (see diagram) to make it 600 mm wide. The front edge was rounded and the top fixed to the carcasses from below. Smaller pieces of parana pine fixed to the carcass form kickplates.

Inspirational kitchens

Country

The country style suits those who enjoy home cooking, collecting and displaying pretty plates, and working in a clutter and bustle. The style is warm and welcoming, with

ABOVE: Worktop and cabinet dimensions.

ABOVE RIGHT AND RIGHT: Modern appliances and the warmth of timber worktops in a country kitchen promise generous hospitality and the freshest home-cooked food in convivial surroundings.

Tip

- A length of old wooden ladder makes a great hanging rack for saucepans, baskets or strings of onions. Suspend items from chains and butchers' hooks.

bunches of herbs drying and bottles of preserves displayed. For those who are less exuberant, the scrubbed and bleached timber, wooden bowls and blue-and-white simplicity of a farmhouse kitchen may be more suitable.

Modern/urban

One cook's attractive piles of pots, pans and collectable clutter may well be another's nightmare of a dust trap. Those who are highly organised and disciplined are driven to madness unless there's a place for everything and everything is in its place. A purpose-built kitchen is best, ensuring that all things have their allotted space, surfaces can be kept spotless and the cook will be in control at all times! Such kitchens are calm and spatially satisfying. There's room for art and even sculpture.

Mediterranean

This is for gregarious, active and hospitable people who like a touch of the exotic and luxuriate in tangible reminders of fabulous holidays and even more fabulous food. For them, entertaining is a relaxation, and is often a spur-of-the-moment affair. The colour in decoration and

in food is often summed up by the Mediterranean look, whether authentic or not. At the other extreme of this same style is the whitewashed, rather spare decoration of the Middle East, with its brass lamps and coffee pots, sweetmeats and honey cakes. Or you can try cool-tiled, shady, vine-laden Tuscan simplicity.

ABOVE: Streamlined and sophisticated, this kitchen is a practical, well-planned combination of function and beauty. The decorative elements are pared down but the result is definitely not austere. Symmetry and order rule, but the hard gleam of stainless steel is softened by the gentler glow of honey-coloured parquetry. The surfaces are all easy to clean.

LEFT: This kitchen takes its cue from the Mediterranean. The focus is on earthy pottery, tiled surfaces, flowers, herbs and brilliant colours.

Tip

- If you don't have terracotta tiles on the floor, lay bright, striped, washable rugs. If there's room, a café-style chair and table will look right and be useful, too.

Kitchen storage ideas

You don't need to redesign a whole kitchen to make it work better for you. Examine your cooking habits and the way you use your kitchen to help come up with specific storage solutions. Cut down on clutter. Think corner cupboards, open shelves, drawer dividers and extra worktop pull-outs, and turn a nearby cupboard into a walk-in pantry if necessary.

With the clever storage ideas pictured on these pages, you will easily find a place for everything, streamline your time and make your kitchen work for you.

ABOVE LEFT: Utilise space between the tops of cupboards and the ceiling and even over doorways. Use high shelving to store things you rarely use.

LEFT: Note how simply this clever storage space for glasses can be made. Cut the shapes, then just glue and screw to the bottom of your cupboard. But first measure between the bowls of the glasses so they slide in and out with ease.

ABOVE: Store your platters side by side so you can get at the large ones, which are often hard to reach when stuck at the bottom of the stack.

RIGHT: Shallow, pull-out drawers are ideal for storing cookware and kitchen gadgets – much better than cavernous cupboards. Even those seldom-used things stowed at the back are easily accessible.

ABOVE: Storage need not be just for storing. Give cupboards glass backs and fronts, and create an attractive room divider which can be easily accessed from both sides whilst still letting in light.

ABOVE RIGHT: Large hanging racks can house all your pots and pans. Make sure the rack is above a bench and not where you will bang your head on it.

Tip

- Pay a visit to a shop specialising in storage fittings. You'll find gadgets and items that will solve many of your clutter problems, plus some that will open up a whole new way of looking at the places and spaces available to you. And don't forget, there's always a ceiling to hang a rack from!

ABOVE: It's surprising how much easier cupboards are to use if you remove their doors. Foodstuffs don't have to be hidden inside cupboards. They are decorative on open shelves and it's easier to see items that are running low and will need replacing soon.

ABOVE: A pantry with doors creates extra space when you attach shelves to the inside because you instantly double the storage area. Use heavy-duty hinges to carry the extra weight. If you install a power point, you can store and use appliances there as well.

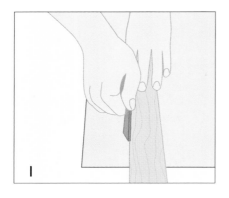

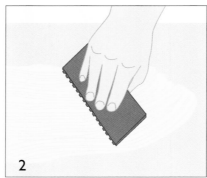

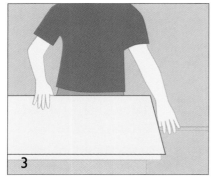

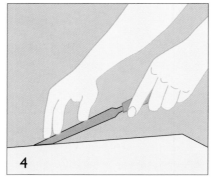

LEFT: Fitting laminate to a worktop.

1 Measure the size of the worktop. Mark the size of the new laminate panel with a felt pen, making it 5 mm larger in length and width than the worktop. Cut along the lines with a laminate cutter.

2 Using a notched spreader, apply the contact adhesive to the surface of the worktop and the underside of the laminate. Allow time for it to dry to the touch.

3 Place the long side of the laminate in position, using a dowel to separate the surfaces. Lower the laminate on to the worktop and slowly move the dowel back. Press the surfaces together with your palm.

4 Trim the edges with a block plane, then file smooth. For the final strokes, hold the file at a 45° angle to the surface.

Fitting laminate to a worktop

You can remove old laminate by working in from the edges with a wide-bladed chisel. Force the chisel between the laminate and the worktop. It doesn't matter if the laminate tears, but you should take care not to damage the particle board underneath.

Fixing drawers and doors

When a drawer with metal side runners sticks, remove the drawer and thoroughly clean both runners. Apply powdered graphite or silicone lubricant. Make sure the screws holding the runners are tight and secure.

Over the years, wooden centre runners can become rough and worn. First smooth the runner with sandpaper, then rub it with crayon or candle wax to help eliminate friction when the drawer slides.

Loose hinge screws cause cabinet doors to sag. If the screw holes have become enlarged, tightening the screws won't help. To reduce the size of the hole, insert a length of toothpick coated with glue, then re-insert the screw.

To work properly, magnetic catches must be in near-perfect alignment. Screws let you adjust a catch back and forth. A sliver of wood, forced underneath as a shim, lets you adjust vertical alignment.

LEFT: Drawers on each side of the hob are ideal for pots and ovenware.

FAR RIGHT: The mobile butcher's block is an asset in any kitchen.

Building a butcher's block

A good chopping board is indispensable. It is even more useful with legs and wheels so it can be used as extra worktop space as well. This mobile butcher's block is a great project for using up any off-cuts of timber, as it requires a lot of short pieces. Even if you have to buy all the materials, it will be considerably less expensive than purchasing a ready-made block.

You may be able to source the hardwood from a demolition site or architectural salvage company; 80 x 80 mm finished is a convenient size. Obviously, the bigger the section you use, the bigger your block will be. If you are using recycled timber, it must be fully seasoned – this is essential. Make sure, too, that there is no evidence of it having been impregnated with any kind of chemical, oil, etc.

You can mix and match different timbers in the block for visual appeal. Look for medium-density timbers (not too hard so they don't blunt your tools) and avoid those with dirt-gathering, gummy veins. Some possibilities would be beech, elm and hornbeam.

Avoid oily timber, as this will inhibit the gluing process. For the same reason, carry out your gluing and assembly work as soon as possible after the timber has been dressed to avoid any dust or build-up of grease from handling.

The block is built in two halves and then bolted together. You may have to spend some time arranging the individual pieces to obtain the best (squarest) fit.

1　Working on a flat bench, lay out one side with two legs and three blocks. When you have them square, drill two holes though their length so you can bolt them together. If you have a long enough drill (an expensive item), you can first glue the pieces together with PVA woodworking glue, clamp them with a sash cramp and then drill through the entire length. Otherwise, drill each piece individually, making sure the holes all line up. Sand off any drill burrs, thread the rods through and, after applying glue to one face of each joint, put on the washers and nuts, and tighten the rods, clamping the five pieces together. Don't worry if the top is not quite level at this stage – you can sand it flat later. The holes in the legs should be drilled large enough to take the nuts (see diagram), and the rods should be cut so that they don't protrude beyond the holes.

2　Repeat step 1 with five block pieces, squaring them up on top of the first section.

3　Glue the two sections together; clamp them securely.

4　After giving the glue 24 hours to set (you can assemble the other half of the block during this period by repeating steps 1 to 3), drill two 140-mm-deep holes through each block of the second section into the first section. Place glue in each hole, then hammer in the dowels. Repeat this for the other half of the block after its glue has set.

5　Drill holes for the six threaded rods that will hold the two halves together in a similar manner to step 1.

6　Cut off and sand any pieces of protruding dowel. Position and glue a spacer to the leg of each completed block half, then glue and bolt the two halves together.

You will need:			
Components	Material	Length or size in mm	No.
Legs	80 x 80 mm finished hardwood	830	4
Blocks	80 x 80 mm finished hardwood	250	16
Spacers	80 x 80 mm finished hardwood	200	4
Bands	150 x 25 mm finished hardwood	370	2
		450	2
Dowels	8 mm hardwood dowelling	150	20
Corner angles	30 x 30 x 3 mm mild steel angles	120	4

Other: handle; brass towel rail; 10 mm threaded rod (buy six 100 mm lengths and cut to suit); 26 nuts; 26 washers; pair of castors (buy a good solid pair with screw-on base plates); a thick-walled length of metal pipe (preferably copper or brass for appearance) with a bore of at least 10 mm and length of 320 mm.

7 Drill a hole through the centre of each pair of spacers, then bolt the metal pipe in place.

8 Shorten two of the legs by the overall height of the castors and fit them.

9 Sand the top of the block and any other edges that are out of line with a belt sander.

10 Mitre the ends of the timber for the bands, and glue and tack them in place. Drill holes in the corner angles to take 60 mm, round-head, black No. 8 screws, then fit the angles, screwing into the mitred corners.

11 To finish, stain or seal the block, use an edible oil, such as vegetable oil, on the top working face. Finally, fit the brass rail.

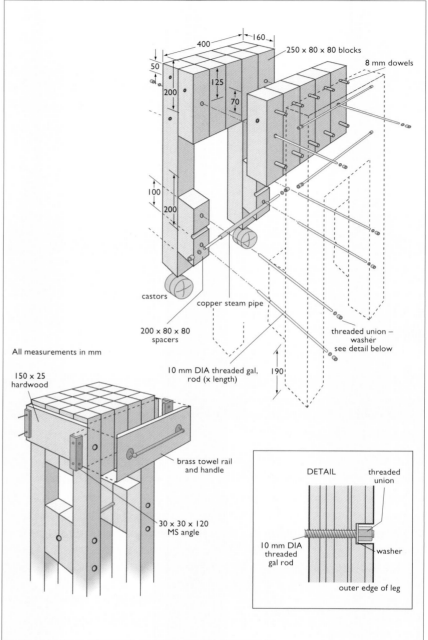

ABOVE: Butcher's block.

LEFT: The island unit can also double as a breakfast bar.

Tips

• You can vary the height of the block to match your worktop simply by using longer legs than those we have specified.

• The key to success with this project is to ensure that all joint faces are clean and square, so take a bit of time over arranging the pieces to get the very best fit.

Bathrooms

Before you begin restyling your bathroom, determine your needs and investigate the options. This may save you much time and effort in the long run.

A bathroom at its most basic consists of an enclosed space and some plumbing fixtures. Yet bathrooms can be among the most complex and challenging parts of a house to design and restyle. The gloomy affairs of yesterday have evolved into the appealing bathing and relaxation rooms of today. Recent trends in bathrooms include brighter spaces, whirlpool baths, luxurious showers, double hand basins, improved lighting, better storage ideas for bathroom accessories and supplies, and bathrooms en suite with master bedrooms.

The best new and restyled bathrooms reflect the way people live today. Life has speeded up considerably in recent decades, and now family members are under more pressure than ever to get up and out of the house quickly. Smart bathroom design can smooth the way by making efficient use of every available square metre while adding visual interest and beauty.

Renovating or adding a bathroom is one of the best home improvement investments you can make. The main benefit is the added enjoyment and pride of

ABOVE: A generously proportioned bathroom in an older house.

ABOVE: Early renovating decisions can help obtain the look you want – such as choosing to keep the wall panelling and pine flooring, then using new panelling for the bath surround for a rustic setting.

TOP RIGHT: White with a touch of warmth added by terracotta tiling and the blue accessories gives a feeling of spaciousness in this small bathroom.

RIGHT: This light, luxurious bathroom has the bath positioned in the bay window so that the bather can take advantage of the garden view.

ownership you'll feel while you continue living in your house. You'll realise benefits if you decide to sell. An adequate number of eye-catching, fully functioning bathrooms is one of the first things people look for when buying a house. The money you spend on a bathroom facelift, expansion or addition almost certainly will increase the value of your property investment.

The key to a successful remodelling is planning. The following pages offer you a systematic approach to the phases of bathroom design, materials selection and construction.

Assess your wants and needs

Before rushing into drawing your floorplans and choosing the fixtures, take the time to determine exactly what you want and need in a new bathroom. You probably have general ideas about this already, but the more thorough and specific you can be from the outset, the more satisfying the final results will be.

Start by taking detailed stock of your present bathroom situation. Consider everything from surface materials to more fundamental issues, such as layout and location. Perhaps new flooring, wallcoverings, vanity tops, cabinets or fixtures would do the trick. Or maybe you'll need to rearrange the layout of an existing bathroom, extend it or create an entirely new one.

ABOVE: Tiling to sill height is practical in a bathroom; the use of colour and pattern here create an Art Deco look.

BELOW: The use of frosted glass on exterior windows and on the screen between bath and toilet ensures privacy without sacrificing light.

Sometimes a bathroom doesn't work well because it has too much space. This occurs most often in houses that were built before the advent of indoor plumbing. When the outdoor privy came indoors, it often was placed in a bedroom or some other space that lacked the correct proportions or scale to function as an efficient bathroom. These old-fashioned bathrooms may contain all the essentials, yet look and feel awkward in actual use, so they offer many opportunities for improvement.

Wants and needs must always be balanced against the budget. Remember not to let your planning decisions get out of touch with financial realities. If you're updating a bathroom to make the house more marketable, make sure you don't overdo it. You could lose money by spending more than realistically you can hope to recover on resale, or by installing unconventional products or materials. If, on the other hand, you plan to live in your present house for the next ten years or more, indulge yourself a little. Remember the trade-off strategy: by choosing, say, standard ceramic tiles from a DIY store as opposed to special tiles from a tile supplier, you'll save money and retain a high resale value. Simple choices can save money that you can put towards a feature you really want, such as a spa, marble vanity top or deluxe shower hardware.

The list of questions on the next page will help you analyse what you need in a new or renovated bathroom. These questions are only a beginning – to get you started in evaluating your situation.

ABOVE: The facelift to this bathroom was achieved with a coat of paint and the installation of new taps and a wooden bath surround.

Take stock of your existing bathroom

- Can two people comfortably and conveniently use the bathroom at the same time?
- Is the basin of adequate size? Would two basins be better?
- Do you use the bath for relaxing soaks, or do you prefer to shower? A built-in shower tray with extra-high sides will render a bath redundant.
- Is the bathroom just for children? Do they like using it? Why or why not? Is it child safe?
- If this is the main family bathroom or a children's bathroom, is it close to the bedrooms? Second bathrooms are sometimes essential, but you might consider one with a shower only, as this can often be squeezed into a very small space. It makes economic sense to place a bathroom next to, or above, a room that already has existing plumbing.
- Does the bathroom relate to adjacent rooms in the way you would like?
- Are there frequent traffic jams in or near the bathroom?
- Is there a door that swings into the traffic path? Doors can be re-hung on the other side of the door frame to make space more efficient.
- Is the room primarily a shower/bath/WC area, or is it also used as a place to shave or apply make-up?

- Are you forever bumping your elbow on a side wall when you brush your teeth?
- Do all the cupboard and entrance doors slide? This will save you a great deal of space, especially if you have a small bathroom.
- Is the WC visible through an open door? A multi-use bathroom will work much better if the WC is separate from it. The addition of partial partitions can help with privacy problems. Also, wall-mounted WCs, bidets and basins make the most of available space and make floor cleaning easier.
- Are there enough light fittings, particularly near the basin and mirror.
- Are there places to hang a towel close to the shower and/or bath?
- Are there allotted spaces for such items as a laundry basket, bathroom scales, towels and a toilet brush and plunger?
- Is there ample convenient storage space?
- Is there a grab handle next to the shower or bath?
- Is there enough vanity-top space?
- Is the bath or shower big enough?
- Are there signs of water damage anywhere?

Level of change

Once you've decided on the kind of bathroom you want, it's time to plot a strategy for achieving your goal. Can it be done with a simple facelift; will it require extending your house; or does it fall somewhere in between? The following five basic restyling categories are arranged in order, from the least to the most costly.

Facelift

If an existing bathroom works well, but needs an infusion of style, it may only need a facelift. This involves re-covering, refinishing or replacing any or all of the existing wall, floor, ceiling and vanity-top surfaces. It also can include replacing the plumbing fixtures and/or adding new lighting, a heater and an extractor fan. With the right combination of well-chosen materi-als, you can make a dramatic change to your bathroom for relatively little money and effort.

Minimal restyling

With a few changes to your existing bathroom layout, you can make a small bathroom function and feel like a larger one. A bathroom as small as 1.5 x 2.5 m, for example, can be divided into sections by adding a wall and perhaps a half-height door, to separate the bath from the WC. Create a sense of expanded space by adding a large mirror or two, installing recessed or strip lighting fixtures, or raising or vaulting the ceiling. When decorating, keep the colours light and the patterns simple.

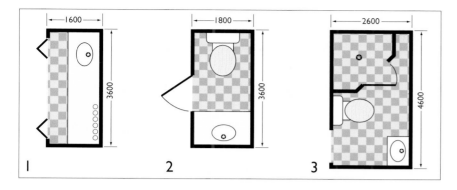

ABOVE: Building an addition.

1 A make-up centre can be installed in an existing cupboard.

2 This half bathroom fits under a staircase or in a coat cupboard.

3 This 100 x 200 mm cupboard space has room for a shower.

BELOW: Black and white is dramatic in a small space.

Expansion

If space is tight, consider expanding the bathroom. You may be able to incorporate all or part of an adjoining cupboard, hallway or bedroom to gain the bathroom space you need. A few extra square metres can make a world of difference.

Finding space

This option involves carving out space from your home's existing floorplan for a new bathroom. To find the space, look first to rooms that already have plumbing – the kitchen or utility room, for example. In multi-storey homes, look to second-floor areas above an existing bathroom, kitchen or utility room. Often, little nooks can be expanded or hidden spaces opened up as shown in the floor plans above. You can make use of space beneath a staircase, for example, or under the eaves in the attic.

Building an addition

If expanding your bathroom or finding space for another one just won't work, you may need to add on to your house. Often, a simple ground-floor extension can yield enough space for a full bathroom. Alternatively, by adding a 900 mm bay window, you might create all the space you need. If you need a new bathroom upstairs, consider using attic space by adding on a dormer. Extra bathrooms and WCs can be fitted into surprisingly small

ABOVE: A half bathroom in an attic can be a convenient solution if you need to add a bathroom, because you often can locate it directly above existing plumbing, making tapping into the supply and drain lines an easy matter.

spaces and can add considerable value to your house.

An important point to remember is that a WC may not open directly on to a kitchen or living room.

Designing or redesigning your bathroom might seem to be a fairly simple undertaking, but because bathrooms are compact, high-activity areas, every small decision is important, every centimetre crucial. Outlined on the following pages are some of the basic space requirements demanded by a range of bathroom products, and aesthetic considerations you might like to take into account.

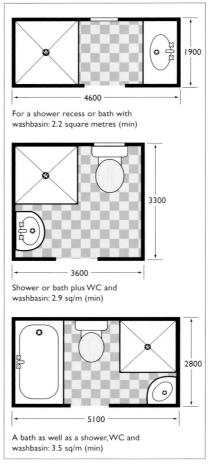

For a shower recess or bath with washbasin: 2.2 square metres (min)

Shower or bath plus WC and washbasin: 2.9 sq/m (min)

A bath as well as a shower, WC and washbasin: 3.5 sq/m (min)

Planning

You should plan carefully before you start spending.

Bathroom layouts

Theoretically, you can build a bathroom as small as you like. In practical terms, however, there are minimum sizes that you should aim for. They are set out here:

- for a shower cubicle or bath with basin – 2.2 sq m;
- for a shower or bath plus WC and basin – 2.9 sq m;
- for a bath, shower cubicle, WC and basin – 3.5 sq m.

If you have no space for a separate utility room, you should allow an additional 0.7 sq m for a washing machine and bath, and 0.5 sq m for a tumble drier.

How to plan your bathroom

Most bathrooms are rectangular or square, so we've concentrated on these two shapes when suggesting possible layouts. The diagrams are designed to help you plan your available space, and determine the size and shape of the fixtures you can accommodate.

Use the examples of floorplans on the following pages to determine your own particular layout, remembering that preventing mistakes at this stage will save you much worry and expense later. (Note that sizes given for fixtures are standard.)

Ventilation

Planning to install a ceiling extractor fan? Then remember that the heat and moisture it removes must be discharged to the outside air – not into the roof space. Flexible ducting must be installed between the extractor fan's outlet spigot and

ABOVE: An all white colour scheme always gives a bathroom a clean, spacious atmosphere. The narrow shelf behind the cantilevered basin looks stylish and the marble and embossed tiles add texture.

ABOVE RIGHT: Bathroom layouts.

RIGHT: Toilet/powder room layouts.

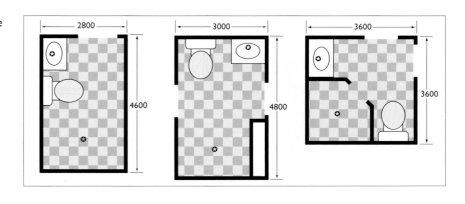

Some important dos and don'ts

- Your local council needs to know what you propose to do, as some of the work may require approval under the Building Regulations.
- Your local council will tell you what its requirements are in specific circumstances. For example, a room containing a WC cannot open directly on to a kitchen or living room.
- Internal bathrooms must have adequate ventilation; you may need a skylight and/or extractor fan.
- Although there is no reason why you should not carry out all the work yourself, unless you are totally competent, you will be better off employing a qualified plumber and electrician.

a roof vent mounted at ridge level. Alternatively, it can be led to an outlet grille fitted into the roof eaves.

Bathroom sizes

Once you've decided on the part of the house the bathroom will serve best and who will be using it, the next basic question is: 'What type of bathroom am I planning?' To find the answer, make an inventory of the shortcomings of your current bathroom. Keep a list of your general wants and needs as you start to become more specific about your restyling plan and what size bathroom you want to create.

Don't rush the process. According to many design experts, you should spend as much time planning your new bathroom as it takes for the construction phase of the project. Visit show homes and exhibitions to gather design ideas, and check out plumbing supply firms for product ideas.

ABOVE LEFT: Storage need not always be built in. Free-standing furniture can be suitable for storing rolled up towels or even books.

ABOVE RIGHT: The richness of dark-stained timber is complemented by white woodwork and hand-painted blue and white striped walls.

ABOVE: A pleasant and practical bathroom with innovative tiled storage.

Avoiding perils

Common sense reduces risks in the bathroom. Here are some simple steps you can take to make your home safer for the whole family:

- Store chemicals, cleaners and medicines in high-level cupboards where children can't see them.
- Make sure cupboards can be locked.
- Install grab rails in the bath and shower.
- Purchase child-proof packaging for dangerous substances whenever possible.
- Make sure that the flooring is slip-resistant.
- If you have a rug in the bathroom, it should have non-slip backing.
- It's best if vanity tops have rounded corners.
- Water heater temperature should not be too hot.
- Never leave a small child unattended in the bathroom.
- Install locks that can be opened from inside and out.
- Provide a sturdy step-stool so children can reach taps and vanity tops easily.
- Shower enclosures must always be of safety glass or acrylic material.
- Remember, you're not allowed to install power points in the bathroom. However, you are permitted to install a low-voltage shaver point. Some of these are incorporated in fluorescent light fittings for mounting over a mirror.

The following describes the three basic bathroom options, along with the minimum size requirements for each.

Half bathroom or cloakroom

A basin and WC constitute a 'half bathroom' or cloakroom. Typically, half bathrooms are located close to the main living areas of the house. They're intended primarily for visitors' use and can provide an invaluable back-up to the main bathroom. Suitable dimensions for half bathrooms are 1.2 x 1.5 m or 1 x 2 m. At a pinch, they can be as small as 1 x 1.8 m or 1.4 x 1.4 m and still work effectively.

A half bathroom is often the most overlooked part of the house. It's tempting to ignore a room that's not used often, but you should think of your guests and the impressions they'll take away from their visit. Because they are generally small, half bathrooms offer a great opportunity to indulge in fun, offbeat or lavish decorating. Also they can provide a lot of convenience in a small space.

Three-quarter bathroom

Equipped with a shower cubicle instead of a bath, a three-quarter bathroom can be squeezed into a space that measures 1.8 x 1.8 m.

If your family prefers showering to soaking, a three-quarter bathroom could solve your morning traffic jams. This kind of bathroom is ideal as a guest bathroom, a bathroom for older children or a back-up for the main family bathroom.

Full bathroom

Typically located close to bedrooms, a full bathroom will contain a basin, WC and bath. The bath may also offer a shower facility, or there may be a separate shower cubicle. The minimum room size needed to accommodate this full range of fixtures is 1.5 x 2 m. Many different floorplans are possible, although it all depends on your particular wants, needs and budget.

At least 20 cm should separate the top of a vanity splashback from the bottom of a medicine cabinet or mirror.

RIGHT: A separate bath and shower are useful in a family bathroom.

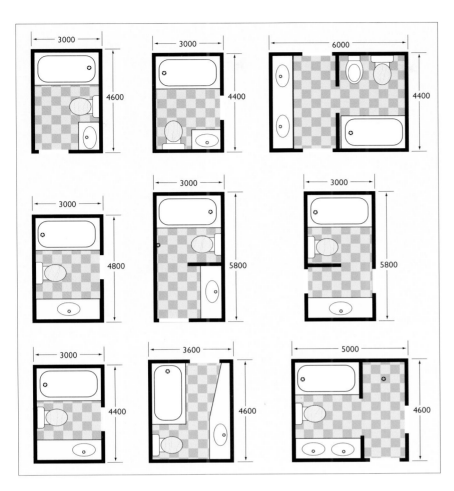

LEFT: Bathroom floor plans.

BELOW: A glass brick wall lets in the light but maintains privacy. The inexpensive vanity provides ample storage for everyday items, while a glass soap jar is practical as well as decorative. The carpet flooring matches the pastel theme.

Allow at least 40 cm from the centre of the WC to any obstruction, fixture or equipment on each side. For clearance in front of the WC, ensure an open floor space of 1.2 x 1.2 m. A good 40 cm of that floor space should extend to each side of the WC's centre line. You should allow at least 2.5 cm between the back of the WC cistern and the wall behind it.

The toilet paper holder should be positioned 15 cm beyond the front of the seat, with the roller 65 cm above the floor.

Minimum interior shower dimensions are 75 x 75 cm, but most people prefer more room. Swinging shower doors must open into the bathroom, away from the shower's interior.

The standard height for vanities is 75–80 cm. Adjust the height upwards for tall users. In bathrooms equipped with two vanities, one can be 75–80 cm high and the other can be 85–105 cm high.

A WC isolated in a separate compartment should occupy a space 90 cm wide by 165 cm deep with a swing-out door. Dividing walls are normally about 15 cm thick (this includes the thickness of the skirting at the bottom of both sides), so allow space for them.

Shapes and sizes

Do lots of homework! Shop around for basins, WCs, baths and bidets so that your choice of shape and material will suit both your taste and your pocket. You'll find that they come in materials including enamelled cast iron, vitreous china, acrylic and fibreglass, while bath shapes can be rectangular or square, circular or oval, even

triangular. You can choose from basins that are wall-mounted, fit on top of pedestals or that are designed to be built into vanity tops.

Then there's the importance of storage. It's wise to work out what you need and choose to store in the bathroom. Certainly toiletries, towels, cleaning materials, soaps, toilet paper and toothbrushes come to mind, but you may want more areas for specialised storage – now's the time to plan them.

It's also the time to work out your lighting needs. All fittings must be located safely, well away from wet areas, and be operated by pull-cord switches, or switches outside the bathroom.

Hand basins

Before you choose a bathroom basin, consider how the basin material will influence its looks, how durable it will be and how much maintenance it will require. Each of the following materials has its own characteristics.

Porcelain-enamelled cast iron is extremely durable and is easy to care for, but it's heavy and needs a sturdy support system.

Stainless steel is durable and unaffected by household chemicals. The steel, however, tends to collect spots from hard water and soap.

Vitreous china has a lustrous surface, is easy to clean and is the most resistant to discolouration and corrosion. However, it is not as durable as other materials and can chip easily if struck by a heavy object.

Fibreglass and acrylic can be moulded into novel shapes, but don't hold a shine as well as other surfaces, nor are they as durable as the other materials mentioned.

Simulated or cultured marble and other solid-surface materials are handsome, but they may chip when struck by a heavy object, while abrasive cleaners may spoil the finish. Shallow nicks and scratches can be removed by sanding gently with fine-grade sandpaper.

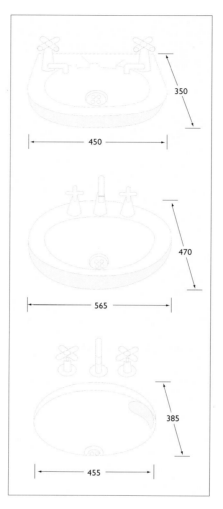

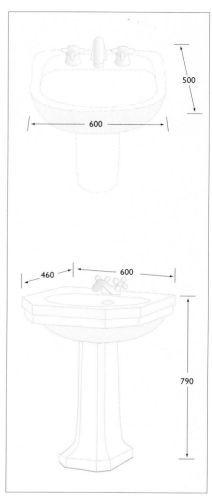

Styles of basin fall into three categories: those that stand on pedestals, those that hang on the wall, and those that rest in vanities. For both pedestal- and wall-mounted basins, you should allow a minimum of 50 mm on each side for elbow room. In front of the basin, you will need a metre, but this can also be the all-important room circulation space.

Pedestal

A pedestal basin not only gives a bathroom distinctive charm, but it also can make a small bathroom look larger because there isn't a wide vanity top around the basin or storage below the basin itself. These advantages are the main disadvantages, too, since pedestal

ABOVE LEFT AND ABOVE RIGHT:
Hand basin styles.

basins make for a lack of vanity space and less storage.

One criticism of many pedestal basins is that they provide little room for putting anything down.

Wall-mounted

Usually designed for compact spaces, wall-hung basins have the advantage of being suitable for squeezing into small bathrooms. However, like pedestal basins, many wall-hung basins provide no facility for storage below, nor do they conceal the plumbing. Often, wall-hung basins are installed in bathrooms designed for the disabled, because they can be mounted at any height and have clear space underneath that allows for easy wheelchair access.

Vanity

Vanity basins have lots of flat surface around them and handy storage below. Their main drawback is that they require the most floor space of any basin style.

Basins in vanities can be attached in a variety of ways:

- A self-rimming or surface-mounted basin sits on the vanity top with its bowl accommodated by a hole cut in the top. The outer rim overlaps the top and forms a watertight seal with it. This type of basin is probably the easiest to install because the hole in the bench top need not be perfect, as it's hidden once the basin has been installed.

- Rimmed basins sit just slightly above the vanity top and have a tight-fitting metal rim that joins the basin and the vanity top. The rim can be chosen with a finish to match the taps being used. The disadvantages with rimmed basins are that the rim joint can be difficult to clean, and they are difficult to install.

- Under-mounted basins are attached to the bottom of the vanity top, giving a clean, tailored look. Under-mounted

basins can be difficult to clean where they attach to the top.

- Integral basins are formed as part of the same piece of material as the vanity's top. Because there is no joint between the bowl and the vanity top, they are easy to clean and no waterproof seal is required. The main disadvantage is that the entire unit must be replaced if any part of it is damaged.

Vanity tops

When it comes to vanity tops, look for something that will stand up to water, soap, alcohol- and acetone-based liquids, toothpaste and cosmetics. Replacing a vanity top, or adding a new one, is a feasible do-it-yourself project, and you don't have to replace the whole cabinet if you don't want to.

Most bathroom vanity tops are surfaced with plastic laminate, tiles, a solid-surface material such as simulated marble, wood or genuine marble or granite.

BELOW: Laminate is widely used on bathroom vanity tops.

although you may have difficulty in matching the quality of a professionally-made example.

Tiles

Ceramic tiles provide an attractive, durable finish for vanity tops. They are available in many colours, designs and textures. Grout lines that trap dirt and encourage mould are a drawback, but modern mould-resistant grouts and sealants help alleviate these problems.

Obtaining professional-looking results with tiles is a challenge for do-it-yourselfers. A slightly irregular look can be appropriate for rustic, unglazed quarry tiles, but other tile varieties demand greater precision. Using sheets of mosaic tile on a mesh backing makes it easier to space tiles evenly.

Solid-surface material

Solid-surface vanity tops offer many of the advantages of stone with few of the drawbacks. Cast from an acrylic resin, solid-surface material demands little maintenance and is extremely durable. Intense heat and heavy falling objects (which shouldn't pose much of a threat in a bathroom) can cause damage, but scratches, abrasions and even minor burns can be repaired with fine-grade sandpaper. The methods and tools needed for working with this material are similar to those for woodworking. Some manufacturers require that a professional install the material.

Solid-surface material is available in a range of colours and stone effects. It comes in flat sheets and as ready-formed vanity tops with pre-moulded basins.

Wood

As a vanity top, wood is attractive, versatile and easy to install. However, it is especially vulnerable to water damage, and its porosity makes it hard to keep clean. Whether hardwood or softwood, it must be well sealed with polyurethane or marine varnish.

ABOVE: Tiles are the most commonly used surface in bathrooms.

BELOW: Floor tiles can also be used on vanity tops.

Plastic laminate

Plastic laminate offers good value and performance. As a result, it is a widely used vanity-top material. Various manufacturers market laminate under different brand names, but they're all basically the same – a stack of thin plastic layers bonded together under heat and pressure. Plastic laminate is easy to clean and resistant to water and stains. On the negative side, laminates can burn, wear thin and dull over time. Hard blows can chip or dent the plastic, and there's no remedy short of replacement.

Available in many colours and patterns, plastic laminate finishes range in texture from high-gloss, glassy smoothness to a mottled, leather-like appearance. Dealers usually have a few standard patterns in stock; you can order others after consulting colour charts.

Do-it-yourselfers can buy pre-fabricated plastic laminate vanity tops or have them made to order with a hole cut for the basin. Installing the finished top is a fairly easy matter. You can also apply sheets of plastic laminate to your own chipboard vanity top,

Special care should be taken to seal around the edges of plumbing fixtures so that water can't seep in.

Marble and granite

Although marble and granite are unrivalled for their beauty, these classic materials warrant careful thought before being used in a bathroom. Marble stains easily. Granite shrugs off most stains, except from grease (especially if it is unsealed). If a solid sheet of stone is beyond your budget, marble or granite tiles may be substituted as a cheaper alternative.

Cultured marble is less expensive and is made from real chips of natural marble embedded in resin. It's available in sheet form and in standard dimensions. Although it is easy to clean, cultured marble must be well cared for. Once scratched, it cannot be resurfaced. Follow the manufacturer's recommendations for the type of finish to apply to cultured marble to protect it.

Taps

Most bathroom taps receive heavy daily use, so don't choose them on appearance alone; you must also consider ease of use, safety and durability. With taps, price is a fairly accurate measure of quality. A warranty is a good indication of high quality.

Tap finishes include chrome, polished brass, coloured epoxy coating, nickel and gold. Polished brass finishes usually are lacquered to keep them from tarnishing. Chrome is the standard finish for most taps because it is durable and is easily cleaned. The best sets are made of brass and come in various finishes and designs.

Before you buy, make sure the tap set is of the proper size and design for your plumbing fixture. Basins and baths have pre-formed holes in their rims to accommodate standard taps and plumbing.

Bathroom taps come in two basic types: pillar and mixer. Pillar taps

are single units, two being fitted to a basin or bath for separate control of hot and cold water. They may be mounted on each side of a basin or next to each other on a bath, depending on the position of the mounting holes. Pillar taps may be equipped with an old-fashioned cruciform-type handle or a more modern knob.

Mixer taps come in a variety of designs, but all have two water inlets (for hot and cold supplies) and a single outlet. All have separate hot and cold water controls so that the individual flows can be adjusted to obtain the desired water temperature delivered from the spout. Some mixer taps have divided flows that keep the hot and cold supplies separate until they reach the end of the spout; others mix the two within the body of the tap. If both hot and cold supplies come from a storage cistern, either type can be used, but if the cold supply

ABOVE: Marble is classic and durable.

BELOW: Gooseneck taps on the basins match that on the bath.

comes direct from the mains, only the divided-flow type is permissible under the Water Byelaws to prevent the possibility of back-siphonage and contamination of the mains supply.

Usually the body of a mixer tap is mounted above the rim of the basin or bath, but some units are available where the body is beneath the rim, leaving only the spout and two controls visible. Some mixer taps also incorporate a control for a pop-up waste, while others may have a shower-hose attachment.

WCs and bidets

The amount of space required for a WC varies greatly from one type to another. However, the average depth from the back of the cistern to the front of the seat is 650 mm. Widths of cisterns range from 350 to 580 mm. For the overall space requirements, you should allow at least 450 mm from the centre of the seat to a large obstruction (to the side), such as a wall or bath. Allow at least 400 mm from the centre of the seat to the edge of a basin at the side.

Bidets require less space because they don't have cisterns.

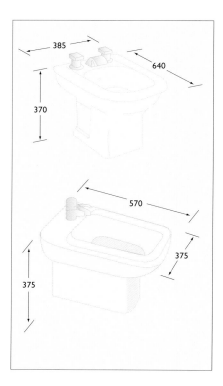

In general, they are about 570 mm front to back and require a 140 mm space behind them. In front of both the WC and bidet seat, you should allow 650 mm (minimum) floor space.

Accessories

These days, you can choose accessories to match any style of bathroom, from Victorian to ultra modern. Some people prefer not to have them matching perfectly, although that is the most obvious way to go. Consider building in the odd shelf with tiles or adding an old, distressed, recycled shelf rather than automatically resorting to matching 'suites' of bathroom accessories.

Showers

Ideally, a square shower should be no smaller than 900 x 900 mm, but a rectangular shower can be as narrow as 750 mm.

Some shower trays are about 300 mm deep and incorporate a seat.

ABOVE LEFT: Bidets.

ABOVE RIGHT: Toilets.

LEFT: This luxurious bathroom has an outlook to the garden and is large enough to accommodate shower, bath and twin basins.

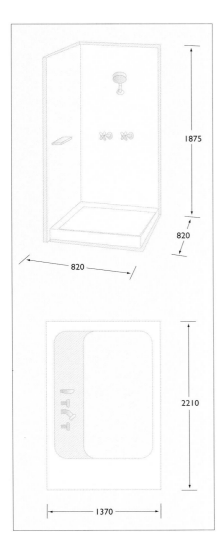

ABOVE: Shower styles.

BELOW: Two types of spa bath.

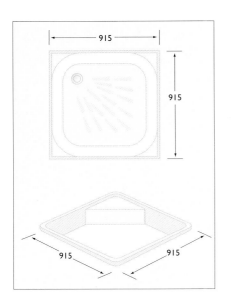

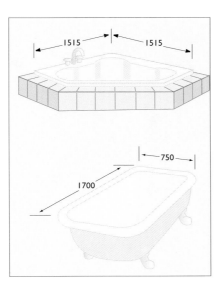

ABOVE: Old and new bath styles.

directional

gooseneck

colonial hand set

overhead

ABOVE: A tiled ledge alongside the bath can also be used for storage

LEFT: Four types of shower head.

These are particularly suited to the elderly. Tiled shower cubicles require ceramic, fibreglass or acrylic shower trays. These are fixed in place before the tiles are applied to the walls and grouted. A silicon seal waterproofs the joint between tray and tiles.

Prefabricated shower cubicles come with a set of fibreglass wall panels that combine with the tray.

Baths

Today you can have the bath of your dreams – anything from the freestanding, old-fashioned cast iron type on legs to a luxurious spa with pulsing water jets. Similarly, you can find a bath to fit virtually any space available. There are corner-style bath/showers that are the space-efficient solution when there is not enough room for a full bath and separate shower cubicle.

ABOVE: Shelving units that glide out work better than drawers, because storage items stay neat instead of getting in a jumble.

ABOVE RIGHT: This bathroom built for two is outfitted with compartments so there's no question where items go. The double vanity houses pull-out towel racks, tilt-out drawers and a rubbish bin.

Storage

In bathrooms, as in kitchens and homes as a whole, it's nearly impossible to include too much storage space. Having easy access to grooming supplies and toiletries is essential near the basin, bath, shower and WC.

Basin area

The basin area can have two primary storage facilities: the vanity and the medicine cabinet. When selecting a vanity, consider how you will use it. Will it store cleaning supplies? Towels? Face cloths? Soaps and shampoos? Cosmetics? All of these items? Your answers will determine the most efficient combi-nation of cabinet space and draw-ers. Some vanities resemble chests of drawers; others are simple base cabinets; most combine drawer and cabinet space. By raising the height of the vanity top, you gain addi-tional storage space below.

If you intend keeping an existing vanity, you may be able to improve its storage capacity by making a few simple modifications. Mount wire racks inside cabinet doors to hold cleaning supplies; add shelves or half shelves to create more space. Take a cue from kitchen cab-inetry and include pull-out features, such as a rubbish bin, shelves and towel rods. If budget and space allow, create built-in nooks for holding your toothbrush, razors and other grooming aids.

A mirrored medicine cabinet above the vanity provides ideal storage for cosmetics and toiletries. Units are available in a variety of styles. Look for examples with adjustable shelves to accommodate items of various sizes, and use cos-metic organisers to keep small items in order. Larger, three-door units provide even more storage space.

Bathing area

Look for bath and shower sur-rounds that have ample built-in niches for storage of shampoos, conditioners, soaps and bath oils. For more storage space, buy a plastic or ceramic shower shelf. You may need to drill and plug the tiles to attach this with rustproof brass screws; other types attach to shower walls with suction cups.

Use wall space at the ends of the bath to mount towel rails. To keep bath salts and lotions handy, you can place shallow shelves above the towel rails or on the back wall, above the bath. If you have a central heating radiator in the bathroom, you can fit it with a clip-on towel rail, which is ideal for hanging wet towels to dry.

WC area

Wall space above a WC is a good place to install a wall-mounted cupboard or a freestanding shelf unit that straddles the WC cistern. If you choose a WC with a concealed cistern, you can box the cistern in and not only produce a neater looking installation, but also provide a useful shelf area behind the WC. This may be an attractive option when the wall behind the WC contains a window.

Other storage tips

Use wall space wisely. Hang towel rails above one another. Top a row of hooks or pegs with a shelf, hanging bath towels on the hooks and stacking hand towels and face cloths on the shelf.

Add shelves wherever practical. This could be almost anywhere in the bathroom, since many shelving products come in a variety of widths and can be cut to any length. Corner shelves take advantage of frequently wasted space. Create an illusion of spaciousness (and more storage space) with glass or mirrored shelves.

Revamp an existing cupboard by converting the bottom half into a chest of drawers or a built-in laundry basket. Install open shelves or cubicles for rolled bath towels in the upper portion.

Bring in items from other rooms. Chests of drawers, china cabinets and antique kitchen cupboards add character and storage space. Just remember to finish wood furniture with a moisture-resistant sealer.

Develop a colour scheme

Creating a good colour palette for your bathroom can be a challenge, but there's nothing forbidding or mysterious about it. The following general guidelines will help.

For the sake of continuity, carry your home's overall personality into the bathroom. Link the bathroom with adjoining rooms by matching colour values (that is, the colours' darkness or lightness) as well as actual hues. For example, if the woodwork on the landing outside the bathroom is painted a high-gloss creamy white, consider using that colour in the bathroom.

Most successful colour schemes use a minimum of three and a maximum of six colours. Three-colour schemes consist of a main colour (the prevalent colour used on most surfaces), a secondary colour (often used on cabinets, woodwork and/or some wall or ceiling surfaces) and an accent colour (the least-used colour to provide interest, variety and balance). The accent is often the brightest or darkest colour in a scheme; use it in at least three places (or on one major design element) to establish a definite presence.

Give thought to the colour of every component: walls, ceiling, window and door frames, skirting, floor, furniture, vanity tops, fixtures, curtains and accessories.

When deciding where to place colours, determine what you want the main focus of the room to be. It is important to remember that the eye is attracted first to the lightest colour. If the walls aren't the main focus, they should not be painted the lightest colour.

White (including ivory and cream) fixtures can not only be less expensive, but they are also easier to clean than dark items.

White comes in many tones, and choosing from among them can be

ABOVE: Framed with mouldings that match the door, this built-in storage unit was carved from space often overlooked in bathrooms – the area between the end of the bath and the wall.

ABOVE: In this bathroom, the mottled grey woodwork complements the muted green walls and pure white floor.

difficult. Decide if you want a cool white or a warm white, then choose one specific hue. Match all the white or off-white elements so that various tones won't be competing with each other.

If you use the bathroom for applying make-up, choose lighter versions of the colours of the clothes that look good on you. The lighter colours will reflect flattering light, allowing you to ensure that your make-up colours are correct.

Vanity-top colours that keep their good looks are lighter mid-tones, greys and beiges. Dark colours have poor reflective qualities; solids tend to show marks; and white shows stains.

White cabinets can make a small bathroom seem larger. Dark cabinets will have the opposite effect. Be sure to use dark cabinets only in a well-lit bathroom.

Planning a cosmetics centre

If your bathroom is large enough, you may be able to incorporate a cosmetics centre where you can apply your make-up, but, because you are not allowed to have power points in the bathroom, a hair drier will have to be used elsewhere. You can always incorporate a shaver point, however.

Purchase drawer organisers for cosmetics, brushes and combs.

Make your bathroom children friendly

Protect your children against potential dangers in the bathroom by heeding these additional safety precautions:

- Keep face cloths and toys beside the bath so you won't be tempted to leave your child unattended in the bath.

- A cushion around the bath-tap spout, as well as edge and corner cushions on cabinets, can help to prevent cuts and bruises.

- Install child-proof locks on all cabinets. Even the WC lid should have a latch.

- Use only non-breakable drinking tumblers in a bathroom. Store them where children can reach them without having to climb precariously.

- Add slip-resistant strips in front of the basin and bath. Anchor rugs with non-slip pads or double-faced carpet tape.

- Make sure grab bars inside the bath and shower stall are low enough for children to use.

- Choose taps and handles that are easy to use and that have rounded edges.

- Locate towel rails or rings 15 cm or less from the bath or the door to a shower cubicle so children don't have to reach too far for them.

ABOVE RIGHT: A children's bathroom should allow space for toys.

RIGHT: A well lit bathroom with slat blinds to control the amount of natural light.

Light it right. If possible, light the cosmetics centre to duplicate the lighting in the place where you will spend the most time. That is, if you work in a setting with fluorescent lighting, your make-up centre should have fluorescent lighting. The best make-up centres allow users to switch easily from one type of lighting to another, but these can be expensive.

Ensure the proper distance between yourself and the mirror. When applying eye make-up or lipstick, it may be difficult to get close enough to the vanity mirror, so supplement it with a good freestanding mirror.

Carry out a facelift

Small changes can add up to major results. A well-planned facelift will not only bring a fresh, updated look to an older bathroom, but also it can make a small bathroom look and feel more spacious.

Facelifts normally involve paint, wallpaper, vanity-top surfacing materials, light fixtures and accessories. They also can help solve spatial problems. Using space better and minor adjustments to doors, accessories and cabinets improve the way the bathroom functions.

Take a moment to consider what kinds of problems you experience when using the bathroom in question. Simply correcting what bothers you can make a big difference and may not always require major changes. For example, if the bathroom door hits fixtures or obstructs cabinets, you might improve matters by changing the direction in which it opens. If you need to keep costs down, don't relocate fixtures, especially the WC. Sometimes turning the WC so that it faces in a different direction (which can be done by changing the waste-pipe connector) can give you more room to manoeuvre. Also, you can angle the vanity into a corner. If there's a severe shortage of space, install a smaller vanity – or a pedestal basin – and a WC with shallow cistern.

When you carry out a bathroom facelift, re-evaluate the room's storage potential. If the room is more than 1.5 m wide, you may have space to add a cabinet or shelves at the end of the bath. Shelves above the WC or on the back of the door also help.

Make a small bathroom feel large

You don't have to increase the area of an existing bathroom to make the space seem larger and work better for you. Just keep the following ideas and areas of improvement in mind. Some of them fall into the facelift category, while others require more extensive restyling strategies:

- Light. Install adequate lighting to eliminate shadowy corners. Create an illusion of height by focusing low-wattage, indirect lighting on the ceiling.

BELOW: The easiest way to give a room a facelift is with paint. In this case, white contrasts with coffee-toned wallpaper and bench tops in aubergine and chocolate to make an unusual but striking colour scheme. The main storage area, reflected in the mirror, is decorative as well as functional.

- Downsize. Swap large fixtures for smaller ones. Switch a bath for a corner shower, or a bulky vanity for a sleek pedestal basin.
- Design. Use no more than two dominant horizontal lines. The top of a dado rail, for instance, establishes one line. Aligning tops of doors, windows, mirrors and bath/shower enclosures establishes a second line.
- Minimise. Don't mix a lot of materials; stick with one, such as tiles for floors, walls and vanity tops. Get rid of clutter. Choose wallpaper patterns that are light and small in scale. Reject frilly curtains and furry mats.
- Reflect. Use large mirrors to make walls look like windows.

Re-enamel the bath

Pedestrian as it may seem, re-enamelling an old bath can go a long way towards brightening a tired bathroom. A new coat of epoxy paint can cover up an unsightly colour or chipped finish without the mess and expense of replacing the whole fixture. It's a job for professionals, but it can be done without moving the bath. The job takes 4–6 hours, after which the new finish should cure for a few days before the bath is used.

Renovate

Renovation goes beyond cosmetic changes to encompass replacing fixtures, changing the layout, adding lighting, enlarging or replacing windows, and making any structural changes. You'll save money if your plan calls for replacing, rather than moving, the bath, basin and shower. You'll have to balance your need to move any fixtures against your budget.

Space-stretching strategies

As the smallest rooms in most houses, bathrooms pose some of the biggest decorating and restyling challenges. Every centimetre of space must count. Putting one or all of the following ideas into practice will help you create a stylish, affordable, efficient bathroom.

Go for more vanity space

Forget balancing grooming items on the edge of a small basin. Augment the available space by extending the vanity as far as possible on both sides. You'll obtain even more space if you extend a narrow piece of the vanity top over the WC (remember not to block access to the cistern).

Increase storage

Just as older homes never have enough cupboard space, older bathrooms invariably lack storage. In addition to the other storage ideas in this chapter, replacing a narrow medicine cabinet with a wider one and/or building cabinets above the bath for seldom-used items are good storage solutions.

Add light

There's no better way to bring daylight into a bathroom than by adding a skylight, if the location

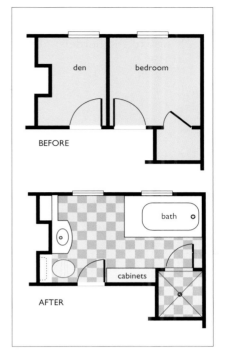

ABOVE: Here, space for a bathroom was gained by knocking out a wall.

BELOW: The installation of a bay window added light and an alcove for the bath in this renovation.

allows it. Be careful – condensation on skylights can cause moisture problems, especially during winter in colder areas. It is important to buy only a high-quality unit and make sure it's installed according to the manufacturer's specifications.

Putting in a skylight requires installing framing between the bathroom ceiling and the roof to create a skylight shaft. Shafts that flare outwards towards the bottom admit more daylight. Paint the shaft white for maximum light transmission and to give the illusion of space, or paint it a colour that will give the bathroom a warm glow.

Divide and conquer

One popular approach to making the most of existing bathroom space is to divide it into compartments. Separating the bath, shower and WC from the vanity area with a wall and half-height door creates a division of functions and enhances privacy. This can make it possible for the room to serve more than one user at a time.

Expand

If the amount of space in an existing bathroom simply won't do, borrow extra from adjoining areas. Look first to cupboards and other spaces that abut your current bathroom's 'wet wall' – the wall that

already contains plumbing pipes. It's far less expensive to install fixtures when you can connect them to nearby pipes. If you want to expand a main bathroom, think about leaving the WC and bath in their original locations and expanding adjacent space to accommodate the basin (or basins) and dressing room. That way, you will save money and labour by not moving the plumbing fixtures that are the most difficult to relocate.

Carve out space for a new bathroom

Facelifting, renovating and expanding can do only so much good if what you really need is another bathroom. Before concluding that you need to build an addition to your house, however, examine the existing floorplan. You may find some under-used space where a new bathroom would fit in well.

ABOVE LEFT: Before – This tiny bathroom, only the length of a bath wide and slightly more than that long, needed to be made both functional and visually much larger. It had only three small windows – two of them high up, and no storage at all.

ABOVE: After – The new grey and white colour scheme is streamlined and works perfectly in the small space. The high windows were replaced with a flat skylight. The use of small tiles on the bath and walls and two large mirrors facing one another help the space look larger. The new built-in vanity created much needed storage space.

But where should you look? Often, a half bathroom near the family room can take the burden off a one-bathroom house, as can installing a self-contained shower cubicle in a bedroom. An under-used utility room is a good candidate for conversion because it will be equipped with plumbing already. Look, too, at areas close to the bedrooms. A vacant corner of the master bedroom is a likely spot for an additional bathroom, provided that the bedroom has one dimension that measures at least 5 m.

Another possibility is to divide a large existing bathroom into two smaller bathrooms, providing access to one of them from the landing. Alternatively, you could transform a small bedroom into a full bathroom, then (if necessary) add another bedroom in another part of the house, such as the attic or downstairs.

Creating a bathroom in an existing space doesn't have to be a major project that leaves you in debt for decades. If you're careful, practical and place new fixtures near an existing soil stack, the cost will be reasonable. The main question is where you'll locate the WC. If the new fixture cannot easily be plumbed into an existing soil stack, the resulting complications can add a large sum to your restyling budget. If you can't arrange for a new

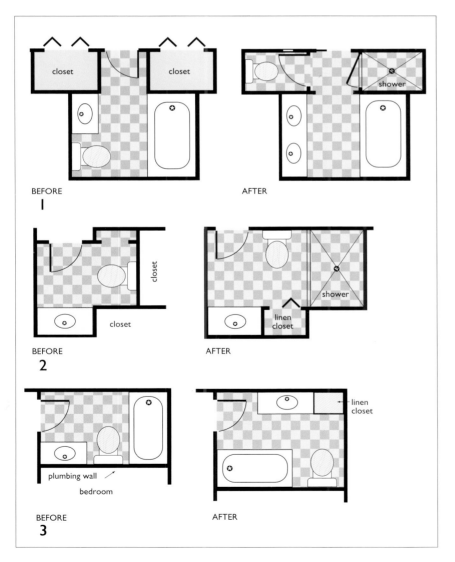

BEFORE — 1 — AFTER

BEFORE — 2 — AFTER

BEFORE — 3 — AFTER

LEFT: Plans for expansion:

1 Built-in wardrobes between bedrooms and bathrooms provide an opportunity for expansion. Simply annex one (or both) wardrobes.

2 By expanding into the wardrobe space, this small half bathroom was transformed into a full bathroom with a large shower and linen cupboard.

3 The plumbing wall in this small bathroom was moved 450 mm into an adjacent bedroom, creating enough space for fixtures to be placed opposite each other. Moving and adding plumbing were less expensive than adding on to the house.

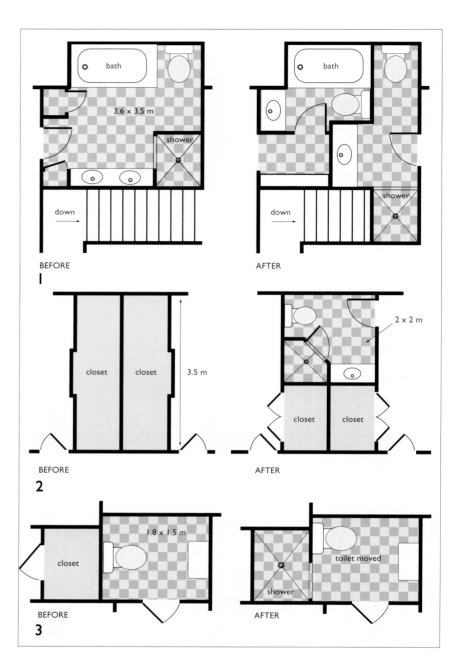

ABOVE: Plans for finding space for a full bathroom:

1. In this project, a large master bathroom was divided into two bathrooms. One opens on to the master bedroom, the other on to a second bedroom.

2. Two back-to-back wardrobes yield enough space for a modest bathroom with shower and two reduced-sized wardrobes.

3. This powder room was transformed into a full bathroom simply by relocating the toilet and adding a shower in what used to be wardrobe space.

bathroom to be adjacent to an existing one, try to site it directly over the kitchen or utility room below, to simplify access to existing pipework.

Ease of access is essential. Many home owners fail to consider this and position the new bathroom in an out-of-the-way place. Size, too, is very important. Fitting all the necessities of a bathroom into too small a space is an unwise investment. If you don't have the necessary room, think about adding on.

Make it stylish

A remodelled bathroom is the perfect place for design flourishes. Because bathrooms are smaller than most other rooms, the quantities of materials required are relatively modest, so you may be able to splash out on extra features and fancier materials without breaking your budget. Here are a few design suggestions to help you make your new bathroom a comfortable, even inspiring, place to be.

- Create drama and impact in a modest-sized bathroom with special tile designs.
- Make views within the room interesting. The least costly way is to use mirrors.
- Allow subdivided spaces to share light and air. Add an internal window or transparent glazing to the walls of divided spaces.
- Don't skimp on windows. Light and ventilation are especially important in bathrooms.

Surface materials

A restyled bathroom that looks good, but doesn't work from a practical standpoint is bound to disappoint its owners. Assuming that you've designed the room's layout to meet your wishes and needs, the next most important factor is the finish materials – the surfaces, fixtures and flourishes that set the room's style and determine how it will hold up over time.

Your top priority should be choosing materials that will be appropriate to the way you and your family will use the bathroom. Beyond that, the best idea is to equip your bathroom with materials, fixtures and features that have become standard in new, comparably-priced homes. If you're planning to live in the house for a while, however, make the materials as personal as you please, since resale will be less important than enjoyment value.

This section discusses bath and shower enclosures, floors and walls, and materials that are available to cover these surfaces. Some materials have more than one application, but may function better on one surface than another.

Bath and shower surrounds

Any surface material for a bath or shower surround should be applied on top of water-resistant wall material. The most common type is

water-resistant plasterboard. A more durable and popular product is fibre cement, which is also water resistant. Fibre cement products may be more expensive than plasterboard, but the added expense gives you a foundation that you know can stand up to the moist environment of the bathroom. The surface material itself must be waterproof, not just water resistant.

Various manufacturers offer pre-fabricated surrounds made of fibreglass, acrylic, vinyl, plastic laminate and synthetic stone. However, you should avoid buying a one-piece surround (typically made of moulded fibreglass) unless you choose a unit that can be moved into the bathroom through available openings. Multi-piece surround kits that can be assembled inside the bathroom are also available.

If you decide you want to create your own bath or bath surround, you will have a choice of the following surface materials.

Solid-surface material

For durable, stylish, easy-to-care-for shower enclosures, solid-surface material is hard to beat. Although sometimes pricey, today's options in this category have a lot to offer.

ABOVE: A basic white tiled bathroom with little ornamentation can be transformed into a warm room simply by adding colours. Here, brightly coloured wall panelling, striped wallpaper, and whimsical soap dishes and holders add sparkle without major changes to the bathroom's design.

ABOVE: Ceramic tiles are a logical choice in bathrooms.

Nothing beats this smooth acrylic surface for ease of cleaning, and the material lasts a lifetime.

For do-it-yourselfers, solid-surface bath and shower kits offer easy installation. These kits generally consist of pre-cut panels and curved corner mouldings. They are designed to go with standard fixtures; non-standard installations require professional help.

Ceramic tiles

Waterproof, durable and easy to maintain, ceramic tiles are a logical choice for bath and shower surrounds. There is one drawback: mould can attack the grout, making it difficult to clean.

Small mosaic tiles come bonded to mesh sheets. These sheets go up faster than single loose tiles, because you don't have to set each piece individually.

When using tiles in the bathroom, it is essential to choose a waterproof grout. You also need to make sure there is a waterproof seal between the tiles and the bath or shower tray. This can be achieved by applying a bead of silicone sealant, or you can add a ready-made plastic sealing strip. Alternatively, use quadrant tiles.

Fibreglass

Fibreglass is waterproof, durable and easy to clean. Many companies manufacture three- and five-piece shower/bath surround units in various sizes. Installing these units isn't difficult if your walls are straight and plumb and have been properly prepared. Most kits consist of two moulded end panels and one or more central panels.

Floors

Before installing a new floor, check the condition of the subfloor (the material between the floor covering and the floor joists) and the supporting joists. Decayed subflooring, especially around the WC and bath, is a common problem in older houses. Spot repairs may be adequate or you may need to replace the entire subfloor. This is an ambitious undertaking, so consult a professional if you're not sure.

You'll have to pry up a bit of the existing floor covering to inspect the condition of the underside of the subfloor. Prod around the base of fixtures and cabinets with an awl or a screwdriver to establish if there are any soft spots.

When choosing floor finishes, remember that your bathroom is the site of daily family traffic, and perhaps even the occasional bath overflow. Look for a durable material that is both attractive and, in particular, slip resistant.

Floor tiles

Properly installed, tiles are one of the most durable flooring materials. They're a good choice for bathrooms because they're waterproof, easy to maintain and stain resistant. Ceramic tiles are available in a wide range of sizes, shapes and colours, and come plain or decorated, glazed or matt. The grout that fills the gaps between tiles can be white or tinted a colour. You can use the grout lines as a design element by choosing a coloured grout that contrasts with the tile. As with wall tiles, make sure the grout is waterproof. Quarry tiles must be sealed to resist staining, and your supplier will advise you on this.

As a bathroom floor covering, however, tiles have some drawbacks: they're hard and cool underfoot, and without a textured surface, they can be slippery.

Laying a tiled floor can be a good do-it-yourself project, although it requires patience and care. All tiles must be installed on a level, clean subfloor. Most tile suppliers have all the necessary materials and equipment, and should offer advice for do-it-yourselfers. Always choose tiles designed for floors. Tiles manufactured for walls and worktops are not suitable for use as floor tiles.

Warm floors

Ceramic tiles, vinyl and wooden floors are popular flooring choices for the bathroom, but they can be quite cold in winter. The best way of overcoming this problem is with one or more strategically placed rugs. For safety, to prevent them from slipping, it is best to secure them with rug underlay.

Resilient flooring

This category includes various types of vinyl and rubber flooring in sheet and tile form. Resilient flooring is soft underfoot, yet stands up to heavy traffic and resists water penetration. It's available in an array of colours, patterns and textures. At the bottom end of the price range, vinyl is the least expensive flooring option. High-end vinyl products are comparable in cost to a good carpet or wooden floor.

Vinyl composition tiles (combining vinyl resins with filler) cost the least. Rotovinyl (a printed pattern covered by a clear topcoat) costs a bit more. Top-of-the-range inlaid vinyl (vinyl granules fused together in a solid pattern that goes through to the backing) is the most durable.

Solid rubber tiles are another option. Because rubber tiles are used mainly in industrial and commercial applications, you may need to work through an interior designer or contractor to obtain them. Installation is difficult, so you will need to employ professionals.

Resilient flooring can be installed over most other materials as long as the floor surface is smooth, clean and solid.

Marble

The costliest of surfacing materials, marble provides a smooth, classic covering for floors. It comes in colours ranging from neutral grey to pastel rose and can have either a polished or satin finish. Although marble is durable, it can be slip-pery when wet, so think twice before using it in or around showers and baths.

You can purchase marble in large, thick slabs or in smaller tiles. Slab marble is difficult to install, and its weight may require the reinforcement of the structure beneath. Consult a professional before choosing marble.

In general, marble tiles are 10–12 mm thick and may be square or rectangular. They are less costly than large slabs. The price of marble varies greatly and, because it is so heavy, is often dependent on how far it must be transported.

BELOW: Marble feels luxurious and is extremely durable, but it can be slippery when wet so you should ensure there are non-slip floor mats in place if you use it around the shower or bath.

Carpet

While it's comfortable underfoot, carpet has several drawbacks in the bathroom. Stains from cleaning products and make-up can be hard to remove, and poor ventilation in the room can cause moisture to collect and mould to grow. As a rule, carpets are more practical in dressing and grooming areas of the bathroom than in wet areas.

If you do choose carpeting, look for types that are described as being suitable for bathroom use. These will resist mould, won't retain odours and will be less prone to water absorption and staining.

Wood

Wood floors are common in bathrooms, even though the potential for moisture damage is high. If your heart is set on a wood floor, make sure it's coated with a polyurethane finish to protect it against moisture penetration. You might consider using a simulated wood product made of plastic laminate that has the look of wood, but the water resistance of a laminate floor. Avoid boards that have bevelled edges, as these form water traps in the floor.

Walls

The quickest way to transform a bathroom is to change the look of its walls. Whether you choose paint, wallpaper, panelling or tiles, remember that a bathroom wall covering must stand up to heat, moisture and frequent cleaning. Mixing and matching materials for their strengths in different areas works well, especially if the bathroom is divided into compartments.

Paint

Paint is the least expensive covering for walls and ceilings, and it's the most easily changed for cosmetic make-overs. Besides choosing a colour, you'll also need to settle on a finish type, from flat to high gloss. Gloss and semi-gloss finishes work best in bathrooms because they repel water and are easily cleaned. Gloss paints exaggerate all the lumps and bumps on a wall, however, so they must be applied to a flat surface.

ABOVE: The faux marble finish in warm, earthy, ochre shades teams beautifully with the black and gold to achieve an elegance and style with a minimum of expense.

ABOVE LEFT: As long as you choose moisture-resistant paper, wallpaper can be used effectively in the bathroom as shown here, but on the panelling below dado height, paint is a more practical choice.

Bathroom surface materials

Floor, wall and wet-area coverings must be moisture tolerant, otherwise they won't stand up well in a bathroom. Look for durable materials that won't trap moisture or encourage mould and that can be cleaned easily. With flooring, avoid materials that become slippery when wet. Keep an eye on costs: finish materials demand a major portion of the budget of a bathroom restyling project.

Type	Life	Maintenance	Comment
Flooring			
Wood	Indefinite	Moderate	Not highly recommended
Vinyl	20+ years	Easy	Recommended
Laminate	10+ years	Easy to moderate	Yes, but avoid laminates with wood-based cores
Carpet	11 years	High	Not recommended
Marble, granite	Indefinite	Easy	Yes
Ceramic tiles	Indefinite	Easy	Highly recommended
Wall covering			
Paint	5–10 years	Low	Mould-resistant additive
Wallpaper	7 years	Low	Moisture resistant
Ceramic tiles	Indefinite	Relatively low	Highly recommended
Mirrors	Long life	High	Highly recommended
Solid-surface material	Indefinite	Easy	Highly recommended
Wet areas			
Ceramic tiles	10–15 years	Moderate	Yes
Plastic-laminate wall panel	10–15 years	Easy	Yes
Marble, granite	20+ years	Easy to moderate	Yes
Solid-surface material	Indefinite	Easy	Highly recommended
Glass	20+ years	Easy	Safety glass essential

Whichever paint you use, be sure to follow the manufacturer's instructions for preparation and application. Most surfaces must be primed first to ensure proper paint adhesion.

Wall coverings

All bathroom wall coverings should resist moisture and withstand frequent washing. Ordinary wallpaper is not the answer. Vinyl coverings (particularly vinyl laminated to fabric) withstand bathroom conditions much better. Wall coverings can be applied to a solid, clean surface.

Wood

Wood adds a natural warmth that complements many interior design schemes. As a wall-surfacing material, it can come in the form of pre-milled dado rails, tongued-and-grooved boards, veneered plywood and melamine-surfaced hardboard (often simulating a boarded finish). Hardboard panels coated with melamine are ideal for bathrooms, because the melamine is water resistant and easy to clean. Make sure any exposed wood is either painted or protected with polyurethane varnish.

┌─────────────────────────────────┐
│   Tip   │
│   │
│ • Never allow tile adhesive or │
│   grout to dry on the face of the│
│   tiles. Be sure to wipe it off as│
│   you go with a damp sponge –   │
│   otherwise it will set   │
│   permanently.   │
└─────────────────────────────────┘

BELOW: Regluing loose tiles.

1 Remove taps and spout.

2 Take out loose tiles.

3 Sand off old adhesive.

4 Apply new adhesive.

5 Fix in place; grout.

6 Polish finished job.

Ceramic tiles

Ceramic tiles are attractive and durable. They won't fade or stain, they are cleaned easily and are not merely water resistant, but when installed correctly, fully waterproof. Tiles can be expensive, but their advantages make them well worth considering for at least some areas in a bathroom.

As with tiles intended for floor use, wall tiles come glazed and unglazed, plain and patterned, and in a wide palette of colours. Be sure that you use only wall tiles for walls and floor tiles for floors.

Glass bricks

Glass bricks can give a sleek, modern look to a bathroom. Not only do they transmit light, but they also preserve privacy. They can be used to create walls and 'windows'. Glass bricks are very expensive,

however, when compared with other materials you might use. The cost can vary depending on the complexity of the job, labour costs and the bricks you select. It is a difficult job for do-it-yourselfers to do well. For professional results, it's best to call in a bricklayer.

Making bathroom repairs and alterations

Refitting loose tiles

Refitting a few loose tiles in your bathroom (or kitchen) is not very difficult. The materials are readily available from tile suppliers and DIY stores, and you can hire any special tools you need.

First establish the reason for the looseness. One possible cause is that the previous subsurface preparation was faulty. The subsurface

1

2

3

4

5

6

must be dry, clean, flat and firm. In some cases, it should also be sealed; for example, bare gypsum plaster must be thoroughly sealed with a proprietary stabilising solution or tile adhesive primer.

A leaking pipe can also cause loss of adhesion. Evidence of this will be a wet or damp subsurface. Unless you are competent at plumbing work, it will be necessary for you to call in a professional to rectify this problem.

Another explanation could be that the wrong adhesive was used or insufficient was applied. Adding fresh adhesive and regrouting should fix this.

A final possibility is that the grouting could be deteriorating and allowing moisture to seep behind the tiles. If this is the case, once you have refitted the offending tiles, rake out and regrout all the joints for complete peace of mind.

1 If you have to remove tap covers or spouts, you'll need a pair of pipe grips or an adjustable spanner. Wrap a cloth around the fittings to avoid damage.

2 Now remove the loose tiles, taking care not to drop them. An exact replacement could be difficult to find.

3 As always, good preparation is essential. Carefully scrape the old adhesive off the backs of the tiles and the subsurface. Clean both surfaces with a strong detergent, which must be rinsed off.

   If the subsurface is painted, scrape off any flaking paint. Avoid using a chemical stripper, as this may leave a residue that could weaken the adhesive. If the surface is uneven, smooth it with a suitable filler. Roughen the surface with sandpaper for a better bond. Then allow the patch to dry thoroughly.

4 Spread adhesive evenly over the area to be tiled. In hard-to-reach areas, as shown here, apply in thick dabs to the corners of each tile. Press each tile into position,

working from the bottom up. Insert spacers (matchsticks were used here) between the tiles to maintain even joints. Make sure that the tiles line up with the existing tiles. Wipe off excess adhesive.

5 When the adhesive has dried, press grout firmly into the joints with a putty knife. Sponge off excess immediately.

6 When it is dry, polish the area with a dry cloth to achieve a truly professional finish.

Fixing a fitting to a tiled wall

Fixing fittings to tiled walls is easy if you know how to do it properly. Remember, screws should be used, not nails, and those screws should be brass to resist rust.

Regrouting tiles

While your tiles may well last a lifetime, the grout between them will need to be replaced every few years because it can become discoloured with dirt and mould.

BELOW: Fixing a fitting to a tile wall.

1 Place the fitting in position and check for level. Stick some masking tape to the wall where the mounting screws will be located and mark the position of the holes with a felt pen on the masking tape.

2 Mark vertical and horizontal lines through the centre of the proposed holes. Use a 3 mm masonry drill bit to bore a pilot hole 25 mm deep and take care that the drill doesn't move off centre while you are doing this.

3 Enlarge the pilot hole using a drill bit that will fit the plastic plugs you are using. Tap the plugs in with a hammer and cut any waste off with a sharp knife.

4 Position your fitting so the two sets of holes line up and screw the fitting firmly in place on the wall.

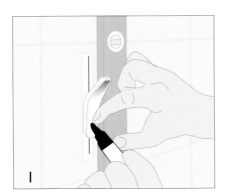

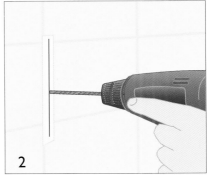

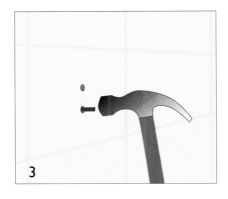

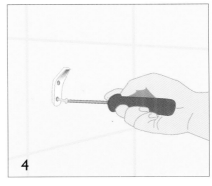

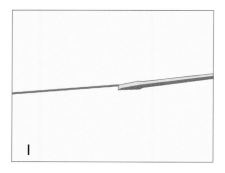

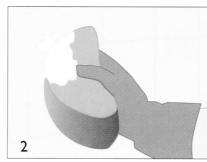

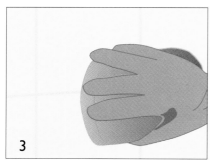

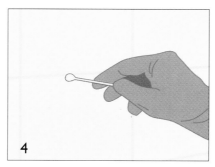

ABOVE: Regrouting tiles.

1 Scrape out the old grout using a large screwdriver or a grout rake. Be gentle, making sure not to damage the edge of the tile. Brush out loose bits of grout with an old toothbrush.

2 Mix the grout as recommended on the packet and apply it with a moist sponge. Work the grout firmly into the joins and wipe any excess from the face of the tiles.

3 Wash the sponge repeatedly with clean water and wipe the tiles clean while the grout is still wet. Do not have the sponge too wet or you will remove the grout from the joins.

4 While the grout is still wet, draw a small dowel, pencil or knitting needle over the join to give a smooth surface to the grout. This will give your grouting a professional finish.

Sometimes gaps can occur because standard grout has been used instead of waterproof grout. Follow the steps pictured here for a professional result.

Replacing a showerhead

In some cases, changing a shower fitting is so easy that you'll wonder why you never did it before. You need to be very careful when tackling anything to do with the water supply. Although it is perfectly feasible for you to alter the existing plumbing by cutting into, replacing or extending pipes, you need to be sure that you know what you are doing, because you may end up flooding your home, or that of your neighbour. It is also possible that you could create a potential health hazard by unwittingly contaminating the water supply.

If alterations need to be done, you may be better off calling in a plumber. And if you are in doubt about the Water Byelaws, check with your water supply authority.

Shower arms and roses come in a variety of shapes and finishes; many have specific uses. For exam-

ple, by varying the number and diameter of holes in the shower rose, some actually save water. This is useful if water bills are excessive, or if the water pressure is low.

Another innovation is the 'bubbling' shower rose. This mixes air with the water to provide the illusion of a fast-running shower. There are other shower roses that produce pulsating jets of water, which vary in intensity and volume, and are claimed by the manufacturers to be therapeutic as well as stimulating.

If your existing shower rose is too low, you can replace it with one on an adjustable arm.

To examine the best range, visit plumbing supply stores, builders' merchants and DIY stores, or collect manufacturers' catalogues from magazine advertisements. Check the size of your current shower fitting connection to make sure the one you choose will screw on to your wall outlet.

If you have problems fixing on to the existing outlet, you may need to buy a suitable adaptor fitting. Your plumbing supplier will be able to advise you on the possibilities.

1 To remove the existing shower fitting, place an adjustable spanner on the collar at the base of the fitting and unscrew it (in an anti-clockwise direction).

2 Wrap a layer of PTFE tape around the thread of your new shower fitting or the wall outlet. This helps ensure a watertight connection.

3 Screw the new shower fitting to the wall outlet, remembering to place the backplate in position as you do so. Be very careful not to cross-thread the connection. This occurs when the fitting is put on crookedly and can damage the thread, which will then need replacing.

4 Adjust the fitting for height if necessary, then turn on the shower to check performance.

1

2

3

4

LEFT: Replacing a showerhead

1 Unscrew the old fitting.

2 Wrap thread with PTFE tape.

3 Screw on new fitting.

4 The finished job.

BELOW: It may seem obvious, but the use of mirrors will make a small space appear larger. This utility room leads off a small bathroom. The white tiles bordered with terracotta and the clever positioning of the mirror give both rooms a light, spacious feel.

Clearing blocked drains

Severely blocked drains call for a the attention of a professional. Fortunately, most drain problems you can often deal with yourself.

First you must realise that your home has three types of drain: branch waste pipes from fixtures such as basins and WCs; a vertical soil stack, to which the branch waste pipes are connected; and underground drains, to which the stack is connected and which carry the waste away into the main drainage system – or in rural areas, a septic tank or cess pit.

A problem can originate in any of the three, so your immediate task is to locate the blockage. Invariably, it will be in or next to a connection that makes a turn, or in a trap at the outlet from a fixture.

To pinpoint the problem, open a tap at each basin, bath or other fixture, but don't flush a WC – it could overflow. If only one fixture fails to drain, the problem is right there or nearby. If two or more fixtures won't clear, something has lodged itself between them and the soil stack. And if no drains work, the blockage is further down the line, either at the foot of the soil stack or in the underground system itself.

If you remember that waste water flows downwards through pipes of increasingly larger diameter, you can find an obstruction that you will almost certainly never see.

Basins

Hair, bits of soap and other debris can block a basin outlet. To remove a pop-up waste plug, you may have to turn and lift.

A plunger with a moulded suction cup is ideal for unblocking traps and branch pipes.

If a basin has an overflow outlet, plug it with a cloth and make sure

the plunger seals tightly over the waste outlet. Then work it up and down to dislodge the blockage.

If a plunger won't work, try an auger or an opened-out wire coat hanger. Thread it down and through the trap to clear the blockage.

If augering doesn't do the job, place a bucket under the trap, remove it and flush it through. This also allows you insert the auger into the branch pipe.

Baths

Make sure the outlet itself is not blocked with hair or soap. Try the plunger treatment, blocking the overflow drain with a wet cloth.

If the plunger doesn't work for you, manoeuvre an auger or opened-out coat hanger down into the trap.

If all else fails, you need to dismantle the trap. Bail out the bath and place a container beneath the trap before removing it.

WCs

Use a plunger similar to, but larger than, a basin plunger over the outlet in the pan. Work the plunger vigorously. This could take a fair amount of some time so don't give up too soon.

If the WC doesn't have water in the pan, fill it to the rim. Spread petroleum jelly on the plunger's rim to ensure a good seal. If a plunger doesn't work, use an auger.

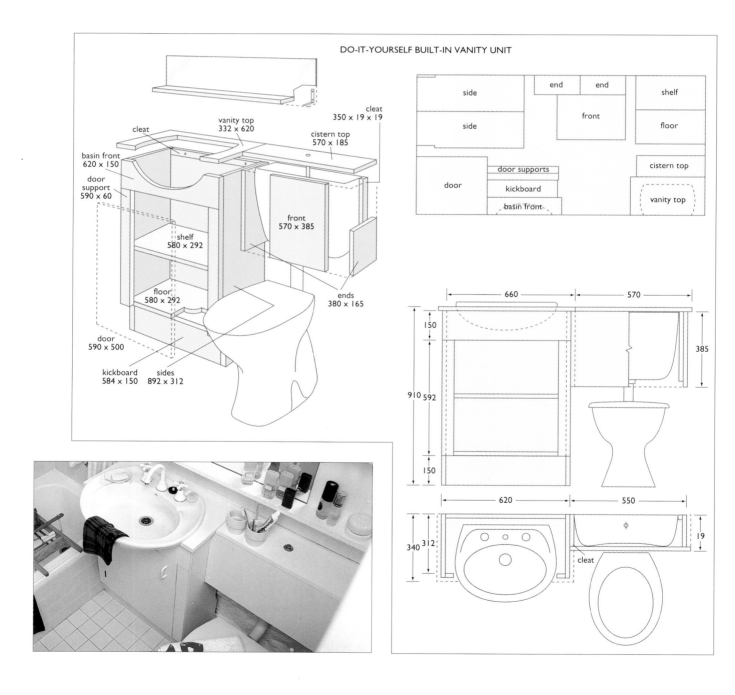

DO-IT-YOURSELF BUILT-IN VANITY UNIT

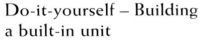

Do-it-yourself – Building a built-in unit

Building vanity units and boxing in WC cisterns creates a streamlined appearance, as well as providing more storage space, especially in a small bathroom such as the one picture here.

We boxed in the cistern, which was adjacent to the vanity unit. By closing the gap between them, we tied the two elements together to help cut down on visual confusion in the confined space.

You should be able to get all the components to make this built-in unit out of one 2400 x 1200 mm sheet of 19-mm-thick melamine-faced chipboard (see cutting diagram). Obviously, you may have to tailor the dimensions to accommodate the available space and cistern size. Use any scrap material for shelves above the cistern. Don't forget that you will need to finish all cut edges with iron-on laminate strips. Include end panels where the unit does not abut a wall and the sides will be exposed.

An efficient medicine cabinet

Storing medicines calls for a special type of shelving: it needs to be small in scale and shallow. This

LEFT: Building a built-in unit.

FAR LEFT: Building in the vanity unit and WC cistern creates a streamlined appearance as well as providing a storage shelf.

ABOVE: Building a built-in unit.

1 Line up the two basin cupboard sides and mark the position of the shelf, kickplate and cupboard floor, as well as that of the basin front.
2 Drill and screw through the sides into the edges of the horizontals.
3 Use aluminium corner strips to strengthen the internal corners, especially for the vanity top itself.
4 Attach the facing components using 25 mm lengths of 9 mm dowelling.
5 Hinge the door using 35 mm concealed hinges or similar.
6 Screw a 3 mm plywood back to the rear edges of the unit. Conceal any screw heads with snap caps where necessary.

For easy cleaning, all components were made from 13-mm-thick plastic-laminated chipboard. Cut out as many components as possible with a pre-laminated edge to the front. Finish all other visible raw edges with iron-on laminate strips. To finish the outer faces of the doors and conceal the sawn edges of the sides, top and bottom, score and cut suitable panels of plastic laminate and use contact adhesive to fix them in place.

Cut out all the components listed in the box below left and indicated in the diagram. Assemble the three boxes with wood glue and 30 mm panel pins. Although the photograph shows mitred joints, it is easier to use butt joints, and the dimensions given are for the latter. Carefully punch and fill the nail holes and retouch with enamel paint to match. Fit the 50 mm butt hinges and spring door catches, and drill through the doors to fit the door handles.

You can leave the cabinet doors plain, as pictured, or make them more decorative by adding a 'frame' of wooden moulding or plastic beading. Alternatively, they could be faced with mirrors.

cabinet opens halfway through its depth, so its compartment-type shelves are not too deep. They allow a clear view and easy access to the contents.

You will need these components cut from 13 mm plastic-laminated particle board:

Item	Size (in mm)	No.
Cabinet sides	625 x 135	2
Cabinet top/ bottom	474 x 135	1 each
Cabinet shelves	474 x 122	2
Cabinet back	599 x 474	1
Door sides	625 x 135	4
Door top/ bottom	222 x 135	2 each
Door fronts	599 x 222	2
Door shelves	222 x 122	6
Door shelf fronts	222 x 30	8

Other: iron-on plastic-laminate strip edging; 1 sheet or off-cuts plastic laminate; wood glue; 30 mm panel pins; four 50 mm butt hinges; two spring door catches; door handles.

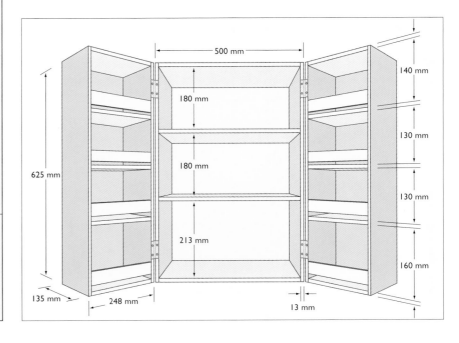

Build a bathroom

Make a set of wooden accessories to create a bathroom with stylish appeal that complements a range of decors and reflects your individual sense of creative flair.

Vanity unit

Cut the components as you proceed, not beforehand.

Begin by gluing 150 x 19 mm boards together to make the side, door and top panels. Use sash cramps and PVA wood glue for the job. Make the two side panels in one 1700 mm length, the two door panels in one 1300 mm length, and the top 1100 mm long.

Then cut them to the actual lengths listed on the right. Glue and screw all battens in place as indicated on the diagram (side bottom batten 75mm up). Draw the shape of the cut-out required for your basin on the underside of the top. Glue and screw the top battens (not shown on diagram) to the underside to correspond with its sides. These will reinforce the edges of the cut-out. Bevel the ends of the outward-facing door battens.

Cut 20 x 12 x 150 mm rebates down from the top of the inside rear corners of the back uprights to take the back rail. Glue and screw the four uprights to the ends of the side-panel battens.

Make the cupboard bottom, cutting out 50 x 20 mm notches that will take the uprights. Turn the sides upside-down and screw the bottom in place underneath the lower side battens.

ABOVE LEFT: The finished medicine cabinet.

LEFT: Medicine cabinet components and dimensions.

ABOVE RIGHT: The timber vanity unit combines with the other components to offset this bathroom's painted surfaces.

You will need for the vanity unit:			
Component	Material	Length in mm	No.
Side board	150 x 19 pine	825	6
Door board	150 x 19 pine	640	6
Top board	150 x 19 pine	1100	4
Side batten	50 x 19 pine	450	6
Door batten	50 x 19 pine	450	4
Top batten	50 x 19 pine	500	2
Corner upright	50 x 40 pine	825	4
Front upright	50 x 19 pine	745	1
Door stop	100 x 19 pine	650	1
Front rail	100 x 19 pine	950	1
Back rail	150 x 19 pine	950	1
Back rail	150 x 19 pine	570	2
Plinth side	150 x 19 pine	1070	1
Splashback	150 x 19 pine	1030	1
Splashside	75 x 19 pine	450	2
Bottom	12 mm plywood	990 x 550	1

Other: PVA wood glue; wood filler; clear satin polyurethane varnish; 30 and 50 mm countersunk screws; 30 mm lost-head nails; two magnetic cabinet catches; two cabinet knobs; four 50 mm brass butt hinges; 4500 x 19 mm scotia moulding.

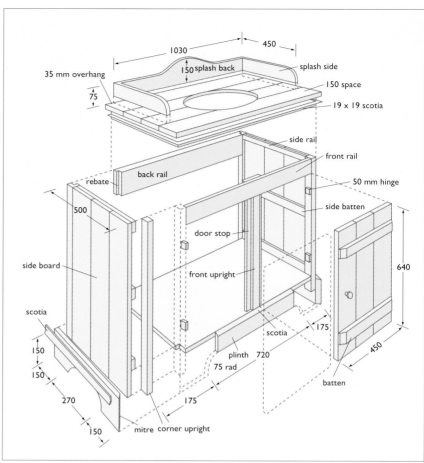

ABOVE: The right vanity unit can be one of the most elusive of household items, especially if you prefer the country look. One solution is to make it yourself. You can do this by following the step-by-step instructions here.

ABOVE RIGHT: The vanity unit components.

Cut 20 x 12 mm rebates into the ends of the back rail, then glue and skew-nail the front and back rails into place.

Make the curved cut-outs in the plinth sides and front as indicated, using a jigsaw. Mitre the corners, and glue and nail the plinth in place. Trim around the plinth's top with scotia moulding.

Glue and screw the doorstop and front upright together, flush at the bottom, and fit in place.

Similarly, cut the curved splashback and sides, and mitre the corners before screwing them in place from under the top.

Cut out the hole for the basin, using a jigsaw. Sand the edges of the vanity top to a rounded profile – or use a router. Fix the top in place by gluing and pinning the scotia moulding to its underside and the tops of the side panels.

Attach the doors with their hinges and screw magnetic catches to the inside of the cupboard, at the bottom. Fix the door knobs in place.

Make sure all fixings are set below the surface, fill their holes and sand before applying three coats of semi-gloss varnish.

Wall shelf

Cut out all the components as illustrated in the diagram. Use a jigsaw to cut the two shaped ends. Give the edges a rustic look with a spokeshave or plane.

Drill and insert three equally-spaced, 30-mm-long, countersunk screws through the back into the rear edge of the shelf, and two through each of the sides into the shelf ends.

Drill four 16 mm peg holes, 40 mm up from the bottom (see dia-

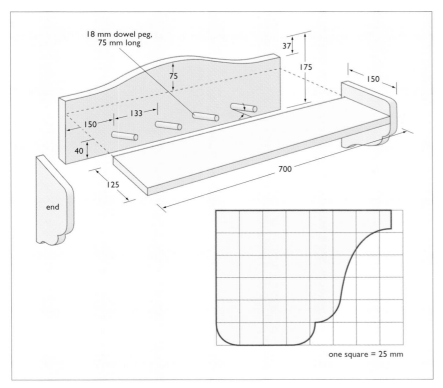

gram for spacing). Allow the drill to rest against the bottom of the shelf as you make the holes. This will give the pegs an even upward tilt. Glue and insert the pegs.

Sand and varnish before fixing to the wall by screwing through the upper back.

Light shades

Cut the 19-mm-thick block to the dimensions on our diagram, trim the edges with a plane to make a simple chamfer, or a router for a decorative shape. If you prefer, trim the four edges with scotia moulding.

ABOVE LEFT: Details of the wall shelf.

ABOVE: A well-lit mirror is essential in the bathroom and a do-it-your-self one will save you money. With their perforated shades these wall brackets will give a perfectly diffused light to your vanity area. Make the fitting, screw it together and have it professionally wired in place.

LEFT: It's a handy occasional shelf anywhere in the house, but in the bathroom you'll find it ideal for hanging and folded towels. It's compact enough to position wherever you need it.

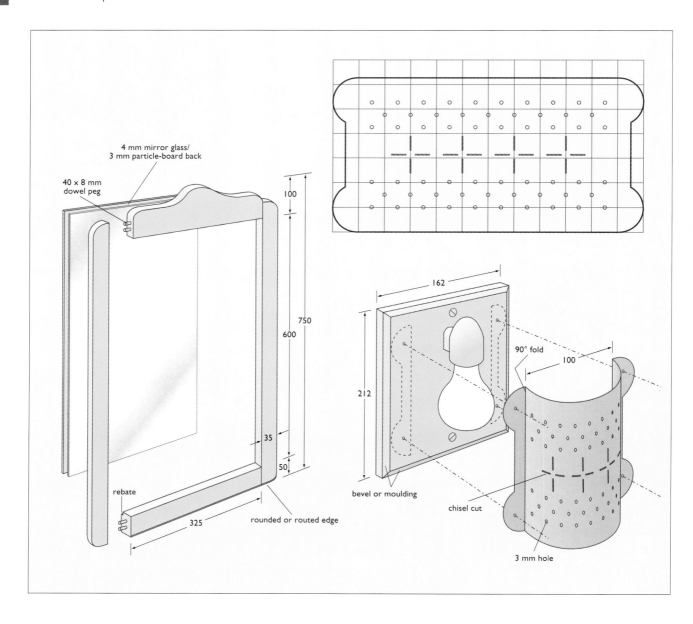

**4 mm mirror glass/
3 mm particle-board back**

**40 x 8 mm
dowel peg**

100

750

600

35

50

rebate

325

rounded or routed edge

162

212

90° fold

100

bevel or moulding

chisel cut

3 mm hole

ABOVE: **Mirror and light
shades details.**

Make the shade using a 20-gauge aluminium sheet. Cut it according to our cutting diagram, using tin snips, then file the edges to remove any sharp burrs. Use a nail punch to make the holes, and an old wood chisel for the slots. Again, remove any burrs. Use steel wool to give the shade a buffed patina, and drill the four fixing holes. Bend the sheet over a round surface, such as a paint tin, to produce the 100 mm diameter, then fold the mounting flaps on either side over a hard, clean edge to form a 90° angle.

Mirror

Begin by cutting two 700 mm side pieces of 35 x 19 mm pine. For the top, use 100 x 19 mm, and for the bottom, 50 x 19 mm. Cut both to a length of 325 mm.

With a jigsaw, shape the top piece, making it 50 mm high at the ends and the full 100 mm at the centre. Similarly, round off all the corners with the jigsaw.

Cut a 10-mm-square rebate into the rear inside edge of each of the frame pieces to accommodate the mirror glass and back. Make the

mm timber, cut out the four components, using our diagrams as a guide.

Drill 12-mm-deep holes for the paper rail in the position indicated in the side cutting diagram. Assemble the holder by drilling and screwing through the ends of the sides into the ends of the cleat.

Glue and pin the shelf to the top of the sides and cleat, checking the inside width against the length of the rail. Fill, sand and varnish.

Toilet seat

To calculate the dimensions that are shown on our diagram, measure the WC pan and add a 30 mm overhang to the front and sides. You will have to draw the seat and lid to the actual size on cardboard, observing the suggested dimensions.

Glue and clamp four 100 x 19 mm boards together to produce timber panels large enough for both the seat and lid. You can make the rear seat and lid components from single lengths.

Mark out the components using your cardboard pattern, and make the curved cuts with a jigsaw. Cut out the opening in the seat to suit the shape of the WC pan. Reinforce the glued joints in the seat with corrugated fasteners (wiggle nails) inserted into the end grain of the timber. Round off all edges by sanding.

Both the seat and lid will need to rest on 20-mm-diameter (approximately) rubber feet screwed to their undersides. To ensure that the rear sections are aligned with the seat and lid, you will have to add wooden spacers of the same height as the feet, glued and screwed to the undersides of the rear sections.

Hinge the two pairs of components together (using piano hinge for the seat). Glue and pin the packing to the undersides of the rear components.

Drill and fit countersunk coach bolts through the rear section of the seat to correspond with the

TOP: Give every bathroom accessory the country look. The shelf and sides of the paper holder have irregularly shaved edges to match the wall shelf.

ABOVE: A timber toilet seat completes the country look. It is not an easy thing to make. Details depend on the style of the toilet bowl.

ABOVE RIGHT: Paper holder and toilet seat details.

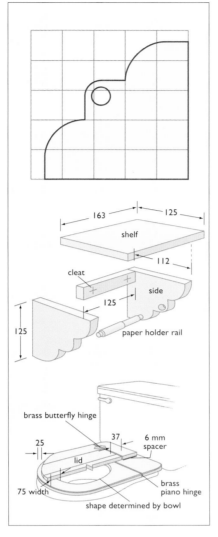

corner joints by drilling two 20-mm-long, 8 mm dowel holes into each piece. Now glue and assemble the frame.

You can round the front edges of the frame with an electric sander, but you will achieve a better finish with a router.

Have mirror glass cut to size, and fit it with a 3-mm-thick plywood backing into the frame rebate. Use panel pins tapped into the inside edge of the frame to hold the back in place.

Toilet paper holder

For this, you will need a sprung rail from an old toilet paper holder. From a 450 mm length of 150 x 19

fixing holes at the back of the pan. Glue and pin the two sections together (the seat rear section will cover the coach-bolt heads).

Sand and apply three coats of polyurethane varnish. Secure to the pan with wing nuts.

Pelmet

The wooden pelmet adds the finishing touch to your new, country-style bathroom. All you will need to make this pelmet is a length of 200 x 19 mm timber that matches the width of your window, with an additional 60 mm added at each end for overhang. Use your jigsaw to cut the curved shape and then sand all the edges. Coat with polyurethane varnish.

Drive nails into the top of your window frame and then insert corresponding screw-eyes into the back of the pelmet, as indicated in the diagram.

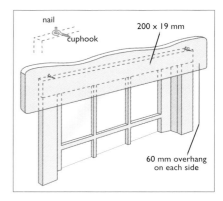

TOP: This pelmet will dress up any window.

ABOVE: Pelmet detail.

LEFT: The natural timber walls, old tiles and stained glass windows, although combined with modern fittings, give this bathroom a country look.

Utility rooms

More than any other room in the house, the utility room is a workplace. Because it is purely functional, you have to take a practical approach with its design. Spatial efficiency, adequate storage and ease of maintenance are the main considerations. Regardless of the period or style of your house, the utility room aesthetic comes from slick, easily-cleaned surfaces, tidiness and the comforting feeling that the home is being kept in order by this household nerve centre. It's pretty logical really. To do the work, it has to work.

Planning

Utility room essentials

Even if you can't afford the space for a big utility room, you should plan to include as many of the following items as you can (some of them you just can't do without):

- Washing machine. Compare the benefits of various models in terms of price, space, energy usage, water efficiency and load capacity, according to your requirements.
- Tumble drier and/or airing cupboard. Also, if you have a back garden, a clothes line outside.
- A sink for scrubbing stains and handwashing delicate items.
- Storage for detergent and bleaches, and anything else that is kept in the utility room.

ABOVE: When not in use the ironing board can be folded into the cupboard.

LEFT: Utility rooms are, of necessity, practical, but they can be attractive as well.

RIGHT: With plenty of space, you can have a large utility room with areas designated for specific tasks and storage.

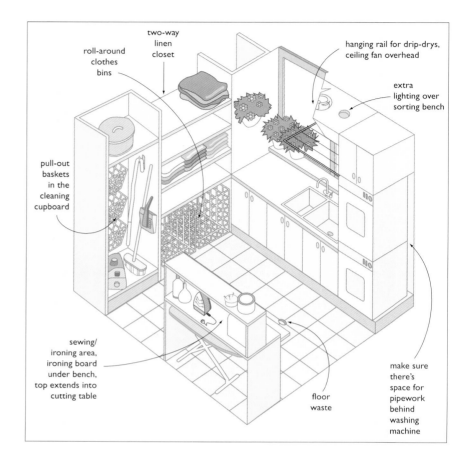

two-way linen closet

roll-around clothes bins

hanging rail for drip-drys, ceiling fan overhead

extra lighting over sorting bench

pull-out baskets in the cleaning cupboard

sewing/ ironing area, ironing board under bench, top extends into cutting table

floor waste

make sure there's space for pipework behind washing machine

- Worktop space for sorting. If you haven't got much room, this sorting area could be a fold-down or pull-out table.
- A place for drip-drying. This will need drainage, so the easiest thing to do is put a hanging rail over the sink and drainer. This also provides somewhere to hang freshly-ironed clothes.
- Space for ironing. This includes the ironing board, iron, storage for sprays and somewhere to stack or hang the ironed clothes. The ironing board can fold out from the wall, or swing out from or sit under the worktop.
- Linen storage. This should be positioned close to the sorting space and, ideally, should be two-way, with direct access from the hall or the bedroom.
- A washing sorter. This is simply a divided bin or basket for organising clothes into different machine loads.

- If you have the space, the utility room is also a good place to create a mending centre and put the cleaning cupboard.
- Remember that good ventilation and lighting are an absolute must in an utility room.

Space-saving ideas

The washing centre on the right is tucked away in a handily-located cupboard, so it's easy to get to and hide away. Although it doesn't take up much space, it's packed full of good ideas that you can use in any utility room.

As well as a hanging rail above the sink, there's provision for drip-drying dresses or gowns that are too long to fit above the worktop. The drips are caught by a drip tray.

When the hanging space is not required, the worktop drops down to become a sorting and folding table. Even the sink converts to valuable worktop space.

Tip

- Store the most used boxes, bottles or sprays so that they're within easy reach – not tucked away beneath the sink.

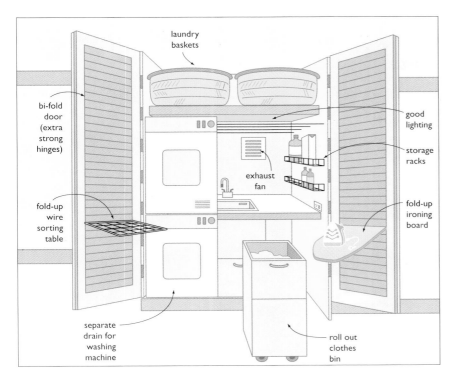

laundry
baskets

bi-fold
door
(extra
strong
hinges)

good
lighting

storage
racks

exhaust
fan

fold-up
wire
sorting
table

fold-up
ironing
board

separate
drain for
washing
machine

roll out
clothes
bin

ABOVE: This galley layout combines the utility area with convenient storage.

ABOVE LEFT: Careful planning is required for a small utility room to work efficiently.

BELOW AND BELOW LEFT: The table folds down into position when the hanging rail and sink are not in use.

High-necked taps (also called gooseneck taps) make it easier to remove a bucket from under the spout without drowning yourself!

Colour co-ordinated appliances look great, and nowadays some manufacturers offer washing machines and driers in a choice of colours. Investigate the possibilities through local retailers and bear them in mind when planning a decorating scheme for your utility room. Don't forget that once you buy, you're stuck with the colour you choose, so be absolutely certain it's what you want.

ABOVE: A rail over the sink is handy for freshly ironed clothes or for allowing wet items to drip dry.

ABOVE RIGHT: Tall cabinets make long items such as mops and ironing boards easily accessible and see-through, pull-out baskets make smaller items easy to find.

BELOW: Work flow plan.

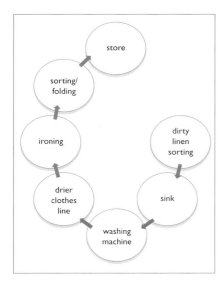

The labour-saving utility room

The days have long passed since washing was done with a copper and scrubbing board. Apart from having an efficient design and layout, there are other labour-saving devices and tricks for your utility room to help you get through the loads of washing and ironing faster. Although it's important to create a room that's pleasant to be in, it's even better to create one that you don't have to be in for too long.

Work flow

Work flow is simply arranging things so that the work follows a logical, smooth progression, rather than requiring numerous trips across the floor. A utility room doesn't need to be big to work efficiently; in fact, the less distance you have to travel, the better.

Washing machines

Fully automatic washing machines are no longer a luxury, and there are many available at reasonable prices. Some machines also double as tumble driers – an extra space saver in a small utility room. Make sure the appliances are large enough for the household – washing a few large loads is more efficient than washing a lot of small ones.

Clothes driers

A tumble drier must be vented to the outside, either permanently or by hooking the vent hose through a window. An airing cupboard is great for drying damp clothes.

Utility room sinks

A deep sink is more versatile than a shallow one, and twin sinks will give you the option of soaking in

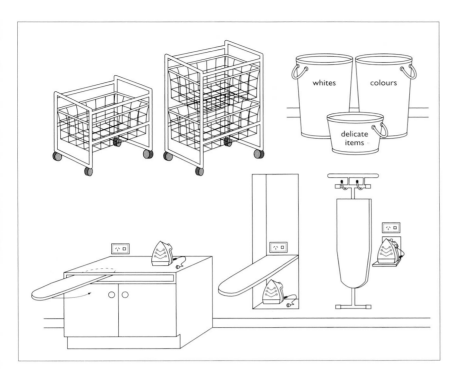

LEFT: Utility room storage ideas that save time.

Wire drawer frames/baskets on castors can be wheeled from room to room or drier to ironing board. They are available from large hardware stores and storage shops.

A divided clothes basket, or two or three separate containers, will save you from having to sort the wash into loads later on.

Unless you can leave it up all the time, you'll need somewhere to put the ironing board so it's convenient to use.

one while handwashing in the other. Different finishes are available, but stainless steel is easiest to clean if you use the sink for dirty jobs, such as cleaning the barbecue grille or washing paint brushes.

Taps

Lever-action handles are simpler to turn on and off; high-necked taps make it easier to fill buckets without splashing water everywhere.

Surfaces and finishes

These should be waterproof and easy to clean, as well as bleach resistant. Non-gloss paints will help prevent condensation, and wallpapers should be vinyl, scrubbable and suitable for the wet. Save finishes from flood damage by installing a separate outlet for the washing machine.

Lighting and ventilation

There's no reason to put up with a dark, stuffy environment in the utility room. Make sure all work surfaces have adequate lighting above them, and install an extractor fan to remove moist air efficiently.

Deciding what you need

These questions and answers can help make using the utility room less of a chore in your home.

Q Is everything positioned so that work flows in a logical order?

A If not, consider rearranging things so they are; plumbing fixtures are usually located together, so this often only involves rearranging the storage or putting up some extra shelves.

Q Is the washing machine fully automatic? Is it large enough?

A If necessary, trade it in for a better model.

Q Is everything stored exactly where you actually need it?

A Arrange things so they are.

Q Is the laundry basket divided to save you from sorting out the wash later on?

A Cut a plywood divider to fit the basket, or simply use two baskets instead of one.

Q Do you have to hook the waste pipe from the washing machine over the edge of the sink?

A Buy a plastic washing-machine standpipe that can be connected

Storage ideas

The easier everything is to get to, the better. Make sure you have a place for things where you actually use them.

Items you'll need storage space for:
Washing powders, bleaches and so on, soiled clothes and clean clothes.

Items it's useful to have storage for:
Iron and ironing board, linen, sewing and mending equipment, cleaning materials, mops and brooms, vacuum cleaner, raincoats, wet shoes, gumboots (use the utility room as the 'rainy-day' or 'works' entrance), vases (and other flower-arranging bits and pieces), potting and gardening equipment, and luggage and/or sporting equipment.

ABOVE: The lattice inserts make the mellow look of these cupboards more interesting. Make sure the wood is well sealed from moisture.

TOP RIGHT: A little imagination can produce an attractive as well as practical utility room. Here, a farmhouse dresser effect has been created complete with inset sink.

BOTTOM RIGHT: You can buy solid frame doors such as these or use plain ones and glue on timber mouldings to give the same effect. Paint them to protect against the wet and fit the room's colour scheme.

to the sink waste pipe; it may prevent the risk of expensive flood damage.

Q Have you enough space for sorting clothes?

A Install a pull-down sorting table.

Q Could you install a two-way linen cupboard that opens from the utility room and the hall?

A Employ a professional carpenter or do it yourself.

Q Is the ironing board positioned for quick and easy access?

A Investigate the alternatives. You could keep it in its own cupboard, or make it fold away.

Q Is the lighting and ventilation good enough?

A Put in an extractor fan and/or additional task lighting.

Utility room styles

Thoroughly modern, old-fashioned utility rooms

Just because you want your utility room to be up-to-date, labour-saving and low-maintenance doesn't mean you have to miss out on old-world charm – it's simply a matter of choosing the right finishes.

Small utility rooms

A utility room doesn't need a large space. When it comes to the crunch, you can use the smallest room in the house, and find space somewhere else for the ironing board and broom cupboard.

The minimum requirements are around one square metre of floor space for the washing machine and drier (if mounted on on top of the other), and a little less than that will take care of the sink. If you can manage it, you'll be better off arranging some space for sorting

dirty clothes into loads and folding clean ones, thus making even a small space an efficient one.

Use light colours, which reflect more light, to make the room seem larger. It's also handy to have direct access to the clothes line outside.

Dual-purpose utility rooms

Inspired renovating can turn an old utility room into a multi-purpose work room that will be a pleasure to use. If there's space in your utility room, here are some great ideas to adapt.

Imagine the luxury of having a complete sewing centre with see-at-a-glance wire-basket storage for fabrics and patterns beneath the worktop. The utility room is the ideal place to locate a sewing machine: it's close at hand for mending tasks, and the ironing board is always at the ready.

By building a timber framework along one wall, you can create a 'take-away' system for clean clothes in one stack of wire baskets, and allow for multiple storage in others. A fold-away ironing board frees floor space when it's not in use, while fixed shelves beside and above it make an ideal linen store, conveniently placed so you don't have to trek through the house with piles of towels or sheets.

A high shelf takes care of off-season storage, and in the lower section you can add a bin for clothes and linen waiting to be washed. A drying rack with a collection of assorted coat hangers gives clothes a chance to dry wrinkle-free and cuts down ironing time. Walls painted with washable paint and floors covered in hard-wearing rubber help to provide a good-looking room, which needs very little maintenance.

ABOVE: Here a utility room has effectively been combined with a downstairs WC.

RIGHT: If you have the space, the utility room can be fitted out with enough storage facilities to keep everything well organised and allow sewing and ironing to be done with ease.

Tip

• Hard water is hard on your wash because it doesn't always rinse well and leaves a detergent residue behind so clothes feel stiff. In hard water areas, add a few tablespoons of baking soda to the load.

Liberate the utility room and double its duty

Happiness is a utility room and work centre with plenty of light and oodles of space. A tiny utility room has more good features than you'd imagine at a single glance. The three major units – washer, drier and sink – can be ranged along one wall to minimise the cost of plumbing in. Open cupboards can be used to store frequently used linen. An ironing board will tuck into a cupboard, and all the necessary ironing paraphernalia can be stored within it.

Building a utility room and sewing centre where every morsel of space is used to its best advantage isn't difficult. Standard cabinets can be fitted in where space permits and then laminated worktops added.

Best dressed in the utility room

For the swishest of all utility rooms, a combination utility/dressing room

ABOVE: The galley-style layout can work as well in a utility room as it does in a kitchen.

RIGHT: The wall opposite the laundry appliances provides plenty of storage for children's clothes and sports equipment.

must surely be the ultimate in dignified living. The secret here is that every item has a given place, so the clutter is actually a picture of organisation.

Even in a small room, every bit of space can be called into service to achieve a look of busy order that will make you want to keep up the good work. The walls can do wardrobe duty, modified by the addition of hanging rails, with the area under the worktop used for folded items and a tailor-made shelf-system on the opposite wall for shoe racks.

Hide-away utility areas

Utility location need not be confined to the conventional areas, such as adjoining the kitchen or bathroom. Any house with a staircase has a little gold-mine of unused space just waiting for conversion into a compact family utility area. Just one weekend's work could create an efficient workplace from the wasted triangle beneath the stairs.

How you arrange the utility area depends on your individual priorities, but by using the sleight-of-hand approach, you can easily incorporate all the necessary features into the empty space and all but invisibly.

You can use louvred doors to conceal built-in shelves and allow access to the wedge-shaped space above from folding doors on one side. The under-stair area can house mending, ironing and cleaning gear, as well as the washing equipment.

A coat of paint will give a cheery welcome when the doors are open. If the doors themselves are finished in a clear polyurethane and are splash safe and easy to clean, they will complement the surrounding ceiling and floor.

If you utilise the under-stair space in this manner, the house loses no effective floor space and the utility area need only be visible when it is in use.

The open-and-shut case

With a little planning and perhaps some remodelling, a long, narrow cupboard can provide almost as much useful space as a small room – if it's filled efficiently. Build in a smart slide-out bin for soiled linen between the washing machine and tumble drier. A laminated top, flush with the appliances, will provide a surface for sorting and folding. And with storage, it's a good idea to make your shelves adjustable. That way, you can create specific places for jars and packets of different sizes. Folding doors give the finishing touch, taking less room than conventional doors.

ABOVE: Ranging your units and appliances along one wall of your utility room makes good use of limited space and can cut down on the cost of plumbing in.

ABOVE: With the sturdy drying rack extended, damp washing can be conveniently air-dried in the utility room.

ABOVE RIGHT: The drying rack folds away leaving a handy storage shelf.

FAR RIGHT: Drying rack patterns.

Do-it-yourself – Make a wooden clothes drying rack

This compact clothes drier is a useful addition to any utility room. It features a sturdy pull-out rack for hanging clothes and a storage shelf. Choose a timber which best suits your utility room. Pine would be suitable for most situations, but beech is an alternative. If you want a painted finish, you can use an MDF panel for the shelf. Use the diagrams on the following pages to make and assemble the rack.

Making the shelf

Cut the two pieces for the back (A) from 19-mm-thick pine to 180 x 625 mm. Glue the two pieces edge to edge with PVA glue and cramp lightly. Remove any excess glue with a damp rag. When the glue has dried, trim the panel to the finished length of 615 mm. If using 18 mm MDF, cut out the finished back to 360 x 615 mm.

On a piece of 19 mm pine or 18 mm MDF, plane an edge straight and square an end. From the edge and end, draw a 200 x 375 mm grid of 25 mm squares using a soft pencil. On this, draw the shape of the end panel (B) shown on the gridded pattern. Mark the centre point for the 3 mm pilot hole shown on the gridded pattern and drill the hole to a depth of 10 mm. Cut the end panel to length with a tenon saw, and cut on the waste side of the curved line with a jigsaw. Sand the edges of the panel smooth with 120-grit sandpaper.

Plane an edge and square an end for the second end panel (B). Using the first end panel as a template, mark out the shape of the second end panel. Cut the second panel to length and shape, then sand the edges smooth as before.

From 19 mm pine or 18 mm MDF, cut out the top of the shelf (C) to 200 x 700 mm. Round over the front edge and both ends with an 8-mm-radius round-over bit in a router, and plane the round using a block plane. Round over the front curved edges of the end panels (B) using a router or spokeshave or Surform file.

Draw on scrap pieces of 19 mm pine or 18 mm MDF the shape of the rack rests (D) and both parts of the latch (E and F), using the full-sized latch pattern, carbon paper and a pencil. Cut these parts to shape using a jigsaw, and sand

You will need:					
Finished size*					
Part	Thickness (mm)	Width (mm)	Length (mm)	**Material**	**Qty**
A	360	615	19*	Pine or MDF	2 or 1*
B	175	370	19*	Pine or MDF	2
C	200	700	19*	Pine or MDF	2
D	19	75	19*	Pine	2
E	19	45	12	Pine	1
F	25	65	19	Pine	1
G	19	395	12	Pine	2
H	19	305	12	Pine	2
I	19	305	12	Pine	4
J	19	305	12	Pine	4
K	19	164	12	Pine	2
L	19	164	12	Pine	2

Supplies: 7 m of 10-mm-diameter dowel; 30 mm lost-head nails; 15 mm panel pins; three 25 mm, No. 8 round-head wood screws; two 50 mm, No. 8 round-head wood screws; wood filler; PVA wood glue; 120-, 150-, 180-, 220-grit sandpaper; satin-finish polyurethane varnish.

curved edges using 120-grit sand-paper. Drill the holes in (E) and (F) as shown in the latch pattern.

Sand the surfaces of all the parts of the shelf using 150-, 180- and 220-grit sandpaper.

Glue and nail the end panels (B) to the back (A), using 30 mm lost-head nails and PVA wood glue. Punch the nail heads below the surface and stop with a proprietary wood filler. (A small pilot hole should be drilled when nailing into the MDF. to prevent the surface from splitting) Align the top (C) with the back and centre it. Glue and nail it to both the back and the end panels.

Glue and nail the back rest (D) inside the rack housing, 240 mm beneath the underside of the top (A), as shown in the diagram.

Make the folding drying rack

Using 12 x 19 mm pine battens, cut 16 rack slats (G, H, I, J, K and L) to the lengths listed previously. (Label and sort the different slats as they are cut.)

Carefully mark the centre points for the holes on the rack slats (G, H, I, J, K and L) from the dimensions given on the rack slats diagram. Note that there are three different hole sizes. The smallest fits the mounting screws, and the largest 10-mm-diameter hole gives a clearance hole for the 10-mm-diameter dowel. These holes are determined by the size of the dowel used. If you use a 10 mm drill, it may be necessary to increase slightly the size of the clearance holes with a round file to

accommodate the 10 mm dowel. Ensure that the holes are drilled square with the face of the rack slat.

Remove the sharp edges on the ends of each rack slat with 120-grit sandpaper. Sand all rack slats to a final smooth finish.

Cut the 10 mm dowel into 610 mm lengths using a tenon saw. You need 11 in total. Ensure that all dowels are identical in length. Fine-sand each dowel.

Assemble the drying rack following the three steps shown on the rack assembly diagrams. Start with slats G and H, which are screwed to the inside of the shelf, and insert the centre dowel to make the first cross. Next insert the top and bottom dowels in part H. Then add slats I and J and the dowels needed for the second and the identical

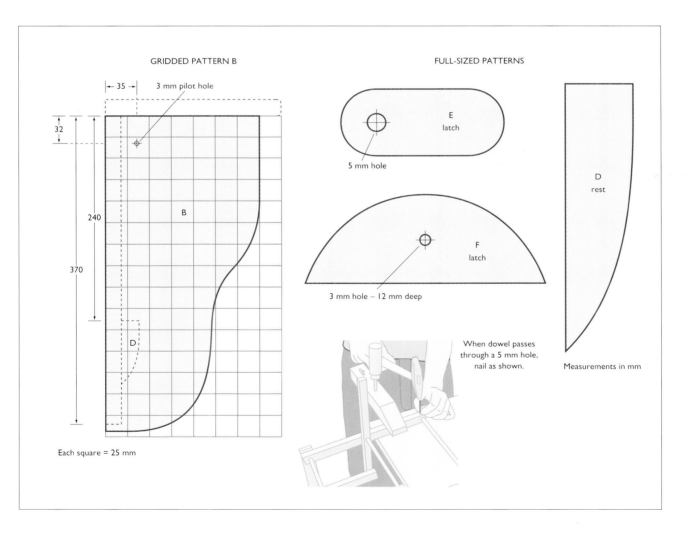

RIGHT: Drying rack assembly.

FAR RIGHT: Rack and shelf components.

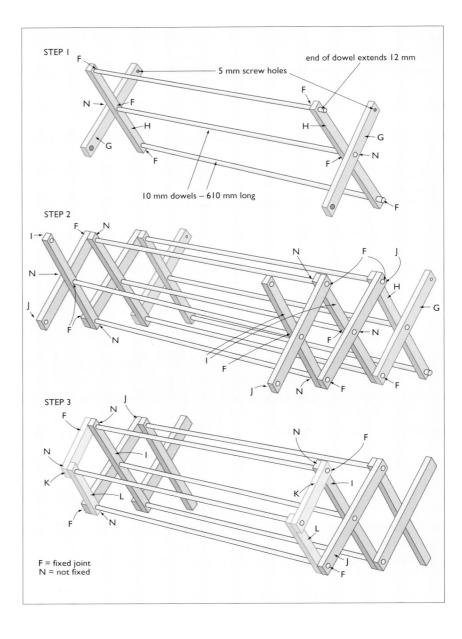

third crosses. Finally, for the last rack section with slats K and L and the dowel. When a dowel passes through a 10 mm hole, fix the dowel in place by driving a 15 mm panel pin through the slat and the dowel as shown. (It is helpful to remember that in the outer slat, the dowels are free to turn at the centre and fixed at the ends, but this arrangement is reversed in the inner slats.)

Assembling and finishing

Using 25 mm, No. 8 round-head screws, attach the assembled rack to the inside of the shelf (the screws fit into the pilot holes previously drilled in the inner faces of the end panels). Fold the rack into the space beneath the shelf and mark the position of the half-round latch (F). Nail and glue the latch to the underside of the shelf. Screw the toggle (E) to the half-round latch.

Two coats of polyurethane varnish give a simple and satisfactory finish (rubbing down with worn 240-grit sandpaper between coats).

Simply secure the shelf to the wall using two 50 mm, No. 8 round-head screws.

Tip

• Dismantle a project before applying a finish. With the drying rack, unscrew the rack from the shelf and expand it before applying the finish.

RACK SLAT DRAWING

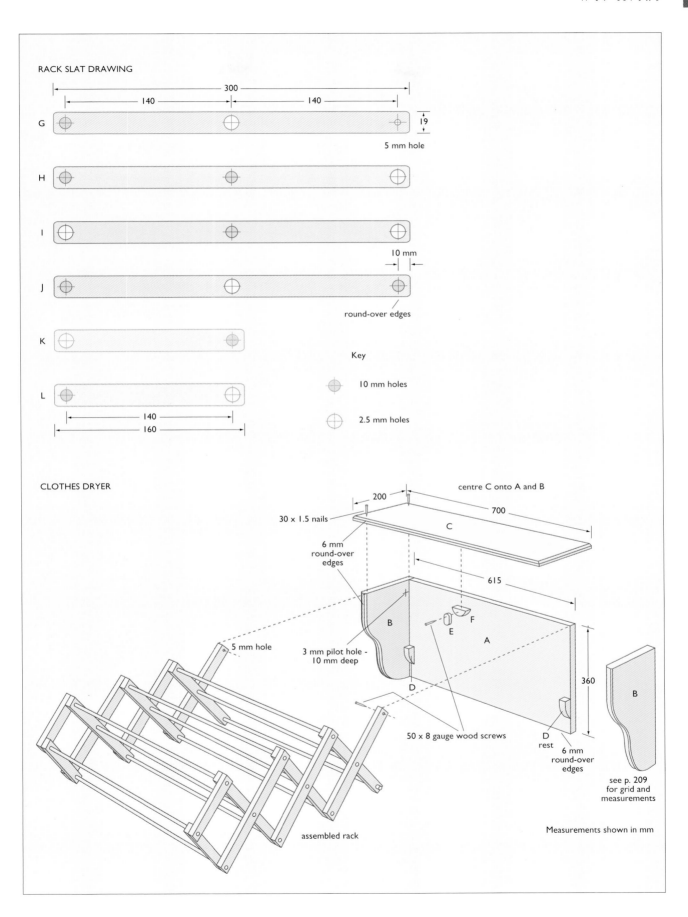

G 300 140 140 19
5 mm hole

H

I 10 mm

J round-over edges

K

L 140 160

Key

10 mm holes

2.5 mm holes

CLOTHES DRYER

centre C onto A and B
200 700
30 x 1.5 nails
C
6 mm
round-over
edges
615
5 mm hole
B
F
3 mm pilot hole -
10 mm deep
E
A
D
50 x 8 gauge wood screws
360
D
rest
6 mm
round-over
edges
B

see p. 209
for grid and
measurements

Measurements shown in mm

assembled rack

Paint, Painting and Wallpaper

Choosing the colour scheme for your home is potentially the most exciting and rewarding aspect of home improvement and renovation. Painting is often the most inexpensive way to achieve the total transformation of an interior. The wrong colour scheme badly applied, however, can destroy the proportions of a room.

Colour affects our moods, and personal preferences are highly individual, but don't let your emotions rule when you are choosing your colour scheme. Consider the colours (and neutrals) not only in their own right, but also in respect of other colours, materials and textures in the room before you decide on a forest green kitchen or a bright red dining room. It may seem obvious, but a small, dark room will appear smaller and darker when painted in a dark tone. The same room will be unrecognisable if you choose neutral creams and white, and restrict the darker colours to the skirting, door frame, windows and architrave.

Apart from standard paints, there is a variety of colour washes and stains available that produce interesting finishes when used with decorative paint techniques such as rag rolling, stippling and combing.

Wallpaper can also create an amazing transformation, especially when complemented by the right colours for the surroundings. Many modern wallpapers are pre-pasted, easy to apply and come in a vast range of designs.

Yellow tones generally have an uplifting effect on our moods. They are bright during daylight hours and give a warm glow in artificial light, as shown here. Handpainted furniture is an easy do-it-yourself project and can give a facelift to old pieces to harmonise with refurbished surroundings.

How colour works

Knowing how to use colour effectively can make all the difference when you come to put the finishing touches to your renovation. If you are unsure, you can always seek professional advice.

ABOVE: The stencilled design lifts the russet coloured walls.

BELOW: Orange-striped walls are contrasted with a blue-and-white checked cloth.

Colour has three aspects:

1 Hue, which gives the colour its name (e.g. red, yellow, blue);
2 Chroma, or intensity, which relates to its brightness or dullness. If all the colours in a room are low-intensity, or dulled, they will create a comfortable, back-to-nature mood that is ideal for family rooms;
3 Tone, which relates to its lightness or darkness, such as pale pink or maroon.

Colour schemes

You will find that most decorating colour schemes fall into the following broad categories:

• Monochromatic. This is when one hue is used throughout a room, but in varying tone and intensity. There should be deep coloured areas, mid-tones and highlights. This scheme works well in small rooms because it doesn't break up the space.

• Harmonious. Most rooms are styled in a harmonious colour scheme, that is, colours that have a common thread, rather like a family where all the children have varying degrees of their parents' traits. For example, colours based on yellow or on blue. Some of the colours have a low intensity (some are quite dull), which actually makes the bright colours seem brighter in comparison. This is a good scheme, even for beginner decorators, because it's logical and easy to apply – a particularly restful scheme for any room.

• Primary. Only primary colours (i.e. red, yellow and blue) are used. This scheme makes a great impact and is particularly effective in modern houses and children's rooms.

• Complementary. This scheme is based on opposing colours (e.g. red and green, yellow and purple, and orange and blue). This is an unusual scheme, but it works well when one colour totally dominates the other, the secondary colour being used only for small details, such as flowers, cushions or crockery.

All colours can be used in different ways: for example, bright and clear, pastel and soft, dark and moody. Reds vary from fire-engine bright, through pastel-like pink, to dark maroon. These variations are achieved by mixing them with black and white.

Tints are colours that have white added. By increasing the amount of white, you create pastels: for example, red and white make pink, orange and white make peach.

Shades are colours with black added. Blue and black make navy, red and black make maroon, blue, yellow and red make olive.

Different colours in different rooms

If you can see from one room to another, it will be more restful to work with colours that are in harmony with each other.

Primary colours

Red, yellow and blue are the primary colours. They cannot be made by mixing other colours together. They energise a room. If you use them together, one of them will have to dominate the others. All other colours are mixtures of the primary colours.

Secondary colours

These are made be mixing equal quantities of two primary colours together. Red and yellow make orange, yellow and blue make green, and blue and red make purple.

Tertiary colours

Tertiary colours are made by adding all the primary colours together in different proportions. Russet is mostly red with a touch of blue and yellow. Olive is mostly blue with a touch of yellow and red. Citrine is mostly yellow with a touch of red and blue.

The more colours you mix together, the duller a colour becomes. When teamed with primary or secondary colours, tertiary colours intensify the bright colour.

Colour psychology

You may choose colours to reflect your personality or to enhance the mood of a room. Even small touch-

es of colour in fabrics furniture and accessories can give a lift:

- Yellow – cheerful, supports intellect, optimistic;
- Blue – serene, nurturing, rejuvenating, peaceful;
- Red – passionate, enhances appetite, energetic, powerful;
- Green – relates to renewal and rebirth, cooling, calming;
- Purple – a spiritual colour, ethereal, fantasy;
- White – purity, peace, cleanliness, romantic.

ABOVE: The different hues of bold yellow brighten and warm this modern living room.

Take the pain out of painting

Painting can be a messy, time-consuming job, but you can make quicker work of it with these clever tips.

Before you start to paint

Glue a large, flat paper or plastic plate to the base of the can to catch any drips and to prevent the paint can from sticking to newspaper or the dust sheet.

Before pouring paint into a paint tray or kettle, line the container with a plastic bag and then discard the plastic when finished.

Painting special areas

- Doors. When painting doors, place several layers of folded newspaper on top of the door before closing, so that the paint won't 'lock' the door.
- Furniture. Place a plastic meat tray or foil dish under each leg to protect the floor from the paint.
- Stairs. Paint every second step one day. The next day, or when the paint is dry enough to walk on, paint the other steps. This will enable you to continue to use the staircase.

Paint brushes and rollers

To paint small areas accurately, place a rubber band around the

ABOVE: The right colour can be selected from a swatch or mixed to your requirements.

RIGHT: Detail adds interest to a pastel colour scheme.

be sure to remove it before the paint dries to avoid peeling off the fresh paint.

Cleaning brushes and rollers

Clean paint brushes easily without staining your hands by placing them inside two strong plastic bags with water or white spirit and squeezing the brushes through the plastic to remove the paint.

When water-based paint has hardened on a brush or roller, soak it for 15 minutes in a solution of equal parts water and white vinegar, then wash it in a strong detergent solution.

Storing paint

Place a large rubber band around the tin at the level of the remaining paint, so you can tell at a glance how much you have left for the next time you need it.

Dip a wooden stick in the paint and attach it to the outside of the can with a rubber band. This stick can be used to colour co-ordinate fabric, borders, cushions and so on.

Lay a sheet of aluminium foil or plastic food wrap on top of the paint before replacing the lid to prevent a skin from forming.

Storing brushes

Wrap brushes in thick brown paper to protect the bristles. If you use paper bags, secure them at the top with sticky tape or rubber bands.

You will damage brushes if they are left to sit bristles-down in cans or jars. Lay them flat or drill holes in their handles and hang them up.

Banish paint odours

Leave a small bowl of sliced onions in the room to absorb odours. Alternatively, fill a large bowl with water, add one tablespoon of ammonia , and leave in the room for ten hours. You can also add one teaspoon of vanilla essence to each 600 ml of paint that you use.

bristles of your paint brush, just above the line of paint. This prevents the bristles from spreading out, thus making the brush more controllable.

Pat the brush against the inside of the tin before lifting it out to remove excess paint.

If you're called away from painting, place your brush or roller in a plastic bag. This prevents it from drying out.

Protection from paint

To protect yourself, wear old clothes and cover your face, neck and hands with a thin layer of petroleum jelly. Use tissues to wipe it off later.

Place a canvas tarpaulin or a heavy dust sheet over floors. This will absorb paint better than plastic.

Cover furniture with old shower curtains or old sheets.

To protect windows and window frames, press strips of wet newspaper on to the glass and simply lift it off when the job is complete. Alternatively, use masking tape, but

ABOVE: Here, wallpaper is used effectively above the picture rail, but paint is more practical on the area below it.

Preparation and painting

Painting is the most popular and instantly rewarding form of decorating. After all, in the whole world of home making, what can be more exciting than seeing a room transformed by a new colour? Just as importantly, painting is about making your house look fresh and being able to maintain it in a pristine condition. Anyone who is involved in the trade, however, will tell you that painting is about 90 per cent preparation and 10 per cent painting. Your carefully and creatively selected colours will only be as good as the surfaces to which they are applied.

LEFT: Some of the tools of the trade

1 Wallpaper steamer	**10** Flexible paint scraper
2 Detachable blade scraper	**11** Combination shave hook
3 Assorted brushes	**12** Triangular shave hook
4 230 mm roller tray	**13** Wire brush
5 10 mm wool roller sleeve	**14** Safety glasses
(230 mm)	**15** Masking tape
6 Drop sheet	**16** Sanding block
7 Dust masks	**17** Caulking gun
8 Point scraper	**18** Wet-and-dry sandpaper
9 60 mm scraper	

Tips

- Paint pads are an alternative to rollers and brushes. Each comprises a rectangle of mohair pile with a foam reservoir behind. They can be used with oil and emulsion paints, and are good for covering large areas and getting into corners.
- Mix paint with a flat stick, preferably one with holes drilled in it.
- Spray painting, using aerosol cans or an airless spray gun, is only warranted when you have intricate items, such as cane furniture and louvre doors, to cover. Overspray is always a problem.
- You can obtain steam wallpaper strippers from tool hire shops.
- A shavehook is good for ripping off softened paint with a downwards motion.
- A heat gun is a useful investment if you are planning large-scale paint removal.

KEY: BRUSH ROLLER SPRAY

What paint to use where

Imagine going to all that trouble and having the paint start peeling about a year after you've applied it. That would mean going back to the heavy-duty preparation stage. For a lasting job, study this chart carefully.

Estimate the amount of paint you will need by calculating the wall area to be covered and checking it against the coverage column on the chart.

Windows require the same amount of paint as if they were solid wall. Moulded doors need one-and-a-quarter times the amount.

If you're trying to cover a dark colour, you'll need two undercoats.

Product	Use on	Application	Coverage	Wash up	Touch dry	Re-coat	Benefits
Interior							
Vinyl matt emulsion	Interior walls and ceilings	Brush Roller Spray	Approx 13 sq m per litre	Water	20 min	2 hr	Excellent resistance to wear; will not shine when lit from an angle; ideal for hiding surface imperfections.
Vinyl soft-sheen emulsion	Interior walls and ceilings	Brush Roller Spray	Approx 13 sq m per litre	Water	20 min	2 hr	Good stain resistance; good washability.
Vinyl silk emulsion	Interior walls, ceilings and woodwork	Brush Roller Spray	Approx 13 sq m per litre	Water	20 min	2 hr	Suited to all wet areas such as utility rooms, bathrooms and kitchens; excellent steam and stain resistance.
One-coat emulsion	Interior walls and ceilings	Brush Roller Spray	Approx 9 sq m per litre	Water	2–4 hr	Not necessary	Ideal for hiding surface imperfections; one-coat coverage saves time and effort.
Kitchen & bathroom emulsion	Interior walls and ceilings	Brush Roller Spray	Approx 14 sq m per litre	Water	30 min	3–4 hr	Designed to prevent mould on all interior surfaces; scrubbable finish for areas where frequent cleaning may be needed.
Satin-sheen gloss	Interior walls and woodwork	Brush Roller Spray	Approx 15 sq m per litre	White spirit	2–4 hr	16 hr	Suited to hard-use areas, walls in steamy areas, doors, architraves and all timber trims, interior metalwork.
Liquid gloss	All interior and exterior surfaces	Brush Roller Spray	Approx 15 sq m per litre	White spirit	3–4 hr	16 hr	Suitable for children's toys, cots etc; hard wearing; long life.
Non-drip gloss	All interior and exterior surfaces	Brush Roller Spray	Approx 12 sq m per litre	White spirit	3–4 min	16 hr	Has a jelly-like consistency for easy use without dripping; hard wearing, very resistant to dirt and water; requires no undercoat; suitable for use on both wood and metal surfaces.
Preparation							
General-purpose primer	Interior and exterior surfaces	Brush Roller	Approx 12 sq m per litre	White spirit	20 min	2 hr	Seals and primes wood, metal, plaster, brick, stone and concrete prior to applying an oil-based top coat.
Acrylic primer undercoat	All bare timber surfaces (excluding tannin-rich types, such as cedar and oak)	Brush	Approx 14 sq m per litre	Water	20 min	2 hr	Convenient primer/undercoat for timber; fills grain; easily sanded.
Oil-based undercoat	Interior and primed exterior timber plaster and masonry	Brush Roller Spray	Approx 16 sq m per litre	White spirit	4 hr	16 hr	Suitable for all interior and properly primed exterior surfaces; excellent hiding power with good sanding properties.
Sealer binder	Porous interior and exterior masonry, plaster, cement sheet	Brush Roller	Approx 12 sq m per litre	White spirit	6 hr	16 hr	Seals porous surfaces and binds kalsomine or thin powdery paint films; provides a sound foundation on which to apply subsequent coats.
Stain sealer	Interior and exterior surfaces	Brush Roller Spray	Approx 14 sq m per litre	Water	30 min	2 hr	Sealer that helps prevent staining from substances such as smoke, oils, tar, bitumen and creosote bleeding through subsequent coats.
All-metal primer	All common metals except zinc and galvanised metals	Brush Roller Spray	Approx 12 sq m per litre	White spirit	5 hr	16 hr	Anti-corrosive primer for all common metals; ideally suited as a primer for clean scale-free steel.
Oil-based primer	All bare timber	Brush	Approx 16 sq m per litre	White spirit	6 hr	16 hr	Suitable for all bare timber and tannin-rich timber; available in pink or white.

Note: Coverage rates are approximate only and will vary according to the method of application and the porosity of the surface. Touch-dry and re-coat times are approximate and will vary with the temperature, humidity and product. Always check the directions on the can.

Interior preparation

When you can't wait to see the final effect, preparation will seem like the boring part. Everything you do in the preparation stage, however, will help to create a solid base on to which you can lay any decorating scheme.

Vital preparation

1 Wash old painted walls with a solution of sugar soap to remove any grease and dirt.
2 Rinse well with clean water and allow to dry.
3 Fill any cracks with a non-shrinking, pre-mixed filler and allow to dry.

4 Sand walls smooth, removing any dust with a brush or a dry cloth. Remember to wear a mask as this job can get very dusty.
5 If the surface was previously painted with a high-gloss paint, sand it lightly before filling to provide a key.
6 If you want to apply a glaze to the surface, mix the paint with a scumble medium (available from art or specialist paint shops). This extends drying time and makes paint more translucent.

Unfortunately, surfaces cannot always be prepared so easily. Shown on the following pages are the main trouble spots – the potential problem areas to watch for.

Tips

- Don't press too hard on the roller, otherwise you'll leave ridges in the paintwork.
- Extra-long-pile rollers are for heavily-textured surfaces. For smooth surfaces, use medium- or short-pile rollers.

BELOW: Peeling paint on chalky surfaces
This occurs when layers of old paint beneath the surface break down, as in the case of kalsomine.

1 Scrape surface back. Sand thoroughly.
2 Wash with sugar-soap solution and then wash again to provide a clean surface.
3 Seal with sealer binder, then fill.
4 Sand before undercoating and painting.

BELOW: Cracks in ceilings
These might appear to be just hairline – they need to be investigated with the point of your knife.

1 Open up cracks. Brush dust from cracks.
2 Fill with good-quality filler.
3 Sand before sealing, undercoating and painting

ABOVE: Lifting plaster on ceiling or walls

Tap for hollow sound. Behind a small bubble
may be an avalanche of falling plaster.

1   Open up the bubble as far as is necessary.
2   Remove all loose plaster with a scraper to
    establish solid edges.
3   Dust away all loose particles in order to give you a
    stable surface.
4   Sand, then paint with a sealer binder. Undercoat and
    paint.

ABOVE: Cracked cornice

A feature of many old houses, cornices should be treated
with kid gloves. Inspect them carefully for damage.

1   Scrape out the crack with a scraper point.
2   Fill the gap at the bottom of the cornice using a
    cartridge of flexible caulking filler.
3   Sand cornice grooves with sandpaper rolled
    into a cylinder.
4   Seal, then undercoat before finishing with ceiling
    paint.

ABOVE LEFT: Detailed plaster work

Because the grooves get clogged up with successive
layers of paint, you have to try to re-establish the
plaster's crisp lines.

1   Pick out loose paint with a pointed tool before
    sealing with a sealer.

ABOVE: Chipped joinery

Nothing looks worse than paint slapped over a chipped
surface. Camouflage is the name of the game. Make it
even with two-part epoxy filler.

1   Scrape and feather the edges of the chip, then fill.
1   Sand filler and painted joinery to an even finish.
1   Seal with a general-purpose primer.

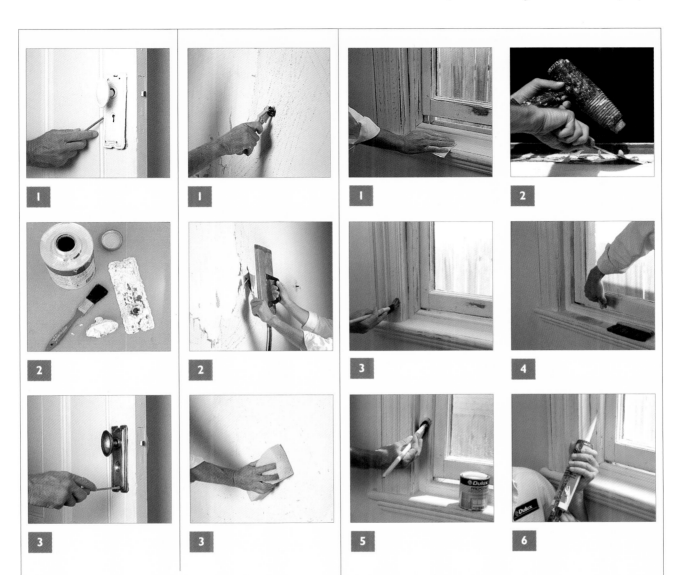

ABOVE LEFT: Painted door furniture

Whether it requires stripping or not, don't try to paint around it. Remove it.

1 Break paint seal with a razor and remove hardware.
2 Apply stripper in coats and wash off in between with steel wool and hot soapy water.
3 Replace polished hardware after you have painted the door.

ABOVE RIGHT: Wallpaper

Strip plain papers with a sponge, water and cellulose paste. Painted and impervious papers are more difficult.

1 Scratch paper at regular intervals with a blade or scraper.
2 Fill steamer with water. Apply it and scrape. Proceed slowly and methodically.
3 Wash down thoroughly before sealing with sealer binder.

ABOVE: Battered windows

Depending on the seriousness of the condition, consider using a hot air gun. Windows have to look immaculate. All attention focuses on them because they are a major architectural feature.

1 Sand off loose particles. Wipe down to remove dust and chips.
2 Remove paint build-up (likely to occur on the outside) with a hot air gun.
3 Seal with a general-purpose primer or wood primer/undercoat.
4 Fill, sand and brush down to make clean before proceeding.
5 Seal a second time to lock in the fillers.
6 Fill crevices with a flexible filler, using a caulking gun.

See pp. 225–26 for advice on preparing specific surfaces for painting.

Pointers for painters

Preparation, the choice of the right tools and how to use them are important, especially if you are inexperienced at painting. This section shows in detail how to choose the tools, how to maintain and store them, how to apply paint and how to fix problems.

Choosing a brush

A well-made natural-bristle brush has some distinct advantages over a nylon-bristle brush. A natural bristle – usually from a pig or boar – has minute indentations all along its length. These indentations actually catch the paint and hold it on the brush. Early nylon bristles were smooth, so the paint virtually slipped off the brush. However, newer and more expensive nylon-bristle brushes have small indentations manufactured into the strands, making the finish they give more acceptable.

In general, nylon brushes are fine for use with acrylic paints on rough surfaces, such as brickwork and cement, but on finer surfaces, such as an interior wall, they may leave brush marks. Therefore, it is worth investing in a quality natural-bristle brush for interior work.

The next factor to consider when choosing a brush is the length of the bristles: too short, and the paint will simply fall off the brush; too long, and the bristles will flip backwards and forwards, which can waste paint and tire your hands and wrists.

The third and final important aspect of brush selection is the thickness of the bristles. A very thinly-packed brush will not hold paint well and simply make for more hard work.

Watch out for brushes with bristles set in vulcanised rubber; this setting can dissolve, allowing the bristles to loosen and drop out. Epoxy resin is the best setting.

Choosing a roller

When it comes to selecting a paint roller, the same rules apply as those for choosing a paint brush: natural material covers, such as mohair or lambswool, offer a finer finish and a longer life than synthetic covers. Of course, you will have to pay more for the advantages of using a natural fibre.

Roller covers are available in different pile lengths to suit the texture of the surface to be painted. Deeper piles are more suitable for coarse surfaces, such as cement render, brickwork and stucco, while roller covers with finer piles are best for interior walls and ceilings.

Always wash new brushes and rollers in mild detergent before use. A new roller should be rubbed between your hands to remove excess fibres. A new brush should be flicked back and forth a few times to remove any loose bristles.

The best way to apply paint

The technique you use when painting will affect the final finish. Haphazard strokes up and down,

ABOVE: The light, strong wall colour harmonises with the crisp white.

RIGHT: The best way to apply paint.

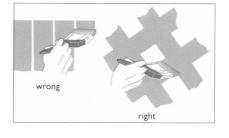

wrong

right

back and forth across the surface will produce an uneven finish of dense and sparse areas. The best technique to use for both roller and brush painting is the lattice pattern, which forms a criss-cross coverage over a square metre. The gaps are filled by feathering the edges of the paint without applying any more. This is a good way to make your paint go a lot further, too.

How to hold your paint brush

To hold a brush correctly, you should grasp the handle completely in your palm. To do this, hold out your hand as if to shake another, place the handle in your palm, running parallel to your thumb (which should be pointing upwards), fold the fingers and then the thumb over the handle and work the brush by wrist action only. According to the experts, arm tiredness when painting is directly related to incorrect brush grip; by using your wrist, you should be able to paint more effectively for longer, and with much less strain.

Storage tips

The best way to store brushes and rollers after washing is by hanging them from a hook or line in your garage or workshop. Brushes may also be stored flat in a drawer, but rollers should always be hung to prevent a flat spot from forming in the cover's pile. Wrap roller covers and brush bristles in plastic food wrap or brown paper to protect them from dust after they have dried completely; any trace of dampness may promote fungal growth on the fibres.

Loading up

When loading a paint brush, dip the bristles up to one-third of their length only into the tin; any further and the unused paint tends to slide back into the handle and clog the bristle base.

When loading a roller, ensure that the entire surface of the roller is covered in paint. However, do not overload the roller, as this may lead to spattering.

How to prepare paint surfaces

A quick cosmetic cover-up won't do; proper preparation is vital. Incorrect preparation can lead to new paint peeling, blistering and wrinkling. Here's how to prepare your surface to ensure a professional quality finish.

New woodwork

Softwoods such as pine need a primer with a high oil content. Hardwoods are often greasy when new, so the primer should be thinned with white spirit before application. Alternatively, use aluminium wood primer. Too much oil and the paint may not coat or dry very well. Before priming, ensure that the timber is completely dry, as new timber is often damp. Sand lightly, dust off debris and fill knots or veins with a suitable filler.

Previously painted woodwork

If the surface is in reasonable condition, with no peeling, blistering or wrinkling, it will require only light sanding and washing. If it is badly damaged, the affected areas must be sanded smooth and spot-primed. Large areas of paint damage require complete removal by chemical stripping or using a blowtorch and scraper. Once the old surface has been thoroughly removed, sand, dust and prime.

New concrete

Wait a minimum of three months to allow thorough curing and settling. After this time, wash the surface with a solution of zinc sulphate (1 kg to every 4 litres of water), then seal with a concrete sealer. This

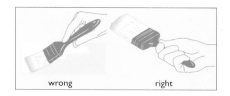

wrong   right

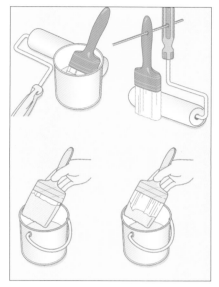

TOP: How to hold your brush.

ABOVE: Storing brushes and rollers. Loading up.

Tips

- Keep an old egg whisk for stirring paint. It's efficient and easy to clean.
- To strain lumpy paint, stir the paint well and pour it through an old kitchen sieve into a clean paint kettle or large jar. Empty the lumps on to newspaper and allow to dry before disposing of the paper. Wipe the sieve clean with white spirit. Return the paint to the can.
- If you're a messy painter, wear an old shower cap when painting a ceiling. For even greater protection, you can wear a cheap plastic raincoat with a hood.
- It's best to use acrylic paints if oil-based paint and white spirit affect your skin and cause an allergic reaction.

ABOVE: The use of a stencil provides an effective border.

BELOW: These timber kitchen cupboards are painted in a matt finish. The russet colour against papered walls is unusual and effective.

prevents oil-based paints from seeping into the concrete. Acrylic paint may be applied immediately after the curing period without using a sealer.

Previously painted concrete

Remove peeling and flaking paint with zinc-sulphate solution (see as for new concrete) and a stiff wire brush. If the surface is powdery, apply a concrete sealer or two coats of PVA bonding agent diluted with five parts water.

New plaster and fibrous plaster

Newly-set plaster surfaces should be allowed a drying-out period; check with the plasterer or builder. Lime can be a problem in new plaster, so a coat of zinc-sulphate solution (see as for new concrete) is advisable. If painting with an oil-based paint, use an alkali-resistant primer. Acrylic paint needs no primer.

Previously painted set and fibrous plaster

Sand the surface and coat with cement sealer before attempting to paint with either oil-based or enamel paint. Flaking paint must be removed by sanding, and patches should be filled with a suitable plaster filler. No sealer is required for acrylic paint.

New iron and steel

Apply a rust-inhibiting primer to new iron and steel surfaces. Remove all dirt and grease before priming to ensure paint adhesion.

Previously painted iron and steel

If the paint is cracking and flaking, remove the old surface by sandblasting or using a blowtorch and scraper. You can use a chemical paint stripper, too. Remove rust with a wire brush; treat affected areas with rust-proofing agent and metal primer.

Stripping paint from timber

Very often, a battered, but worthy, piece of furniture can be transformed by stripping off paint, sanding and sealing or waxing.

If you can, apply chemical stripper outdoors and always wear protective gloves and goggles. Don't breathe in the fumes and, if the stripper comes into contact with your skin, wash immediately.

A well-prepared job when painting or varnishing will always deliver better, longer-lasting results. This is particularly true when it comes to removing paint from furniture and woodwork. Removing it with a chemical stripper is the best way to achieve a good result.

1 Apply the stripper strictly as directed on the container.

2 Leave the stripper for the recommended time, then remove the loosened paint with a scraper. Don't be tempted to press too firmly with the scraper or you may damage the surface of the piece. Scrub with a stiff brush and water.

3 Wash down with a hose before the surface dries to remove all traces of stripper. Repeat the process until all paint has been removed. Let the surface dry thoroughly, then sand ready for the new finish.

Applying paint

Even coats of paint and smooth surfaces are only obtained with practice. In this section, we discuss types of paint and stain, care of brushes and offer solutions to common problems.

Using acrylic paint

Acrylic paint is great for interior walls as it's so hardwearing and easy to clean. It's thicker than oil-based paint and dries more quickly, so it's best not to cover too large an area in one go. You can avoid brush marks if you apply it correctly.

1 Apply a long stroke of paint horizontally, then brush it up and down and from side to side, beginning at the top.
2 When you've covered the surface, smooth it with light, vertical brush strokes, lifting the brush at the end of each stroke to avoid overlap marks.

ABOVE: The green colour of a Granny Smith apple makes a strong contrast to the walls of soft daffodil yellow.

Using oil-based paint

Oil-based paint is perfect if you want to achieve a glossy finish for timber panelling. Don't be frightened by bold colour – enjoy it!

Even coats and smooth surfaces are only obtained with practice. You should always use a primer and undercoat on wood, and take the trouble to apply two thin coats of gloss, rather than one thick one. Don't allow the paint to dry on the brush, but clean it at once with white spirit, otherwise the hard residue will ruin it.

1 First, spread out a dust sheet. Then, starting at the top, paint three or four vertical strokes about 500–600 mm long, leaving a gap between strokes.

2 When the paint on the brush is used up, don't reload, but make horizontal strokes to spread the paint you've already applied.

3 After five minutes, gently stroke the near-dry brush over the painted surface, lifting it at the end of each stroke.

Staining timber

Read the instructions on the container carefully, as each type of stain is applied in a slightly different way. Take time to sand all the surfaces to a fine finish before applying the stain. You'll find that blue and green give good results on pine.

1 Begin sanding with 120-grit sandpaper, change to 180-grit and finish with 240-grit. Use a cork block and always sand with the grain.

2 Wear rubber gloves when applying the stain with a 50 mm paint brush, making long parallel strokes. You can apply the stain liberally, but make sure the depth of colour is even.

3 The stain will leave a slightly roughened surface, which should be smoothed with 600-grit wet-and-dry abrasive paper that has been dipped in the stain.

4 Finally wipe over the surface with a soft, dry cloth, using long parallel strokes.

Colourful wood stains allow the grains of different timbers to show through. Furniture looks particularly good when treated this way.

Cleaning brushes

Be sure to clean your paint brushes thoroughly every time you use them, and especially before the paint dries on the bristles. If you have used acrylic paint, wash the brush thoroughly in clean water and detergent or soap. Remove oil-based paints with white spirit or brush cleanser, the bristles should then be washed in warm soapy water and dried. Mould the clean, damp bristles to their original shape and, when dry, wrap them in brown paper held with an elastic band. Hang them bristle downwards or store them horizontally.

ABOVE: You can achieve wonderful effects by using a combination of opaque paint and the lovely softness of a stain in a similar way. Here it's 'solid' paint on the door and stain on the cupboards.

How to fix what goes wrong

It can be disheartening to find, even after you have carefully followed instructions, that you still have problems with paint application and finish. Identify the problem and use the chart below to find a solution.

Name	Symptoms	Cause	Remedy
Bitty surface	Bristles, grit or fluff under the new paint	Lack of cleaning of surface or painting in a dusty environment	Allow to dry, rub down with fine wet-and-dry paper; re-coat with clean equipment
Bleeding	Staining and discolouration of paint	Tannin stains from tannin-rich timber or residues such as bitumen in surface	Remove as much as possible of residue and stained paint, then seal or prime.
Thickening	Paint increases in consistency and becomes hard to work	Addition of inappropriate thinners or evaporation due to room temperature; lid left unsealed	With old paint or inappropriate thinners, discard paint; alternatively add small amount of thinner and stir with flat stick
Soft surface	Paint is dry, but remains soft	Applied too thickly; presence of wax or oils on surface; mixing of different types of paint	Remove and start again
Receding (or cissing)	Paint separates from surface, leaving bare patches	Presence of grease, wax or silicon; water-based paints have been applied over new oil-based paints	Allow receded paint to harden before sanding back. To prevent, clean surface thoroughly before painting; sand oil-based paints
Curtaining (or running)	Unsightly drifts of thick paint	Paint applied unevenly and too heavily	Allow to set, then sand smooth and re-coat
Discolouration	Dark and light patches or streaks of the same colour, or yellowing	Atmospheric pollutants or moulds and fungus; yellowing due to too much or not enough sunlight	Wash with bleach solution, repaint with acrylic, which will not yellow, or paint that resists mould growth
Lack of drying	Sticky surface	Lack of ventilation; low temperature; excessive humidity; lack of sufficient time between coats	Improve atmospheric conditions; if surface has been impaired, add an additional thin coat
Efflorescence	White crystalline deposits	Moisture continuing to pass through masonry and plaster surfaces	Wash with calcium-chlorine solution and leave for 14 days to check for recurrence; solve the moisture problem
Fat edge	A thick crust of paint adjacent to an edge or corner	Brush deposits extra paint as bristles run over corner	Re-check and spread paint if still wet; allow to harden, rub down, sand smooth and re-coat
Gloss loss	Patches of less shiny finish	Application over an unevenly porous undercoat; unsuitable weather conditions; over-thinning of paint	Rub down and re-coat with full-strength paint
Grinning (showing) through	Underlying coats show through	Too few coats or over-spreading	Use an additional undercoat when making a marked colour change; use a recommended undercoat

Name	Symptoms	Cause	Remedy
Holidays (misses)	Gaps in the paint coat	Poor lighting conditions while working; undercoat too similar to the final colour; careless application	Apply additional coats
Lifting	One coat is softened or disturbed by a subsequent coat	Re-coating before recommended drying time	If in doubt, do a small-scale test before proceeding; if it is too late, cease further work, allow to dry and sand back before re-coating
Foaming	Tiny bubbles that have burst, leaving pin holes	Too vigorous brushing or rolling; applying paint to hot surfaces	If it occurs through several layers of paint, the lot has to be stripped off; otherwise, sand back dried top coat and re-coat
Coarse finish	Unsightly texture that can, but does not always, look like brush marks	Over-working of paint after drying has already commenced	Allow to dry, rub down and re-coat
Saponification	Softened and discoloured paint	Oil-based paints coming into contact with alkalis in the presence of moisture	Alkalis exist in cement, lime, plaster and compressed cement sheet. Make sure they are cured and not damp. Strip and dry the surface before re-coating – preferably in acrylic
Seeding of paint	Small particles of dried paint rather than pieces of grit	Old paint; wrong thinners	Re-coat with fresh, clean paint
Patchiness	Uneven sheen in low-gloss paint that shows up as roughness	Variations in porosity of surface; brushing of semi-dry paint	Sand lightly and re-coat
Wrinkling	Surface dries in a series of fine ridges	Occurs most frequently with heavily applied exterior gloss finishes	Drying can take weeks, but this is essential before you can rub it down with fine wet-and-dry paper. Otherwise, scrape and wipe with white spirit

ABOVE: A terracotta colourwash was used to decorate this dining room. Through the doorway the faux effect of stone blocking makes a dramatic and imposing hallway.

RIGHT: The stencilled frieze in this traditional room works well as an alternative to wallpaper.

Paint finishes

These easy paint finishes give you a maximum reward of exciting effects for minimum effort. The combination of different colours, the particular finishes you choose and the patterns you create with them can be applied to so many things. Walls, of course, are natural candidates, but so are furniture and kitchen and bathroom fittings – you're really only limited by your imagination.

Rag-rolling

Wonderful, decorative effects are achieved by dabbing or rolling cloth over a wet glaze. You can experiment with lace, hessian and towelling. First, paint on your base colour and allow it to dry. Then apply the glaze over it in sections and roll your cloth across it, changing direction as you go. It's best to work in pairs before the glaze becomes too dry.

Combing

Cut even notches in the edge of a squeegee blade to make a combing tool. Paint on your base colour and allow it to dry. Then apply the coloured glaze over the top, one

manageable strip at a time. Draw the squeegee through the glaze in a wavy, straight or random pattern. Continue to work your way across the wall in this fashion. If there are two of you, one can apply the glaze while the other combs through it.

Sponging

This is achieved by dabbing coloured glaze over a dry base colour. Dip a natural sponge lightly into the glaze and dab over the entire surface. If desired, apply second or third colours, leaving them to dry thoroughly after each application. Concentrate the various colours on blank spots, overlapping them occasionally.

Crackle

In this process, the top paint layer is made to separate into a fine crazed or crackled pattern. Apply two coats of base colour, allowing each to dry completely. Then apply an even coat of crackle medium (available from art and specialist paint shops). Allow to dry

ABOVE: A mixture of techniques. The wall was painted in wide stripes with a roller, then each colour was lightly sponged with the other. Basic combing has been used on the corner cupboard in a bold but contrasting colour to make a vivid focal point.

LEFT: Rag-rolling.

BELOW LEFT: Combing.

BELOW CENTRE: Sponging.

BELOW: Crackle.

thoroughly. Apply the second colour with a natural sponge for an overall crackle effect. As the crackle coat reacts with the top coat, it shrinks, taking the top coat with it and thus forming the cracks.

Colourwashing

For this elegant finish, two colours are washed over a dry base coat, one at a time. Apply the first colour with loose, irregular strokes across the wall, leaving patches of the original base coat exposed. Let this dry, and then apply the second colour using the same technique. Concentrate on covering the exposed patches, but allow glimpses of the base coat to show through. This finish looks best when accomplished in pastels.

Dragging

This finish is formed by dragging a dry, soft-bristled brush through fresh glaze, painted a section at a time over a dry base colour. For best results on large areas of wall, work with a partner. While one person applies the glaze, the other can drag the dry brush down or across it. Use two strokes to drag a vertical strip: one in a single motion from the top to the centre, the other from the base to the centre. Stagger the junctions of the vertical strokes as you move across the wall to avoid creating a horizontal marking.

Stippling

To achieve this orange-peel-like finish, apply glaze over a dry base coat. Working in pairs, one partner applies the glaze in vertical strips while the other dabs the fresh surface evenly with a stiff-bristled brush held at right-angles to the surface. Stippling with a rough-textured roller is quicker, although it produces a much softer texture. However, you must first run a clean roller over the wet surface to remove some of the paint.

Stripes

Cut uneven notches along the edge of a squeegee blade. Paint the wall in a base colour and let it dry. Next,

ABOVE LEFT: Colourwashing.

ABOVE CENTRE: Dragging.

ABOVE TOP: Stippling.

ABOVE: Stripes.

FAR LEFT: Darker stripes are hand painted roughly down the wall and the whole wall has been dabbed and streaked with a rag and brush at random in other muted colours.

Tips

- Don't be restricted by the tools suggested here. Hair combs or fingers can substitute for a notched squeegee blade for vastly different effects. And for rag-rolling, try scrunched-up lace, plastic or crackly paper.
- Experiment until you have perfected a technique, working on cardboard or a scrap surface before tackling your walls.

paint the coloured glaze on to the wall with a brush, working in vertical strips so it doesn't dry before you can work with it. Draw the squeegee through the glaze with a straight, wavy or random stroke to the bottom of the wall. Continue across the wall in this manner. Work in pairs, one applying the glaze while the other uses the squeegee to create the stripes.

For best results

For all finishes except crackle and colourwashing, make a glaze by diluting the top coat with a scumble medium (from art and specialist paint shops). This extends the drying time, especially if you're painting large areas such as walls. It also helps the paint hold the brushstroke patterns and creates a translucent finish.

Give walls the look of aged plaster

To give walls the look of aged plaster, try this technique. Purchase matt-finish, water-based emulsion paint in cream, taupe and gold. Paint the walls with a base coat of cream. Thin the taupe and gold paints half and half with acrylic matt medium. Colours will stay vibrant if you thin paint with acrylic matt medium (available from art and specialist paint shops). When used to thin interior paints, it lends depth and sheen to the finished paint scheme.

To apply the thinned taupe and gold paints to the walls, use rags and brushes. A little paint goes a long way. Working on 1 x 1 m sections, alternate patting and dabbing the paints on the wall.

Use a soft touch and run the paint out to the edges. Don't worry if you don't like the way it looks. You can go right over it again. If it's too dark, gradually add more of the light colour.

To complete the finish, create a border using taupe paint, a spray-

on dark grey paint and cream paint. Mask off the ceiling and create a level line along the walls. Then paint the border taupe. After the paint has dried, spray on a light coat of the dark grey paint. (Protect walls and ceiling from overspray.) Complete the look by painting thin feathery lines randomly across the border. Detailing takes a couple of hours.

Do-it-yourself – Stripes

Have you ever wondered how to create fresco finishes in your home? They look great and it's easy! To recreate the living room shown above, all you'll need is some time, paint and sponges. Be adventurous and experiment with other colours – dusky pinks, powder blues and greens all look terrific.

You will need: a suitable undercoat for the walls – a matt emulsion

ABOVE: The end result, softly contrasting stripes.

ABOVE: Paint and a wallpaper frieze set off rag-rolled walls.

---

in a sandy colour would be ideal (the quantity of undercoat and base colour will depend on the size of the room and the extent of the woodwork – check the paint tins for coverage); satin-finish emulsion in a dark yellow, or ochre, a paler yellow and a bluish-green; white emulsion tinted with the bluish-green as an undercoat for the woodwork; a hardboard template (see note below); a pencil; low-tack masking tape; kitchen sponges; containers for mixing paint; a lint-free cloth (an old T-shirt is ideal); a pencil eraser; paint brushes; a white wax candle; 320-grit sandpaper; beeswax; and a soft cloth.

Fresco walls

Note: The template used for marking the stripes was 120 mm wide and the length was just short of the measurement between the bottom of the coving and the top of the skirting. We used smaller lengths made of cardboard for areas above and below windows, doors, fireplaces and so on.

1 Undercoat the walls by applying two coats of the sandy-coloured emulsion. Let each coat dry.

2 Hold the template against the wall and make light pencil marks each side of it. Mark the stripes around the entire room.

3 Using the pencil lines as a guide, mask the stripes with the tape, smoothing it down along the paint edge. Cover the pencil lines with the tape.

4 Add ten per cent water to the dark yellow and mix well. Dip the corner of a sponge into the diluted paint and dab it randomly on to the wall, within the area of the masked stripe. Spread paint by wiping the sponge in a circular motion, side to side and up and down. Using the cloth, dab off some of the paint. Treat every second stripe in this way.

5 When the paint has dried, remove the tape by pulling it off diagonally towards the paint stripe. This will help prevent smudging and paint peeling off the wall. Erase the pencil marks.

6 Add ten per cent water to the paler yellow and mix well. Dip the corner of a sponge into the paint and apply by wiping the sponge backwards and forwards over the entire surface of the wall. Allow to dry. The lighter colour, applied over the walls, softens and reduces the contrast between the stripes.

Woodwork and skirting

1 Using the tinted undercoat, paint the woodwork; allow to dry.

2 Rub the candle in a random fashion over the woodwork.

3 Having combined a small quantity of equal parts of paler yellow and bluish-green, dilute with five per cent water and mix well.

4 Dry-brush the woodwork with diluted paint. Dip the tip of the brush into the paint, dab it on to a lint-free cloth to remove excess paint, then apply it to the woodwork. Allow to dry.

5 Lightly sand the woodwork with the 320-grit paper. Where the candle has been rubbed over the surface, the paint will not adhere. This completes the aging effect and will allow the base colour to show through.

6 Rub beeswax over the woodwork. Polish when dry.

Notes

For the ceiling and coving, we applied the sand-coloured paint diluted to half-strength.

For a more subdued appearance, finish with a wash of the base colour over the entire surface. For example, in this case our base was sand-coloured and the stripes were dark yellow. For a lighter, less bright look, we would have applied the diluted sand-coloured paint over the walls to finish.

Wallpaper

Today, many of us may associate wallpaper with grandma's dingy living room or the wild designs of the 1970s. Although not as popular as in the past, modern wallpapers offer an exciting and vast range of options if you want something different to a painted finish. In addition, many are much easier to apply than before.

Wallpaper can transform a boring room into a charming, inviting place. It envelopes you. It can hide uneven walls, create architectural emphasis and add interest to a surface. Many fabric designs also have corresponding wallpapers, which allows you to create mix-and-match rooms with confidence.

Modern wallpaper includes vinyl, flock relief and embossed finishes. Many types are ready-pasted to allow easy application.

Stripping wallpaper

Most wallpapers can be softened simply by soaking with water, but adding wallpaper stripper to it will make the job much easier. Vinyl and foil-faced papers are water resistant, so you must peel off these facings before applying the diluted stripper to the remaining base paper. Washable paper should be scored with a wire brush or scraper.

1 Protect the floor while you work and wear rubber gloves. Using a large sponge, soak the wallpaper with the diluted stripper, working in sections from the top.

2 Ease the blade of a scraper under the edge of the paper and lift it. If you have difficulty, apply more stripper mix with the sponge.

3 Holding the scraper at a low angle to the wall, push away from you beneath the wallpaper. Take care not to dig into the surface of the wall.

How to wallpaper

Decide how much wallpaper you'll need. This will depend on the size of the room. Your wallpaper stockist can work out how many rolls you need from the height of the walls and their length.

Read the instructions on the wallpaper roll carefully. Clear the room of furniture.

Prepare the walls. Remove old wallpaper (see illustration 1 on page 236). Most old papers are easy to peel, but you may need to hire a steam stripper to remove difficult papers. If you use a steam stripper, wear protective goggles and gloves. Remove excess paste with a sponge and water, then fill any cracks or gouges with filler so they won't show through the new paper.

When the walls are smooth and dry, apply a liberal coat of size to seal them and leave for 24 hours to ensure it is dry.

BELOW: Vertical stripes draw the eye upwards and make this elegant room look taller.

ABOVE: Emphasise interesting details by wallpapering between the skirting boards and picture rails. You can take the wallpaper all the way up to the ceiling to add height to your walls.

Before hanging the paper, measure each wall and use a plumb line and pencil to mark a straight line 48 cm from the corner (see illustration 2). Start hanging here to ensure that the first drop is absolutely vertical and the rest of the wallpaper lines up perfectly.

Unroll the wallpaper and cut the first strip according to the height of your wall, adding 10 cm top and bottom. If the paper is ready-pasted, place the roll in a water trough and slowly draw the length of wallpaper through the water (see illustration 3). Gently place the upper part of the wallpaper against the wall. (After wetting, some papers must be folded and left to stand for a minute or two. Check the manufacturer's instructions.)

Align the edge of the paper with the plumbed pencil line and smooth down with a sponge. Work down, centre to edge, removing air bubbles and wrinkles as you go (see illustration 4). Press the paper into the angle at covings and skirtings, and cut off excess with a sharp knife against a broad filling knife (see illustration 5).

Fixing lifting wallpaper

If the paste has been spread unevenly, you may find that the paper starts to lift and form bubbles. All you need do is apply more paste beneath the paper.

1 Using a very sharp knife, make a cut big enough to slide a filling knife in beneath the centre of the bubble.

2 Lift the edges of the cut carefully with a flat knife blade. Work some paste into the slit using the filling knife.

3 Wipe the surface with a damp sponge to remove any excess paste, pressing the wallpaper down as you do so. Make sure the edges of the cut close neatly.

4 Cover a block of wood with plastic food wrap, place it over the slit and apply pressure for several minutes.

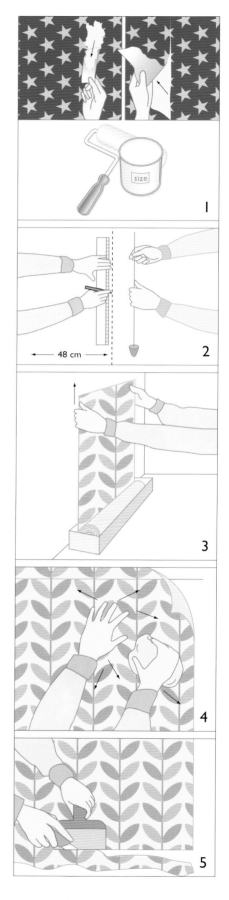

Tips

- Never remove power points when wallpapering – water and electricity don't mix. Instead, hang wallpaper over the point and make diagonal cuts to form flaps that allow the paper to be fitted around the point.
- Change trough water regularly, and keep your sponge clean.
- Pay careful attention to paper soaking times.
- Manufacturers usually specify the correct paste to use.
- If you haven't wallpapered before, don't start in a room that needs a lot of fiddly cutting-in, such as a cloakroom, or where there's not a lot of space to move around.
- Beginners should practise with a small piece of paper – not a three metre drop.
- Paint all window frames, architraves, cornices, skirtings and ceilings before hanging wallpaper.
- Walls in less-than-perfect condition look best when textured papers are used to hide the faults.
- Solid vinyl wallpaper will outlast paint, so use this in high-traffic areas.
- Vinyl papers should always be hung with fungicidal paste, as they can't 'breathe' like conventional papers.
- Clean washable vinyl paper with a mild detergent and water solution.
- Remove grease spots with moist fuller's earth. Stubborn stains may respond to rubbing with stale white bread or a soft pencil eraser. If not, try a proprietary cleaner, but patch-test first.
- If possible, buy an extra roll of paper for future repairs.
- Save left-over scraps of wallpaper for spot-patching. To spot-patch patterned paper, tear roughly into shape, as the uneven edge will help disguise the repair. Plain paper will need a full replacement drop.

ABOVE: The country blue-and-white check wallpaper gives an informal look to this dining area adjacent to the kitchen.

LEFT: This sunroom takes on the air of a conservatory with a lattice wallpaper.

Tip

- Save the ends of wallpaper rolls after a renovating stint, and look out for cheap rolls on sale. Some wallpapers make pretty wrapping paper for birthdays, etc, and they are perfect for lining kitchen and bathroom drawers.

Storage and Furniture

Solving all of the family's storage problems is a bit like painting the Forth Bridge – by the time it's finished, it's time to start again. With proper planning, though, you can clear most of your existing clutter and anticipate any future requirements as well.

Begin by asking yourself whether you really need more places to put things, or just better organisation of what you have. Often, the simple space-engineering techniques shown in this chapter can do wonders for a cupboard's capacity. And remember that you can rotate seasonal items. Try letting things such as a sun shade swap places with the overcoats as the seasons change. Decide where to locate any new units. Keep everyday items at or near their points of use, and once-a-year specials, such as Christmas decorations, in more remote spots.

It might help to survey your entire home, noting and measuring all areas with potential for development, then indicating them on a graph-paper floorplan. If you are left with several options, concentrate on ground-floor storage first – it's much handier than storage upstairs. Finally, select the type of storage you need. Open shelves are relatively inexpensive and easy to install; they also attract dust. Cabinets provide more protection for stored items and are available in sizes to fit almost any space you have. New built-in cupboards offer the most permanent and least obtrusive storage. Also available is an impressive array of ready-made storage units.

Plan spaces carefully, note the sizes of your household items and be sure to allow for the thickness of shelves and dividers. Don't over-plan and don't forget to allow a few centimetres of extra space for removing and replacing items, and enough flexibility to accommodate changes later on.

Storage and furniture are often one and the same thing. Most households require space to display decorative pieces as well as storage for everyday items. The shelving unit pictured here serves multiple functions as a display unit, a bookcase and a room divider.

Storage

If you cannot tailor storage to suit your needs, a reassessment of your existing storage capacity may be the solution. Cleaning out unwanted items can create a surprising amount of space.

Organising existing storage

Tailored storage not only makes everything easier to get at, but it can also increase the capacity of a cupboard or a cabinet by as much as a third. This means that modifying three cupboards would effectively provide you with a fourth – without the trouble of building it.

The diagram of the bungalow below may assist you in room-by-room planning of your storage. Study the layout, make an inventory of the things you want to make places for, then adapt it to suit your own needs.

Plan spacings carefully. Tables later in the chapter give typical sizes for many household items. Don't forget to allow for the thick-ness of the shelves when planning your storage area, and dividers when you are using them.

Make sure you don't over-engineer. It's better to be flexible, as you may change your mind later on about layout and the items you want to store.

The Ten Commandments of better storage

1   Don't be a hoarder. Discard unwanted items or those you haven't used for years.

2   Consider built-ins whenever possible for maximum and most efficient use of space.

3   Exploit odd spaces such as corners, next to fireplaces and so on, to build or place furniture.

TOP: Space under stairs is ideal for storage.

ABOVE: Shelving across one wall maximises space.

RIGHT: Organise your storage space.

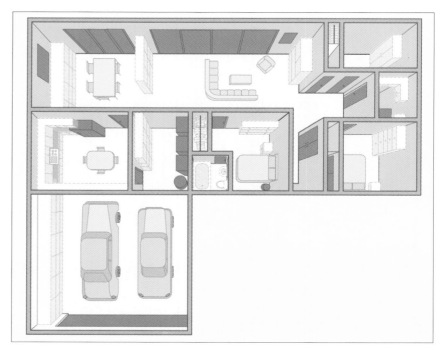

4   Don't waste under-stair space. Enclose it for extra storage or turn it into a small home office.

5   Extend built-in units to the ceiling. Finish with coving.

6   Save floor space with sliding, rather than swinging, doors.

7   Boost wardrobe space by creating a walk-in wardrobe, fitted out with both hanging space and shelving.

8   Make extra space for storage in your roof by creating an attic room or simply by placing boards across the joists near the access hatch.

9   Consider the space under beds. A series of boxes on castors can provide a surprising amount of storage beneath a bed.

10   Use open shelving – adjustable and/or fixed wherever possible.

Why built-in units

Upgrading the level of comfort of your house improves both its value and your lifestyle. A good built-in unit not only enhances a room by rationalising and organising its contents, but it also improves the look of that room. But whatever a built-in unit achieves, it will have to be made specifically for its purpose and for the space it occupies. Unlike anything you can buy from a shop, a built-in unit takes its form from your needs and requirements. That's why you can adapt the ideas here to suit your home.

ABOVE: The space on each side of a fireplace is useful for built-in storage, which can be both functional and attractive.

ABOVE LEFT: Sewing can be a messy job, but if the sewing machine and all its associated bits and pieces can be stored where the work is carried out it will be easier to set up and put away each time. Cupboards with shelves are the key. These can be prefabricated in white plastic-laminated board or custom-built in the colour of your choice.

LEFT: Shelves built into the end of the kitchen wall in this small apartment are a clever and practical idea.

Where will we put it?

Finding places to store things is a constant battle for most of us. Even if you're not a hoarder, you will still need a place for all the essentials you can't live without. And, as you can see, function and beauty can go hand in hand.

With open storage, place important objects at eye level and less attractive items near the floor.

ABOVE: Insets on a staircase make an effective display space.

LEFT: An office combined with the sewing room must have well organised storage.

ABOVE: Follow the lines of the roof and take shelving right to the ceiling, to create a whole wall of books and ornaments.

ABOVE: Television in a built-in unit is unobtrusive yet accessible.

TOP LEFT: A built-in sideboard with bookshelves above combines beauty and function.

RIGHT: A double bookcase, up to the ceiling, is perfect for a traditional room with high ceilings.

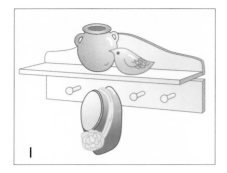

1

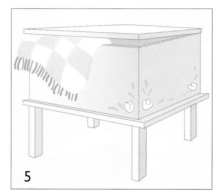

2

3

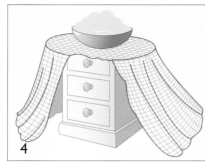

4

5

6

DIAGRAMS THIS PAGE: Furniture combining.

Combining furniture

If space is at a premium, you can stack furniture. Ready-made and flat-pack items offer lots of options.

1 Place coat hooks under a narrow shelf. This is great in a bathroom for towels, bottles and jars.

2 Sit a small cupboard, such as one used for a video recorder, on top of a chest of drawers.

3 Place a long narrow cupboard on top of a bedside chest. Don't forget to screw the pieces together for stability.

4 With a chipboard disc and a cloth on top, a small chest can serve as a table and storage.

5 A blanket or toy box on top of a coffee table of similar size makes great storage for a hallway and saves bending.

6 The top portions of two wardrobes, one of them turned upside down, could make a new and interesting piece of furniture.

Room-by-room storage ideas

When you're planning storage or trying to increase what you've got, consider the general storage commandments. However, you can also use the following clever storage tricks for specific rooms.

Kitchen

Kitchens need to be stacked to the ceiling with storage facilities. This means you have to exploit every storage possibility. Because there are so many different sorts of kitchen items to be stored, there has to be an equivalent range of storage methods: drawers of all shapes and sizes, shelves designed to fill specific needs, racks and rails, trays that rotate and glide.

Consider an overhead rack to hang cookware and create more space in cupboards and drawers.

Install an appliance cupboard to keep appliances within easy reach on your worktop.

Extend wall cupboards to the ceiling for maximum space.

If you have room, install a kitchen island to give you more worktop and under-worktop space.

Add open shelving to spare wall spaces to stock recipe books, storage canisters and jars or other attractive kitchen items.

Investigate the vast range of modular racks, baskets, lazy Susans, hooks, waste tidies and so on to increase storage in existing and new kitchen cabinets.

ABOVE: Specialist storage means having the right type of storage for the job. Here are three types in one cupboard. The wire baskets (on the right) are hooked onto a vertical hanger and slide easily. Plastic bins (on the left) with a lip around the top are available from hardware stores. You will need to build rebates into the sides of your cupboards for them to slide along. In the centre are slide out shelves.

TOP LEFT: Building an island across the corner makes your kitchen much more multi-faceted and gives you more under-worktop storage space as well. The work space, a couple of open shelves and narrow, but deep, side drawers will always be handy.

TOP RIGHT: Finding space for small items may mean building a large shallow shelving unit. All you need is some 90 x 19 mm timber for the sides, 70 x 19 mm shelves and shelf fronts, a 3 mm plywood back and a good-sized door with clearance from the shelves to hang it on.

ABOVE: Now you can fold away your most space-consuming kitchen appliance, as it remains sitting on its own shelf. As this fold-away fitting disappears out of sight beneath the worktop, its parallel-arm system keeps whatever sits upon it perfectly level.

ABOVE RIGHT: Standing plates on their edges means you don't have to stack. Placing your plate rack in a cupboard above the worktop is the best site for it. These racks are home made. The slats between plates are 19 x 10 mm, front and side rails are 32 x 19 mm and the main framing timbers are 42 x 19 mm. Butt joints are simply glued and stapled together.

RIGHT: Open up your over-worktop storage with exposed shelves. Make shelves, sides and shaped brackets from 190 x 19 mm pine. Use 70 x 19 mm timber for the supporting wall battens.

RIGHT: Closing up a doorway provided the opportunity to build in recessed shelving behind the newly installed sink. Shelving tracks and clips make shelf adjustment easy and bottleneck-sized notches keep an even distance between the wine bottles on the upper shelves.

RIGHT: Suspending saucepans above your worktop makes sense. A shelf mounted on decorative brass shelving brackets, commonly available in DIY stores, gives you a wide horizontal surface. This allows your saucepan/towel rail to be far enough out from the wall to accommodate large utensils.

CENTRE LEFT: Revolving corners make maximum use of corner cavities, which inevitably have limited access. Not having a corner door shape cut out of it, this model is completely circular. The central shaft is fixed at top and bottom and comes with two plastic shelves, which can be set at any height.

CENTRE RIGHT: Rounding the ends of cupboards with quarter- or semi-circular open shelving gives you accessible incidental shelving for a few everyday essentials or prized possessions, and curved worktop ends make for easy movement about the work area.

BELOW RIGHT: The use of roller shutters behind the worktop allows appliances to be left plugged in and ready to use. It also means you can tidy up at short notice. Plastic rolling shutters come in brown and white. Their maximum width is 1200 mm, but you can cut the shutter down with a hacksaw for a perfect fit.

ABOVE: Decorative items and bathing accessories are displayed in this bathroom, but a cupboard under the bath provides storage space for more everyday items.

RIGHT: This small country-style bathroom has utilised a small space for the built-in shelves to store rolled up towels. Above the basin is a handy rack for toiletries.

Bathroom

Place open shelving on walls to store towels, shampoos, soaps, oils and bathing accessories.

You should make the most of ready-made hooks, rails and containers to boost storage in your bathroom.

If you have little storage space for medicines and bottles, you can construct a shallow, recessed cabinet in a stud-partition wall.

Build a cabinet with shelves beneath a freestanding basin for extra space.

Bedroom

Parents

Consider taking extra space from an adjoining room to construct a walk-in wardrobe.

Whether you have a walk-in or built-in wardrobe, you can make the best use of space with a combination of double hanging, single hanging, adjustable shelving and a few modular pieces to store smaller items of clothing.

Consult a fitted bedroom furniture supplier to determine the possible options for the space available. When planning wardrobes, it's vital to allow more space than you'll need and make them at least 60 cm deep.

Children

Consider bunk beds to save space or install a mezzanine level in the room if you have the space and budget for it.

Use divan beds with drawers beneath for extra storage.

Buy or build modular furniture that can be constructed in space-efficient configurations to include a wardrobe, shelves and a desk for children's study.

Make use of small boxes, trunks and baskets to store children's toys, books, drawing items, sports equipment and so on.

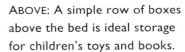

ABOVE: A simple row of boxes above the bed is ideal storage for children's toys and books.

ABOVE LEFT: An open shelving unit in a bedroom can add colour but will only look attractive if it is kept tidy. The wall rack for jewellery and belts keeps the items tangle-free.

BELOW LEFT: This bedroom storage space literally has a place for everything. You do need a big bedroom and a large empty wall space to attempt this level of organisation, however.

LEFT: These tiny built-in shelves will save you from having to rummage for small items in large drawers. Jewellery, watches, hair accessories and scarves can be easily retrieved simply by sliding the shelf out.

FAR RIGHT: A ladder on castors gives easy access to high shelves. The long, shallow shelves are perfect for storing smaller items.

RIGHT: The ideal place for ties and belts is on the inside of the wardrobe door. On their own hooks they save space and are easy to find.

BELOW: Everything can have its own space in a walk-in wardrobe. Vertical dividers create order and the ladder provides access to high shelves.

Fitting more into wardrobes

Typically, a shallow wardrobe of 600 mm deep by 1500–2400 mm wide offers lots of room for improvement. With most, you get a single hanging rail, plus a shelf above it, and a pair of hinged or sliding doors.

Start your analysis of a wardrobe's efficiency with the doors. If they slide, do you find yourself opening one, then rolling both to the other side (and maybe back again) every morning? If so, consider replacing these awkward panels with a set of bi-folding units.

Next, study how space is utilised inside. Chances are, you'll notice that a few dresses and coats fill most of the vertical space between the rail and floor, while the bulk of your clothing hangs down only a little more than halfway. Group garments by size and you'll 'discover' a sizeable empty space beneath the shorter items.

Shallow cupboard designs, with either sliding or bi-folding doors that include a shelf unit, take the pressure off freestanding storage elsewhere. A walk-in wardrobe is the ultimate luxury – the one illustrated on page 252 features two rails on one side to accommodate shorter clothes, creating more hanging space for longer items. You can adapt your built-in wardrobe by using this idea, but keep in mind that the spaces allowed for hanging clothes are the minimums.

ABOVE: Narrow cupboard doors are easier to handle than full-sized ones. Paint them to suit the room and choose knobs to match.

Fitting more into a walk-in wardrobe

Walk-in wardrobes, although larger than their shallow built-in cousins, actually provide less storage per square metre. Subtract the minimal 600-mm-wide corridor needed for access and you can see why. If a walk-in measures just 1200–1500 mm deep and access isn't a problem, you might gain by converting it into two shallow cupboards positioned back to back.

Otherwise, you can install rails along the longer wall or walls, as illustrated. Double-tier rails for suits, skirts and other short items can provide you with half as much again in hanging space.

Shelves – either at the back or along one wall – often will hold all of your folded clothes. It's best to space them about 180 mm apart to minimise rummaging.

And don't neglect shelf possibilities above the rails. Although you may have to stretch to reach them, boxes stored here can hold seasonal or seldom-worn clothing. Install a second shelf approximately 300 mm above the existing one and you won't have to stack the boxes on top of each other.

Dimensions you need to know

You'll be wise to familiarise yourself with a few basic measurements before you take on the re-organisation of a wardrobe. A wooden coat hanger with a heavily-padded jacket on it occupies a space about 500 mm deep. Rails are normally hung 300–350 mm from the wall, but in a tight situation you could cut this distance to 250 mm. The table lists other typical dimensions. Use them as an aid in allocating space in your restyled wardrobe.

Living room

Install built-in furniture and shelving right to the ceiling for TV/stereo equipment.

Use a chest or trunk as a coffee table-cum-storage box.

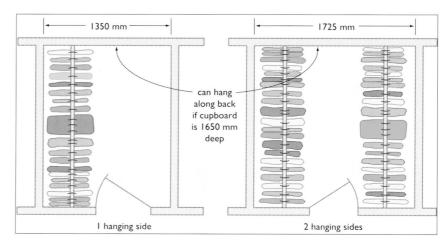

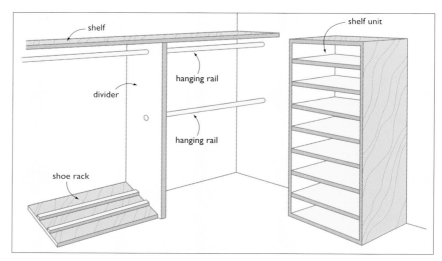

Fill wasted under-window space with a short stack of bookshelves.

Entertaining storage

We all know how our sound and viewing equipment can take over a room. A large part of making a sitting room work is in organising the

ABOVE: Getting more into a walk-in wardrobe.

Wardrobe contents (all measurements are in mm)					
Women's items		**Men's items**		**Accessories**	
Long dresses	1750	Top coats	1270	Garment bags	1450
Dressing gowns	1320	Suits	960	Hanging shoe bags	900
Skirts	900	Travel bags	1050	Umbrellas	900
Dresses	1150	Trousers (cuff hung)	1120		
Dress bags	1220	Trousers (double hung)	500		
Blouses	700	Ties	700		
Coats	1320	Shirts	700		
Suits	750				
Suit bags	1050				

storage of television, video and sound systems. To begin solving your storage problems, work out the best furniture arrangement; from there, establish the appropriate location for your home entertainment equipment. Now decide how best to use the space that you have available.

TOP LEFT: Clearly different-sized items require shelves and cupboards of different depths. A pivoting stand is an excellent extra for the television set.

ABOVE: Extending television turntables that run on heavy-load bearing runners allow the television to be shut away when not in use. These mechanisms are available through specialist hardware manufacturers.

CENTRE LEFT: Grouping different activities into one storage unit is an efficient use of space. This corner unit incorporates an unobtrusive sitting room bar, as well as books, ornaments and sound equipment.

LEFT: Be guided by your site. Here, the below-stairs area is perfect for a triangular format. Even the lowest, least accessible cavities can be used for storage.

ABOVE: Storage units are just boxes, after all. Think about a separate 'box' for each storage category – this one is purpose built for the sound system.

RIGHT: If you can tailor your storage unit to suit your room's style, you will create a finished look that's perfect. Here, it's fine polished timber throughout.

Tips

- Deep cupboards will allow you to store your television, video and audio equipment neatly. Use shallow shelves above for CDs, cassettes, video cassettes and books. This is the most popular storage format.
- Align storage units with the heights of the window sills, doors and coving.

Utility room

Fix a tumble dryer to the wall above the washing machine.

Attach a fold-out ironing board cupboard to the wall. The ironing board can then be folded away when it is not needed.

Make more space in an existing utility room for sorting with a small table, then add a few wall cupboards or shelves for more storage.

Fix hooks behind the door to hang brooms, mops and so on, or install a tall cupboard for them.

Fitting more into a linen cupboard

The trouble with tall stacks of folded sheets and towels is that you have to be a magician to remove the lower ones without crumpling the rest . . . and possibly toppling adjacent stacks as well. The solution – compartmentalise.

The diagram opposite shows a scheme for putting foldables in their respective places. Bulky blankets go on the top, then bath towels, sheets, hand towels and so on.

Drawers and a cabinet also add concealed storage below.

Plan the dimensions according to the items you want to store, leaving a few centimetres of clearance for putting them in and taking them out.

And, as with all storage solutions, keep your arrangement flexible: home furnishings change.

Linen cupboard contents (all measurements are in mm)	
Pillowcases	180 x 380
Blankets	690 x 570
Sheets	
Flat	460 x 380
Fitted	340 x 270
Face cloths	180 x 180
Hand towels	150 x 250
Bath towels	350 x 330
Bath mats	250 x 230
Dish cloths	250 x 410
(Maximum space requirements – folded)	

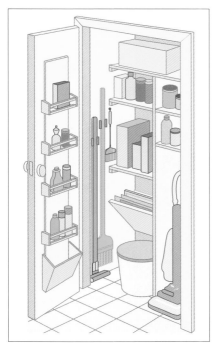

TOP: Fitting more into a linen cupboard.

ABOVE: Fitting more into a cleaning cupboard.

Fitting more into a cleaning cupboard

Compartments can help organise the jumble of awkward shapes that utility storage must accommodate. The cupboard shown here stores an upright vacuum cleaner, provides shelves for an assortment of cleaning products, and holds a mop and broom so they won't fall out when you open the door. Note, too, how a slanting compartment near the bottom of the cupboard reduces the clutter of stored carrier bags.

For even more storage, look to the inside of the cupboard door. Lipped shelves and/or a cloth caddy for vacuum cleaner attachments put this space to good use. And if room in a cleaning cupboard is really tight, consider outfitting it with wire racks rather than wooden shelving. You'll gain storage space and improve air circulation as well.

Cleaning equipment (all measurements are in mm)	
Cylinder vacuum	350 x 430
Floor polisher	300 x 1140
Upright vacuum	350 x 1220
Carpet sweeper	410 x 1370
Broom	250 x up to 1520
Dust pan	280 x 230
Brush	90 x 320
Feather duster	150 x 500
Dry mop	340 x 1680
Wet mop	300 x 1220
Bucket	270 x 30
Cleansers	200–250 x 150–350

Adding new storage

The answer to a storage shortage may be as simple as a few coat hooks near your front door or as complex as an entire wall of custom-made living-room built-in units. Most solutions fall somewhere in between, with open shelving heading the list. If you select the right hardware and master a few basics, you'll never be floored by a shelf project again. Available in a variety of styles and finishes, they make useful additions to any room.

You could also consider building a new cupboard or cupboards. Before you begin, though, consider the almost instant alternative offered by storage you can buy.

Choosing shelf hardware

The success of any shelving project rests quite literally upon its support system. So you should ask yourself these questions before making your choice. What weights must the hardware hold, and what space should it occupy? Can shelves be supported at their ends, or must they be attached along the back edge? Do you want fixed or adjustable brackets? How will you attach the shelves to the wall? Do you really need hardware at all? Wooden battens screwed to the wall are an alternative.

Once you've answered these questions, consider appearance. Styling ranges from utilitarian to hardwood wall furniture. You'll discover that price is a factor, too – hardware can cost more than the wood needed for the shelves.

The box on the next page discusses the most commonly used support systems, but there are dozens of variations. With adjustable shelving supports, for instance, you can choose a painted or anodised finish, different bracket shapes and locking mechanisms, and even special fittings, such as magazine racks.

And while you're selecting hardware, give some thought to buying pre-finished shelving as well. Although more expensive than boards, chipboard or plywood, it saves a lot of tedious work.

Installing adjustable shelf uprights

Adjustable shelving seems to concentrate a lot of weight on the few

Support systems

- Rigid pressed-steel angle brackets hold medium-weight loads. Always mount them with the longer leg against the wall. For heavier duty, choose types reinforced with triangular gussets between the legs.

- Adjustable shelving brackets clip into slotted uprights, allowing you to vary the spacing between shelves to meet changing needs. Various sizes of bracket are available up to 300 mm. Properly installed, this system supports surprisingly heavy loads.

- The simplest (and least expensive) way to hold shelves inside cupboards, bookcases, cabinets and alcoves is to install wooden battens at each end. For longer spans, fix a third strip along the back to support the rear of the shelves.

- For a less cluttered look, you could mount shelves by placing plastic clips into pre-drilled holes. Relatively inexpensive, they'll support medium loads on 20 mm-thick boards up to about 750 mm long.

- Alternatively, you can make end-mounted shelves adjustable with slotted uprights and clips. Again, limit spans to about 750 mm. For a flush installation, you can recess the uprights into the cabinet's sides.

- So-called 'tension' poles (actually they work by expansion) wedge between floor and ceiling where you don't want to make holes in the wall. They're relatively expensive.

- Folding brackets let you drop a shelf out of the way when you're not using it. You can buy a variation of these brackets for spring-loaded installations; the shelf simply pops up when you pull it out of the cabinet.

- Light-duty wire brackets are among the many accessories you can mount on perforated hardboard. Measure the board's thickness before you buy it to make sure that the brackets you buy will fit.

ABOVE: This bookcase, with a deeper central section, is a practical way of providing shelves of various dimensions.

small fasteners that secure the uprights. But those fasteners don't actually bear the load; they simply clamp the uprights to the wall. This means that the strength of a shelving system actually depends more on the fasteners' holding power than it does on their size.

Use plastic wall plugs for light-duty installations. For extra strength, wood screws driven directly into the studs of a timber-framed wall hold much better, but you will need to adjust your design according to the spacing of the studs. Hollow-wall fasteners such as toggles let you put the uprights exactly where you want them.

Armed with the proper fasteners and a screwdriver, drill and spirit level, you can fit the uprights in an hour or so. It is essential that they are positioned so that the brackets and shelving will be level. To do this, use the first as a datum for the remainder. Don't measure up from the floor or down from the ceiling for each one; neither may be level.

Before fitting the first upright, note whether it has a definite top and bottom. Mark and drill the wall for the top fixing only.

Insert a screw or fastener, but don't tighten it until you've plumbed the upright, drilled the remaining holes and installed the lower fixings.

Draw a level line from the upright's top or bottom to locate the last upright in the run.

Position the intermediate uprights, using the line you've drawn as a guide. Maintain an equal spacing between them.

Estimated shelf spacings and spans

Plot any shelf layout carefully, using graph paper and the dimensions supplied here to minimise any 'surprises' later. The span table gives the maximum distance you should allow between supports. It assumes a full load of books, which are the heaviest items you're likely to put on shelves. Don't allow the unsupported ends of shelves to extend more than half the span distance beyond the last support, otherwise they may begin to sag.

With adjustable shelving, you can save space and reduce dusting by tailoring vertical spacings to accommodate your possessions exactly. Just be sure to leave an extra few centimetres so you can easily tip out a book, for example,

ABOVE: The kitchen wall dishrack.

Shelving spans	
Material used	Maximum span
17 mm plywood	900 mm
250 x 50 mm or	
300 x 50 mm timber	1200–1350 mm
18 mm	
particle board	700 mm
13 mm acrylic	550 mm
300 x 25 mm timber	600 mm
10 mm glass	450 mm
(Assumes shelves fully loaded with books)	

Item	Space required
Paperback books	200
Hardback books	280
CDs	160
Over-sized hardbacks	380
Cassette tapes	130
Catalogue-format books	400
Video cassettes	190
Shelf spacing guide (all measurements are in mm)	

(allow a little more leeway if you decide on fixed shelves).

Before determining your final shelving layout, consult the lower table for the spacing required between shelves for several often-shelved items.

Do-it-yourself – A kitchen wall dish rack

Although dishwashers are becoming more common in today's kitchens, they are by no means universal and many of us still wash up by hand. A family meal can generate a lot of washing up, and even with a twin-drainer set-up, there often is not enough space to allow everything to drain and dry. A wall-hung dish rack, positioned above the sink, can solve the problem, allowing washed and rinsed items to drip dry out of the way. You could even use the design simply as a permanent store for your crockery when not in use if your kitchen is short of storage space.

We made our dish rack from lengths of beech, with 13-mm-thick hollow stainless-steel tubing for the rods. It is best to use a hardwood for the construction of the framework, as this allows it to support the weight without looking too bulky. (If you don't feel like going to the expense and trouble of using stainless-steel rods, you can easily replace them with wooden dowels of the same thickness.)

Tip

• Plan your shelving strategy around available space, while bearing in mind the style and function of the room. But don't be afraid to break a few of the conventional rules. You can be ruthless when it comes to maximising space.

You will need for the dish rack:

Item	Material	Length or size (in mm)	No.
End frame front	32 x 19 mm beech	322	2
End frame back	32 x 19 mm beech	830	2
End diagonal	132 x 19 mm beech	425	4
Front rail	32 x 19 mm beech	1200	3
Back rail	32 x 32 mm beech	1200	3
Back spacer	32 x 19 mm beech	1200	3
Top side rail	32 x 19 mm beech	175	2
Middle side rail	32 x 19 mm beech	145	2
Bottom side rail	32 x 19 mm beech	105	2
Top rod	13 mm dowel or s/steel	200	28
Middle rod	13 mm dowel or s/steel	170	28
Bottom rod	13 mm dowel or s/steel	130	28
Back rod	13 mm dowel or s/steel	750	28
Top capping	32 x 19 mm beech	1200	1

Other: 100 mm expanding bolts; 35 and 50 mm countersunk screws; wood filler; lost-head nails for pinning.

1

2

3

4

5

6

7

8

ABOVE: Do-it-yourself − A kitchen wall dishrack.

1 Cut and assemble end frames.

2 Drill holes in front and back rails.

3 Fasten end frames to rails.

4 Assemble rails and rods.

5 Drill and pin rods.

6 Fit spacers.

7 Fit back rods.

8 Fix rack to wall.

1 On your workbench top, draw the shape of the end frames to the dimensions on the diagram and lay lengths of 32 x 19 mm timber on it to the exact lengths and angles of the two sets of four components. Rebate the back verticals into the diagonals and cut half-lap joints at the front angles. Glue and screw the end frames together.

2 The shelves are 1200 mm long. Cut the three 32 x 19 mm front and three 32 x 32 mm back rails to this length and drill 28 holes along the centre of their inner faces. Make the holes 10 mm deep and 13 mm in diameter. Use a dowelling jig for the purpose and mark out the position of the holes using the shelf lay-out plan as a guide.

3 Cut pairs of side rails to length. The three different shelf widths will allow you to accommodate the standard range of plates, but if you wish to store extra-large items, make your own calculations and adapt the design accordingly. Glue and nail the side rails to either the back or front rail of the shelf you are working on.

4 Rods or dowels should measure 130 mm for the bottom shelf, 170 mm for the middle shelf and 200 mm for the upper shelf. Cut these with a hacksaw or tenon saw, depending on the material you use, and tap them into the holes with a mallet. Tap the other rail on to the free ends of the rods. You will have to line up all 28 rods with their holes. Work from one end to the other and, if possible, get someone to help.

5 At four points along each of the back and side rails, drill a fine hole through the rail and the inserted rod end. Pin the rails by punching in nails with their heads removed. This will stop the rails flexing outwards when the shelves are loaded.

6 Add 32 x 19 mm spacers to the back of each shelf. Drill, glue and screw these in place.

7 The back rods are 750 mm long. Drill vertical holes into the back rails of the shelves to correspond with the horizontal rods, as close to the ends of the latter as possible. Slide the shelves down the back rods. The holes will be tight enough to hold the shelves apart at the suggested clearance heights. Next, fit the top rail, with holes drilled to correspond with the ends of the rods.

8 Screw the ends of the frame in place. Countersink screws through the end frames into the ends of the top capping, as well as the front and back of each shelf. Plane the top front corner off the top capping to match the angle of the top diagonal. The

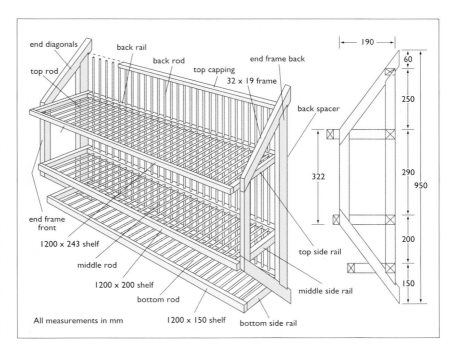

bottom shelf will cantilever by half its depth past the bottom diagonal of the end frame.

Fix the rack to a masonry wall using expanding bolts at two points along the back rail of each shelf, and diagonally through the top of the end frames. Lime the wood and coat with polyurethane varnish to protect the timber. Alternatively, you may prefer leave the wood untreated to take on the traditional patina of water stains.

Do-it-yourself – Build a blanket box

Window seats and blanket boxes make fabulous storage. They are deep enough to accommodate the bulkiest of items – blankets, pillows and big bags, or things you're not ready to part with just yet. We have given you the plans for a blanket box that is large enough to be turned into a window seat if you would prefer.

The blanket box can be built from a variety of woods depending on your preference and pocket. You can even use recycled timber, but this will probably need cleaning up

ABOVE: Take advantage of the space created by a bay window by filling it with extra seating and storage. This seat opens across the front through cupboard doors, instead of having a hinged lid.

ABOVE: If money and space are at a premium, the conventional window seat with a hinged lid is a cheaper style than one with cupboard doors. You have to take everything off it to get into the box, so store only seasonal items there.

ABOVE RIGHT: A blanket box can double as an extra table or seating.

with a plane to a greater or lesser extent, and the widths and thicknesses may vary from those specified. To this end, the sizes given are only meant as a guide.

1 Use a router to cut the rebates in the side rails and the lid frame pieces to the depths shown in the diagram. Mitre the ends.

2 Mitre the ends of the side panels. By gluing and screwing at an angle through the back of the side panels, fit the rails to the side panels. Assemble the sides into a box and fix them by pinning through the mitres of the end side rails (hardwoods will need to

be pre-drilled to prevent splitting when nailing and screwing).

3 After ensuring that the box is square, fit the floor braces. Screw through them at an angle into the side rails, then fit the floorboards into the box and secure them by skew-nailing into the bottom side rails and the braces. Complete the box by screwing brass angle pieces to the corners. (If you are using tongued-and-grooved boards for the flooring, you will need to trim the edges off the two outside boards so that they fit the box.)

4 The lid can be made of plain boards or tongued-and-grooved boards. If you are using the latter, fit them together, then clamp them before making the frame for the lid. Glue and screw the pieces of the lid frame to the underside of the lid, ensure that it is square. Add the lid braces.

5 Screw and glue the hinge mount to the top rails and fit the hinges and lid. The quality of the final appearance of your blanket box will be in direct proportion to the amount of effort put into the final sanding and finishing of the timber. We used a satin-finish polyurethane with plenty of sanding between coats for a smooth finish.

You will need for the blanket box (finished sizes in mm)			
Item	Material	No.	Size
Side panels	Pine (or plywood)	2 pieces	1456 x 275 x 18
		2	546 x 275 x 18
Side rails	Pine	2	1500 x 60 x 45
		2	590 x 60 x 45
Lid boards	Pine	4	1448 x 112 x 18
Lid frame	Pine	2	1500 x 45 x 23
		2	500 x 45 x 23
Lid braces	Pine	2	400 x 100 x 18
Hinge mount	Pine	1	1500 x 90 x 23
Floor	Pine (or plywood)	4	1420 x 130 x 20
Floor braces	Pine	3	500 x 60 x 45

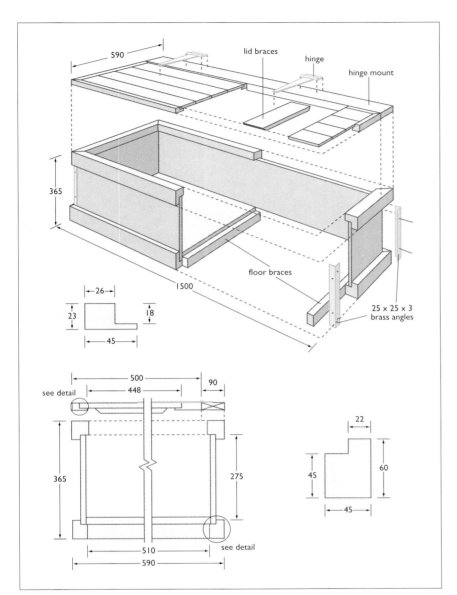

26
23
18
45

500
448
90
see detail

365
275

22
45
60
45

510
590
see detail

LEFT: Build a blanket box.

BELOW: This back-door arrangement is an effective way to keep the house clean and to stop dirt and clutter from spreading into the house.

Back-door bonus

In any house, it is useful to have a place close to the entrance to put coats, boots or shoes and umbrellas. In wet weather, this prevents mud and water from being trailed through the house.

Make a bench as long as you have space for, but you should include a leg and brace support every 1500 mm. Use 40 mm countersunk screws and glue all the joints as you proceed.

Use 50 mm square timber for the framework. As an alternative to the seat slats pictured, our diagram (on page 262) indicates 19-mm-thick MDF for the seat. Because the leg braces have to be cut from a sheet material, making the seat from the same board will produce a substantial cost benefit.

Cut the ordinary braces and the decorative braces from the MDF. Screw through the legs into the back edge of the braces, then drive screws back through the leg into the wall. Use toggle fixings for a hollow partition wall, or drive screws into the studs; use expanding bolts if the wall is built of

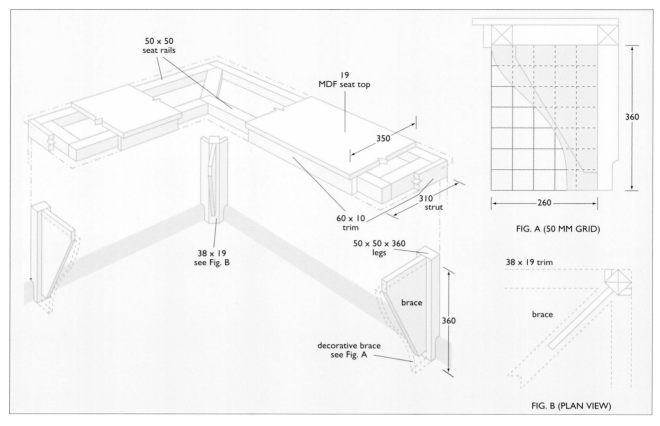

50 x 50
seat rails

19
MDF seat top

350

310
strut

60 x 10
trim

50 x 50 x 360
legs

38 x 19
see Fig. B

brace

360

decorative brace
see Fig. A

FIG. A (50 MM GRID)

360

260

38 x 19 trim

brace

FIG. B (PLAN VIEW)

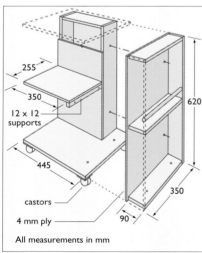

255

350

12 x 12
supports

620

445

350

castors

4 mm ply

90

All measurements in mm

TOP: Back-door bonus.

ABOVE: Mobile storage.

masonry. In the corner, you will find it easier to bolt the leg in place through the 38 x 19 mm trims indicated in the diagram.

Now fix the 310-mm-wide seat frame to the braces. You should add a transverse strut running the depth of the seat at least every 800 mm.

Complete by adding the seat top of your choice.

To make the coat and hat rack, use 300 x 200 mm ready-made wooden shelving brackets. Alternatively, cut braces of similar shape to the decorative braces used for the bench from MDF. Cut a 325-mm-wide MDF back panel to the length you require, and drill and screw through it into the back of the shelving brackets or braces. Fix through the board into the wall. Drill the panel and glue wooden pegs, dowels or knobs into the holes. Or you could add brass hooks for a more traditional finish if you wish. Finally, glue and screw a 250-mm-wide shelf in place.

Mobile storage

A mobile unit will provide a practical and multi-purpose storage facility. For example, it can be used as a kitchen or sewing trolley that can be moved where you want. By adding a pegboard, it can become a workshop accessory, or it can be adapted for use in the utility room or study. Mobile units can be stored out of sight when not in use.

The unit shown here consists of a base with four castors and two 90-mm-deep shelved boxes with plywood backs, which are mounted on the base in one corner. They form a right-angle that provides rigidity to the trolley. The arrangement of the shelves can be as complex or as simple as you want. The best material for this unit is 12 mm MDF or plywood (particle board is also an option, but will require edging).

Six pieces of 326 x 90 mm MDF or plywood are used for the box shelves and ends (extra if more than one shelf is required). Four pieces

of 620 x 90 mm are needed for the sides. The base (and top, if it is required) measures 445 x 350 mm. If an intermediate shelf is to be included in the back section, it will be 350 x 255 mm and will be supported on 12 x 12 mm wooden battens. The 4 mm plywood backing for the boxes needs to be 620 x 350 mm. To stop items falling off the shelves, use dowels, strips of Perspex or thin wooden battens. You could also make a tray 90 mm deep to fit flush behind the boxes.

The fastenings include 18 mm countersunk chipboard screws and 38 mm nails. PVA glue and a suitable paint finish complete the requirements.

1 After checking the box components for square and straightness, assemble them using the screws or nails and glue. While the glue is still wet, nail and glue on the backs to square them up. If you're using dowels, bore holes 6 mm deep in the sides and fit them in place as you're assembling the boxes.

2 Fix the boxes to the base and each other as shown, again using glue and screws. Next fix the top, if any, and/or the intermediate shelf (or shelves) once the

battens have been screwed into position. The best way to secure them is to screw through the plywood into the battens.

Now fit the castors, but remove them again in case they get paint on them. Then fill all the holes and apply a suitable gloss or semi-gloss paint, sanding lightly between coats.

3 When finished, replace the castors, Perspex strips and any other refinements you need, and load up the unit. It will provide years of service.

Do-it-yourself – Build your own bookcase

Most families include at least one bookworm, which normally means books all over the place. Here, we tell you, step by step, how to build an attractive bookcase and, with a little more work, a corner unit. Put a bookcase on each side of the corner unit and you will have a special area for the books and the bookworm. Another option is to fill an entire wall with simple shelving.

The timber used is parana pine, which is easy to work and generally has a knot-free grain that gives an excellent finished appearance. The sizes given are as close as possible to standard, but you may have to adjust them slightly to allow for sizes of timber available.

1 Cut the sides, top rails and shelves to length, then glue and screw the shelves and top rails to the sides, using countersunk screws. The simple box section that you make by doing this must be square, and the faces of the rails and shelves should line up with the edges of the sides.

2 Fix the tongued-and-grooved boards to the back with the flat-head nails.

3 Glue and screw the top in place, ensuring that the overhangs at each end are equal and that the back edge is flush with the face of the boards.

To build your own bookcase, you will need:			
Components	Material	Length or size in mm	No.
Sides	190 x 20 mm parana pine	820	2
Shelves	190 x 20 mm parana pine	770	2
Top	230 x 20 mm parana pine	850	1
Top rail (back)	70 x 20 mm parana pine	770	1
Top rail (front)	45 x 20 mm parana pine	770	1
Bottom rail	70 x 20 mm parana pine	810	1
Front moulding	25 x 15 mm parana pine	810	1
Back	130 x 13 mm pine boards	770	6

It's important that the bottom shelf and the two sides are the same width. All the other components can increase a bit in width without interfering with the construction.

Fixings: eight 60 mm countersunk wood screws; 50 mm lost-head nails; 30 mm flat-head nails; 30 mm panel pins; PVA wood glue.

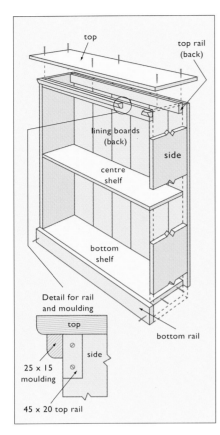

top

top rail
(back)

lining boards
(back)

side

centre
shelf

bottom
shelf

Detail for rail
and moulding

top

side

25 x 15
moulding

bottom rail

45 x 20 top rail

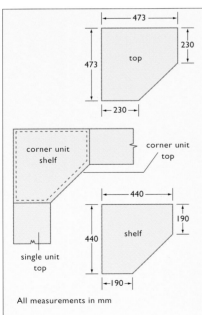

473

230

473

top

230

corner unit
shelf

corner unit
top

440

190

440

shelf

single unit
top

190

All measurements in mm

TOP: The bookcase plan.

ABOVE: The corner unit plan.

RIGHT: The corner unit.

4 Glue and nail the bottom rail to the bottom shelf and the sides, with the lost-head nails, and pin and glue the moulding to the face of the top rail.

5 Either by hand or with an orbital sander, remove all the sharp edges from the timber and form the curves to the moulding and the top's edge (see detail). Stain the bookcase if required, and finish it off with a clear polyurethane varnish or sealer.

Corner unit

This simply consists of two of the bookcases plus an angled unit that joins them in the middle. As the top and shelves for the middle unit are quite wide, they will need to be made by butt-jointing two narrower boards. When assembling the middle unit, fit the top as part of step 1 before adding the top rails, then the back. The top should not overhang the sides, and the two adjoining units should not have an overhang where they abut the middle unit.

As the middle unit is an unusual shape, you should take your time when squaring it up, and compare its fit with a finished single unit.

ABOVE: If you have a large collection of books you may find it easier to have a special area for them. These floor-to-ceiling bookshelves occupy two walls without taking up too much space in the room.

Storage you can buy

Sometimes it makes sense for even an ardent do-it-yourselfer to buy storage units rather than build them. Why spend several evenings cutting, joining and sanding the timber for a simple bookcase, for example, when you can purchase a similar unfinished piece for not much more than it would cost to buy the materials.

You don't have to settle for a utilitarian look, either. You can easily dress up unfinished or drab units with paint, stain or even covering them with fabric.

The chart below shows some of the more common modular, kit and unfinished units. For additional possibilities, check out timber suppliers, department stores and do-it-yourself centres.

Storage unit	Applications	How to choose
	Unfinished bookcases come in modular sizes ideal for lining up or stacking anywhere you need open-shelf storage. Buy steel bookcases from office suppliers.	The better quality wood units have rebated backs and shelves; surfaces should need only light sanding.
	Wardrobes may be wood, metal or particle board; they come in kit form or assembled. For an entire wall of storage, flank a desk with a pair of them.	Better wood and particle board versions have hardwood frames. Avoid flimsy construction and metal cabinets with sharp edges.
	Open-frame steel shelving stands on its own, making it handy for use as a divider as well as against a wall. Shelves may be as deep as 60 cm.	Sturdy posts and nut-and-bolt locking systems minimise swaying. Large units may need cross-bracing or fastening to a wall.
	Drawer cases stack to any height. Some have open sides for built-in arrangements. For a desk, lay a door across two stacks. Note this compact study.	Good ones have rebated fronts and move easily on metal or hardwood guides.
	Plastic trays and bins make inexpensive drawers. To construct a case for them, build a large plywood box with battens inside to support the trays' lips.	Clear acrylic trays let you see contents at a glance. Polyethylene types, available in a variety of colours, hold heavier loads.
	Cubes and boxes offer versatile modular storage. Choose wood, plastic laminate or solid plastic versions. Some interlock with each other.	Well-made wood cubes have reinforced corners all around. If particle board is used, be sure to surface it with plastic laminate.
	Freestanding cabinets made of wood, metal or chipboard provide storage and a worktop. Typically, they're 75–90 cm high and 50–90 cm wide. Keep tools and other bulky gear in filing cabinets. These are readily available from suppliers of office furniture. For workshop use, buy secondhand steel items.	For a quick test of a cabinet's quality, try to pick it up; sturdy ones are heavier. Look, too, for tight, well-fitting joints and seams.

Furniture

The selection and purchase of new furniture adds the finishing touch to your renovations. If new furniture is beyond your budget, consider garage sales and auctions as inexpensive sources. Many old pieces can be transformed with new upholstery or a painted or stained finish.

LEFT: Odd furniture is no longer a problem with slipcovers. They can unify odd pieces by relating them in colour. In this room all the pieces are slipcovered in different fabrics – a solid, a stripe and a floral – with blue as a common link.

ABOVE: Many fabric collections are designed with a choice of patterns, all printed in the same colours so it's easy to match one with another. The frill on these slipcovers is made from a related fabric.

Covering up

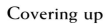

If your furniture needs updating, think slipcovers. They offer a great impact for far less cost than a new suite. They are wonderfully versatile, allowing you to keep changing your decor, which is important if you really have the decorating bug.

RIGHT: This setting looks very grand but it's achievable. Open-backed kitchen chairs could be covered like this and used in the dining room. When slipcovers are this short, small ties need to be attached at the corners to fasten them to the chair legs.

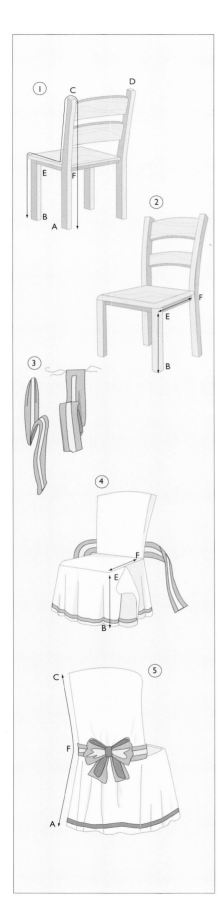

How to make a slipcover

The slipcover shown on this page is supposed to be a loose cover, made from three main pieces of material – one long piece, which covers the front, seat and back, and two side pieces. Ties, added at seat level and tied in a bow, take up any fullness. You should choose firm, washable material.

To find the size of the main piece, measure your chair from the floor at the back (A) to the top of the chair back (C), down to the seat (F), across to the front of the seat (E) and down to the floor (B). Add 1.25 cm at each end for hems. Now measure the width across the back of the chair (C to D), add the thickness of the back of the chair, plus 1.25 cm seam allowance each side. This is the main part of your cover; cut one.

Measure the side of your chair, from the seat (E) to the floor (B), and from the front (E) to the back of the seat (F), add 1.25 cm all around for seams and hem. Cut two. Mark the top of each side piece with a little notch so you know which way is up.

Cut two long strips of material 1.5 m long by 20 cm wide to use for the ties. Hem around the two long sides and one end. Gather the unhemmed end until it measures 8 cm in width.

ABOVE: Create a classic look in your dining room by making your covers out of cotton canvas. White is not impractical in this case as the fabric is machine washable. Slipcovers will never look as neat as upholstery, but they're not supposed to because the fabric is not pulled tight.

ABOVE LEFT: As dining chairs are usually seen from behind, why not emphasise their backs? Details such as the piping and the fringed hem add interest on this mattress ticking cover and the bows ensure it is easy to fit onto the chair.

LEFT: Make your own slipcover.

You will need for the monk's seat:
Recycled fir:
Sides and seat/lid from 4000 x 250 x 25 mm
Front and back frame, top and bottom back, rail and hinge support from 6000 x 75 x 25 mm
Braces and battens from 3600 x 50 x 25 mm
Backing boards from 2500 x 140 x 15 mm
Trims from 1000 x 25 x 20 mm and 3000 x 40 x 20 mm
Lattice from 100 x 100 x 38 mm
Plywood
Front and back panels from 600 x 600 x 4 mm and 9 mm
Bottom 600 x 416 x 9 mm

ABOVE RIGHT: The monk's seat.

BELOW: Plan for the monk's seat.

With right sides together, attach two sides of the side rectangle to the main piece (B to E and E to F), easing around the corner. Sew the other side of the cover in the same way. With right sides together, centre the gathered end of the tie on point F and tack in place.

With right sides together, sew the side panel to the main piece, from A through F to C, repeat for the other side. Finally, hem all around. Turn to right side, press, fit on the chair and tie the bow.

Do-it-yourself – Build a monk's seat

We have called this a monk's seat because it is a little like an old church pew, but whether you call it a deacon's bench or a hall seat, you will find it a useful and attractive piece of furniture. Recycled fir was used to build this one, but you could use any softwood.

The thicknesses and widths of the timber shown on the plans are those obtained after the recycled material had been cleaned up with an electric planer. As these sizes were determined by the amount of planing required, you may find them difficult to match, so we have given you a buying list as a guide rather than a final cutting list. The wood you buy can then be dressed down with the planer to suit the sizes of the plan (70 x 20 mm and 65 x 20 mm, for instance, are both obtained from nominal 75 x 25 mm). You can vary these thicknesses and widths slightly to suit your cleaned-up material. The plans supply all the cutting lengths.

1 If using recycled timber, pull out all old nails. With the planer, clean up the timber until it approximates the specified thicknesses. Cut to length progressively as you build the unit.

2 Prepare two matching pieces for each side and, using a flat surface, glue and clamp them together at the edges. Put them aside for 24 hours to dry.

3 Make the front and back frames by gluing and screwing (use one screw at each corner). Allow time for the glue to set. Using a router, cut the rebates for the lattice and the plywood in the backs of the frames (10 mm for

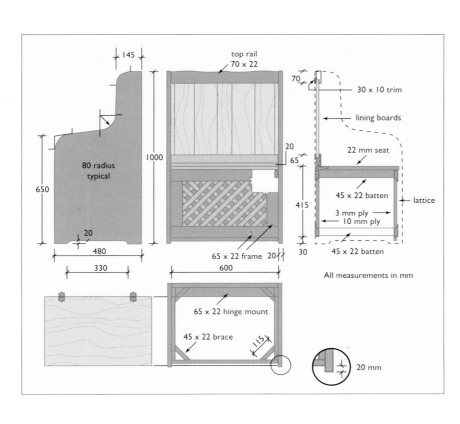

TOP: Storage you can sit on.

ABOVE CENTRE: Detail showing corner brace.

ABOVE: The hinged seat.

RIGHT: One old wardrobe in two pieces.

the back and 8 mm for the front). Turn the frames over and, with the router, put a decorative edge on the inside of the frames, take care not to cut the rebates.

4   The lattice pieces are cut from the 100 x 38 mm timber by setting the cutting guide of a circular saw to a cut of about 6 mm (making strips 1000 x 38 x 6 mm). They are finished with the planer to 4 x 25 mm. The lattice pieces can be fixed diagonally or at right-angles to the frame. Using a short piece as a spacer, lay each strip across the rebates and mark and cut until each layer is in place. Each end piece may need trimming to centre the pattern. Fix the lattice pieces into the frame with panel pins and lay the plywood over the back, allowing 15 mm beyond the rebate for nailing to the frame.

5   Screw the battens to the side pieces, mark out the curves and cut them with a jigsaw. Screwing through the sides, fit the front and back panels, ensure the unit is square, then fit the diagonal braces top and bottom. Finally, drop in the floor and nail it to the bottom battens and braces.

6   Again screwing through the sides, fit the top and bottom back rails and the hinge mount (the back rails will require 15 x 12 mm rebates to take the backing boards). Cut a decorative shape in the top edge of the top rail with a jigsaw.

7   For the seat back, either use rebated or tongued-and-grooved boards, or run the edges off plain boards at 45° with the planer and overlap them. Cut four at equal widths and the middle one to suit the remaining space. Use nails to fix them to the rails.

8   The seat/lid is constructed in the same way as the sides, with two battens underneath. Fix it with a pair of decorative brass hinges. Make sure it bears on the side battens when it closes.

New furniture from old

You may have a period wardrobe in the house. They were built in the days when shoulders weren't as wide and jackets weren't as bulky; modern clothes just don't seem to fit in them. But even the cheaper ones maintain an aesthetic appeal and it's a shame to throw one away just because it is slightly impractical. A better plan is to turn it into something you can use.

For this project, we converted a wardrobe with a single door, hanging space at the top and a drawer at the bottom. The top section became our display cabinet, and the bottom section a coffee table. If your wardrobe is the two-piece type (the top separates from the bottom), then the job will be much easier: it will already be two free-standing units. Chances are, however, that it will still require a base/skirting for the display cabinet, while a couple of pieces of wood on top of the drawer unit — used to fix the top section squarely

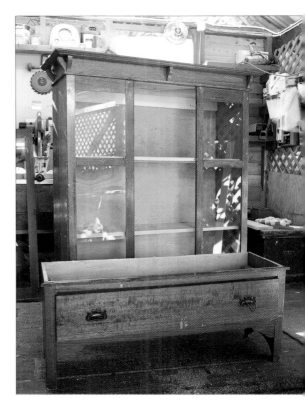

ABOVE: A new display cabinet and coffee table made from the old wardrobe.

BELOW: Old tables such as this one can often be found at garage sales.

shape from the front panels, remove the mirror and, with a jigsaw, cut the frame to the same shape as the other two, adding a rebate with the router.

Note: This may weaken the door frame and require the addition of some battens on the back to strengthen it.

4 Fit 3 mm glass into the rebates (sand first) and secure by pinning lengths of moulding around the edge. Before refitting the front panels, install the shelves. Use a timber that will complement the original (you won't be able to match it), staining it if necessary, and screw fix through the sides, countersinking the heads. Position the shelves, spacing them to coincide with the front-panel frames. The bottom shelf will then form the base of the unit.

5 Replace the front panels and door. You may need to add an extra framing piece across the bottom of the front panels and door to stiffen the unit, although the shelves may be sufficient. To lift the unit off the floor, add a base/skirting. Use the same timber as chosen for the shelves and rebate the corners. Skirting only needs to be on the front and two sides. To get a fixing for skirting, you may have to shorten the door. Check before glazing it.

6 The drawer unit actually remains quite intact because it becomes a coffee table. The back may need to be stiffened by adding a batten along the line where it was separated from the top section, but otherwise it is only a case of adding a table top. Make a top by gluing together lengths of timber, such as parana pine or even old floorboards. Fit the top with a substantial overhang all around (40–50 mm) and then decorate the edges with a router.

If you don't own an old wardrobe, look out for one at garage sales and secondhand shops.

in place — will have to be removed before the table top can be fixed.

1 Lay the unit on its back and, using a hand saw, separate the two parts, cutting as close to the bottom of the hanging section as possible. Put the drawer unit aside and, with the top section still on its back, remove the door and front panel on each side of it. The door and front panels are usually made from a solid timber frame with either a plywood insert or, in the case of a door, a mirror.

2 Assuming the frames are in good shape, try not to disturb the joints. Drill a hole through the plywood in the panels, close to the edge, and, with a jigsaw, cut around the perimeter. This will leave a thin strip of plywood wedged in the slot of the frame, which can easily be pulled out with pliers. Set a router to cut to the depth of the slot from the back of the panel, and turn the slot into a rebate. Use a chisel to square off the corners.

3 If the door panel has a plywood centre, repeat step 2. If it has a mirror in a frame of a different

ABOVE: Refurbished secondhand furniture can endow your rooms with character. Remember, though, that what you save in pounds, you'll probably spend in energy and enterprise. The table and chairs pictured only needed cleaning up and sanding.

RIGHT: This old chair was originally coated with several coats of varnish and upholstered in dreary, dark fabric. It has been transformed by stripping, sanding and re-upholstering.

You will need (measurements are in mm):					
Part	Length	Width	Thickness	Material	No.
A Face frame – stile	860	60	19	Pine	2
B Face frame – bottom rail	380	55	19	Pine	1
C Face frame – top rail	380	35	19	Pine	1
D Cabinet side	860	380	18	MDF	2
E Cabinet shelf	464	371	12	MDF	2
F Shelf battens	371	15	15	Pine	4
G Cabinet back	767	48	9	MDF	1
H Cabinet top	560	430	18	MDF	1
J Door – bottom rail	280	65	19	Pine	1
K Door – middle rail	280	50	19	Pine	1
L Door – top rail	280	50	19	Pine	1
M Door – stile	705	50	19	Pine	2
N Scotia moulding	cut to length		19	Pine	
P Battens	cut to length		10	9	Pine	
Q Punched panels	295	285	26 g	Galvanised iron	2

Supplies: 1.6 m x 200 x 19 mm double-dressed radiata pine; 1200 x 900 x 18 mm MDF board; 1200 x 900 x 12 mm MDF; 1200 x 900 x 9 mm MDF; 8 mm dowel joining kit; 40 x 1.5 mm bullet-headed nails; 25 x 1 mm panel pins; PVA glue; Timbermate stopping putty; two 50 mm butt hinges; eight 8 mm x 4 g countersunk screws; 25 mm x 8 g round-head screws; 9 mm washer; 180, 220 and 360 grit sandpaper; 400 grit wet-and-dry sandpaper; spray cans of auto primer and auto touch-up lacquer; sanding sealer; oil-based all-purpose undercoat; oil-based semi-gloss enamel (we used Dulux Semi Super Enamel Blue River UD 307).

Wood and tin food safe

This is a classic piece of practical and decorative country furniture. Before refrigerators became common household items, most people stored their perishables in a food safe, with either fine wire mesh or perforated tin for ventilation. Use the food safe in the kitchen or as a bedside feature.

We have chosen to use man-made boards rather than solid timber, as it makes the construction of the cabinet easier. If you would like a timber-stained finish rather than the coloured enamel paint we have used, pine could be substituted for the MDF panels in the sides and top of the cabinet. A number of edge-glued pine boards would be needed to obtain the required width for these panels.

Authentic 'punched-tin' panels were made from tinplate, a lead and tin-coated steel that is no longer readily available. We used 26-gauge galvanised steel, but aluminium would also be suitable. To punch out the pattern, you will need to grind a large nail punch to a 60° conical point. If you'd like to design your own pattern with star, curved or tapered holes, a punch can be ground from any tempered tool steel to produce the mark required. A blacksmith would be able to do this for you. Our pattern has two styles of punched hole – it is much easier to use a different weight of hammer to produce each sized mark than to try to deliver consistent light and heavy blows with the same hammer.

Begin with the face frame

1 Using 19-mm-thick pine batten, cut the two stiles (A), top rail (C) and bottom rail (B) to the sizes listed in the panel.

2 Mark out the feet as shown in figure 2 (on page 274) on the bottom inside edge of each stile (A). Use a jigsaw or coping saw to cut the curved shape, then sand the edges smooth.

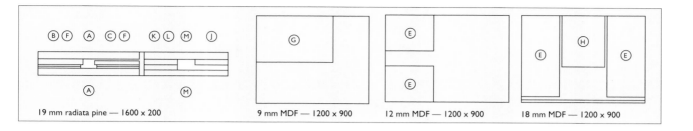

19 mm radiata pine — 1600 x 200   9 mm MDF — 1200 x 900   12 mm MDF — 1200 x 900   18 mm MDF — 1200 x 900

3 Lightly dry-cramp the frame together with the rails in their correct positions against the stiles. Use a try square and pencil to mark the positions of the dowels on the frame. Remove the cramps.

4 Square the pencil lines across the edges of the stiles and mark the centres for the dowels. Then, using the bit from an 8 mm dowel jointing kit, drill the holes for the dowels to a depth of 20 mm. Fit the dowel marker pins in the holes and reassemble the frame to mark the positions of the dowel holes on the ends of the rails. Drill these holes 20 mm deep.

5 Glue, dowel and cramp the rails between the stiles. Check for square and make sure that the assembly lies flat. Wipe off the excess glue with a damp cloth.

Make the rest of the cabinet

6 Cut the two side panels (D) from the 18 mm MDF to the size listed on page 272. Mark out the shape of the feet and cut with a jigsaw. Sand the edges smooth. Using a 10 mm rebate bit in a router, cut a 10 x 9 mm rebate in the back edge of each side panel to take the back panel (figure 3). Remember that the sides are not identical, but are matching pairs.

7 Cut the shelf battens (F) to size. Mark with a pencil the position of the battens on the inside faces of the side panels (D), then nail and glue the battens in position, as shown in figure 4.

8 Cut the two shelves (E) from 12 mm MDF to the size listed in the panel on page 272.

9 Cut the back panel (G) from 9 mm MDF to the size listed in the panel on page 272.

10 Cut the cabinet top (H) from 18 mm MDF, round off the front and side edges with a plane, then sand smooth.

11 Glue and nail the face frame to the side panels (D), using 40 mm lost-head nails. Make sure the outer surfaces are flush. Close the joint by applying light pressure with sash cramps.

12 Glue and nail the bottom and the middle shelves (E) to the battens (F), using 25 mm panel pins. Being careful to make sure the back edges of the shelves are flush with the bottom of the side-panel rebates.

13 Glue and nail the back panel (G) into the rebates of the side panels (D), using 25 mm panel pins and making sure the top edges of the back panel and side panels are aligned.

14 Place the cabinet top (H) in position (the back edge flush with the cabinet back and an even overhang at each side). Mark the position with a pencil. Glue and nail the top to the sides and face frame using 40 mm lost-head nails.

15 Cut the 19 mm scotia moulding (N) to fit under the top of the cabinet with mitred joints at the front corners, then nail and glue in position with 25 mm panel pins (figure 5). Punch all nails below the surface and fill the holes. Sand smooth when dry.

ABOVE: Cutting diagrams.

FAR LEFT: Wood and tin food safe.

Making the door

16 Cut the bottom, middle and top rails (J, K, L) and the door stiles (M) to the sizes given.

17 Using the method previously described for the face frame, mark the positions of the dowels, drill the holes, then glue dowels and cramp the door frame. Wipe off excess glue with a damp cloth and make sure the frame lies flat.

18 Using a 10 mm rebate bit in a router, cut a 10 x 10 mm rebate around the back inner edge of the door frame.

19 Use a sharp chisel to square the routed corners of the rebate.

20 Cut the door battens to size and, using a mitre box and tenon saw, cut lengths to fit the rebate in the door, as shown in figure 1.

21 Fit the door to the cabinet, planing the edges to leave a 1 mm gap all around.

22 Mark the positions of recesses for the hinge plates, 100 mm from the top and bottom of the door. Chisel the recesses and screw the hinges to the door stile and the cabinet.

23 Shape the small swivel catch from an offcut of pine (figure 6). Drill a hole for the 25 mm round-head screw and sand all faces smooth.

Making the punched 'tin' panels

24 Prepare the sheets of galvanised steel by rubbing both surfaces with 400-grit wet-and-dry abrasive paper and washing-up liquid in water. Rinse the panels well under a running tap.

25 When dry, place a panel on a sheet of 19 mm MDF. (Try not to touch the face of the panel with your fingers to avoid contaminating it.) Secure the panel to the board with strips of scrap timber and screws, or use large drawing pins. (The panel will buckle when punched unless held securely to the board.) Centre a photocopy of the design (see page 275) over the top and hold in place with masking tape.

26 Start punching the pattern. When all the holes have been punched, remove the panel from the board. Use a new piece of MDF and repeat the process for the second panel.

27 Drill a small hole in a corner of each panel and hang it on a length of thin wire. Spray the faces of the panels with a coat of grey car primer, followed by two coats of deep grey car touch-up paint, following the manufacturer's instructions on the side of the can.

28 When the panels are completely dry, remove the door frame and place the panels in their rebates. Using 25 mm panel pins, nail the battens in place to secure the panels in the frame (see figure 1).

RIGHT: The template for making the punched 'tin' panels.

BELOW: The plan for making the food safe.

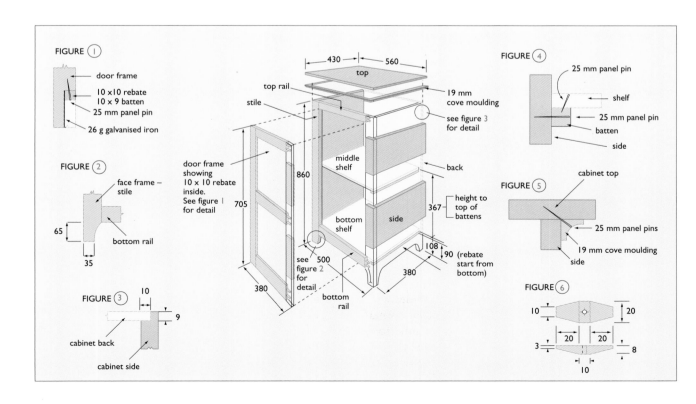

● Heavy punch hole

● Light punch indent

Photocopy the design twice
(at the same size) to match
the pattern. Use a
different weight
of hammer for
heavy and
light punches.

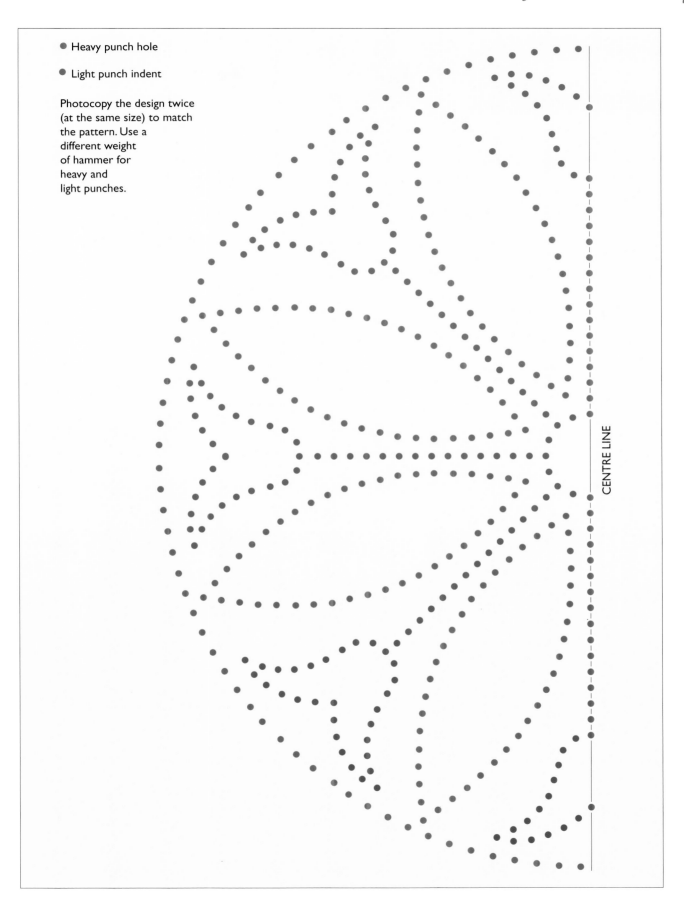

CENTRE LINE

Painting and finishing the cabinet

29 Sand all edges and surfaces with 180- and 220-grit sandpaper. (Unless marked, do not sand the faces of the MDF panels.)

30 Mask any of the edges you do not want to be painted with masking tape.

31 Apply a coat of sanding sealer to all surfaces and, when they are dry, sand lightly with 360-grit sandpaper.

32 Apply a coat of oil-based, all-purpose undercoat and, when thoroughly dry, sand lightly with worn 360-grit sandpaper.

33 Apply two coats of oil-based semi-gloss enamel, sanding lightly between coats.

34 Screw the hinges to the door and screw the door in position. Screw the catch to the face of the cabinet with a thin washer between the rubbing surfaces.

Multi-Purpose Cupboard

You never seem to have enough of the right storage, so we're going to show you how to build a simple unit that you can adapt to your own requirements. It will serve as a bookcase, linen cupboard or even a china cabinet.

Follow the simple step-by-step instructions – you can vary the size, and choose to add doors and drawers if you like.

The ideal material for the unit is MDF, but you can also use particle board. The advantage of MDF is that you can sand the edges to take a paint finish, whereas particle board requires either filling or the fitting of edging strips. As an option, you can make the fronts of the drawers, or storage boxes, out of plywood, then let the grain show through the finish. The frames of the doors can be made from pine.

As you can see from the diagram, we have given you the option of a 300-mm or 500-mm-wide unit. You can, of course, vary these widths to suit a specific opening, but we don't recommend that you increase the width of the doors. Those described are only suited to the 300-mm-wide unit.

The basic unit

1 Screw and glue the two C panels to the two B panels.

2 Glue and screw the B panels to the A panels, driving the screws through the outer face of the A panels (countersink all screws for filling later). Make sure you keep the panels square when fixing.

3 Screw and glue in place the back panel (D) to the A panels and the top and bottom B panels.

Drawer/storage box

1 Glue and screw the C panel to the B panels by driving the screws through the outer face of the B panels.

2 Glue and screw the A panels to the B and C panels by driving the screws through the outer face of the A panels.

3 Drill three 20 mm holes in the face of the front A panel to act as finger grips.

Doors

1 Using a plane or a router, cut a 10-mm-wide, 2-mm-deep rebate on one long face of each of the frame members (E, F and G).

2 Working on a flat surface, fit two E pieces between two F pieces and two G pieces, and glue and clamp (ensure they are square). The rebates should be on the rear, inner face of the frame to receive the glass.

3 Drill two 20-mm-deep holes as countersinks at each joint of the F, G and E pieces, through the outer edge of the F and G pieces. Then, using 60 mm screws, screw them to the E pieces.

Leave the joints clamped together until you are sure that the glue has set.

4 When the doors have been painted, fit the glass, the door knobs and the hinges.

You can fix two or more units together by screwing through the adjacent sides or by making a common back (D panel) and forming them into one unit rather like a room divider or wall unit. Don't be afraid to paint them bright colours – perhaps even a different one for each unit. If you intend to place your unit in the kitchen or bathroom, you should add at least one good coat of a hard washable varnish for extra protection.

For one 250-mm-high drawer or storage box to suit the 500-mm-wide unit:

(you can vary the height to suit your needs, but don't forget also to vary the height of the opening accordingly)

Item	No.	Size
A Panel	2 pieces	462 x 250 mm
B	2	371 x 250 mm
(All 12 mm MDF)		
C Panel	1 piece	438 x 371 mm
(18 mm MDF)		

Eight 40 mm screws for MDF and eight 60 mm screws for doors.

For the 300-mm-wide door:

Item	No.	Size
E Timber	4 pieces	200 x 50 x 20 mm
F	2	1069 x 50 x 20 mm
G	2	987 x 50 x 20 mm
H Glass	1 piece	987 x 218 x 3 mm
J	1	905 x 218 x 3 mm

Accessories: 2 furniture knobs; 4 hinges (there are several hinge types to choose from, depending on whether you want them to be concealed or exposed. Check out the possibilities at your local hardware or DIY store); 16 glass clips or mirror clips.

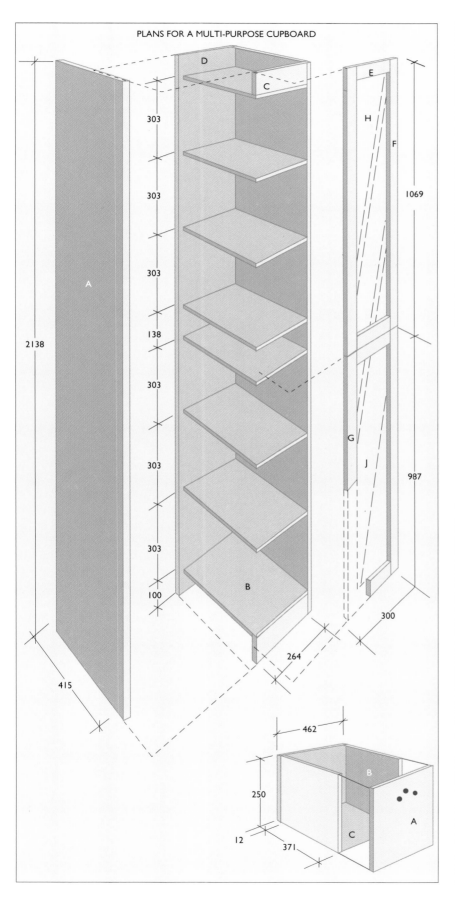

PLANS FOR A MULTI-PURPOSE CUPBOARD

You will need for the 300-mm-wide unit:

Item	No.	Size
A Panel	2 pieces	2138 x 415 mm
B	8	415 x 264 mm
C	2	264 x 82 mm
D	1	300 x 2138 mm
(All 18 mm MDF)		

For the 500-mm-wide unit:

Item	No.	Size
A Panel	2 pieces	2138 x 415 mm
B	8	464 x 415 mm
C	2	464 x 82 mm
D	1	500 x 2138 mm
(All 18 mm MDF)		

BELOW: If you don't want to build your own, you may like to transform an existing cupboard. The louvre doors, painted finish and decorative mouldings on this one show what a little imagination can do.

ABOVE: The newly
upholstered chair.

Upholstered chair

New padding, a buttoned seat and
fresh fabric will turn a plain, old
wrought-iron telephone chair into a
comfortable place to sit while you
enjoy the fruits of your labours.

You will need 60 cm each of two
co-ordinating print fabrics; 60 cm
of calico; medium-density seat
foam 50 mm thick; an electric carving knife; general-purpose glue;
contact adhesive; thick polyester
wadding; brown paper; twine;

seven 15-mm-diameter self-cover
buttons; eight 13-mm-diameter
self-cover buttons; fusible interfacing; matching sewing thread; scissors; a power drill with 13 mm bit;
a 10 cm long upholstery needle; a
staple gun; a tape measure; and dis-
appearing fabric marker.

Covering the chair back

1 Place one layer of wadding on
   the inside of the back of the
   chair and one layer on the outside back. Pin them together,
   following the outline of the
   frame. Trim off excess wadding.
   Glue the wadding together at
   the outer edges.

2 To make the pattern for the
   chair back, pin paper to the
   inside back of the chair. Fold it
   smoothly over the wadding and
   around the outer edge to the
   outside back, pleating the excess
   at corners. Trace around the
   outline of the chair. Add 1 cm
   to all the edges for seams and 2
   cm to the lower edge for the
   hem. Pin paper to the outside
   back and trace the same outer
   edge of the chair frame. Add
   seam and hem allowances as for
   the inside back, then cut out.
   Cut the outside back pattern in
   half lengthways; add a 2 cm
   seam allowance to this centre
   back edge.

3 From one co-ordinating print,
   cut an inside back (if you are
   using a motif print, remember to
   consider design placement) and
   two outside backs. Cut a back
   placket the length of the chair's
   outside backs (plus 1 cm for
   seam and 2 cm for hem
   allowance) by 10 cm wide.

4 Apply fusible interfacing to the
   wrong side of the two outside
   backs and the placket.

5 To sew a chair back cover: press
   the 2 cm centre back facings to
   the wrong side. Stitch four
   evenly-spaced buttonholes on
   each side (to suit the smaller
   covered buttons).

6 Press and stitch a 1 cm single hem on each side of the placket. Machine edge stitch a 1 cm double folded hem at the lower edge of the placket.

7 Place the two back sections face down, side by side. Place the placket, face down, centrally over them, aligning top and bottom edges. Tack the placket in place at the upper edge.

8 With right sides together, pin the inside and outside backs together, positioning the pleats evenly at the corners of the inside back. Stitch and press seam allowances towards the outside back. Machine stitch close to the seam allowance through all thicknesses.

9 Press and stitch a 1 cm double folded hem at the lower edge.

10 Cover the 13 mm buttons following the manufacturer's instructions. Fit the cover over the wadding, and position and sew the buttons to the placket to correspond with the button-holes (see photograph).

Covering the chair seat

11 Using the wooden base as a template, cut the foam with the electric knife.

12 Drill one hole in the centre, surrounded by six evenly-spaced holes in the timber for buttoning. Mark corresponding points on the foam and cut small slits with scissors. Cut a circle of wadding, a circle of calico and a circle of the second co-ordinating print, at least 30 cm larger overall than the base.

13 Run a line of contact adhesive around the edges of the seat and foam. When tacky, place the foam over the seat, aligning the marks on the foam with the drilled holes. Press together. Place the circle of wadding, then the circle of calico over the foam. Thread an upholstery needle with 50 cm of twine and insert from the underside through to the top side. Bring the needle through to one side of the centre hole drilled in the seat, through all layers, leaving at least 15 cm of twine trailing. Take the needle to the other side of the centre hole, catching a little square of calico on top, in the loop of the stitch. Remove the needle from the twine and pull the calico and padding down to form a hollow. While holding the twine ends firmly, staple twice (the second time folding the twine back on itself) beside the drilled holes. Stitch and staple each of the remaining drilled holes in the same way, making sure all the hollows are the same depth.

14 Smooth the wadding and calico to the underside of the seat. Staple the wadding to the timber in at least eight equidistant points. Arrange the calico evenly on the underside, making pleats radiating from the depressions in the padding where necessary. Staple the calico to the timber. Start on opposite sides first, at four equidistant points, and firmly pull the calico before stapling to ensure a smooth result. Trim off the excess calico.

15 Cover the seven larger buttons, following the manufacturer's instructions. Apply the cover fabric to the seat and attach as before with twine and needle, using buttons instead of fabric squares on top. Staple the twine as before. Smooth the fabric to the underside, pulling firmly. Before stapling to the timber, pleat the excess from the buttons where necessary. Trim away the surplus fabric.

16 Using the base as a pattern, cut a circle of calico. Press under a 1 cm seam allowance around the circumference. Staple this circle to the base to conceal seams and staples.

ABOVE: Back view of the upholstered chair.

Tip

• Foam suppliers will often cut the foam to size and shape for you when you buy it.

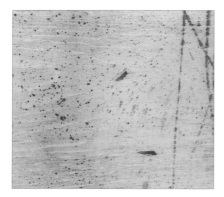

1a

1b

2

Furniture finishes

If you have some items of simple, country-style furniture that you would like to age with an authentic-looking finish, follow these easy steps. You could also use these techniques to give character to

plain whitewood furniture. We show you how to apply a brush finish that simulates a look that normally takes decades to form. You will also learn how to produce the popular crackled and limed finishes, as well as a simple method of gracefully ageing a natural wood surface under a clear finish. Fine-sand all surfaces (using 240-grit sandpaper) before beginning any of these processes.

Five easy steps to a painted antique finish

1 Distress the unpainted surface. Antiques usually have a number of nicks and scratches. Before you start simulating a blemished surface for your new project, consider where it would have received the greatest degree of wear over the years. Use a round-faced hammer to create

dents, a screwdriver to make scratches and a Surform file to scuff surfaces. Gently round the edges and corners using 100-grit sandpaper wrapped around a 25 mm dowel. For a natural, worn look, sand the edges unevenly. Don't overdo it. If a surface would have received little wear over the years, leave it alone. You want to distress the piece, not destroy it.

2 Apply the finish in layers. Be patient. This process requires seven layers. If you want to achieve the perfect, aged look, don't be tempted to cut corners by omitting any one of them.

Wipe on a dark stain (in this case, it was an antique walnut) and remove excess with a soft cloth. Allow to dry. Apply two coats of clear, satin-finish polyurethane varnish. Sand lightly after the second coat

---

How to build up a painted country finish

1 Bare wood

2 Dark wood stain

3 Polyurethane varnish (two coats)

4 Oil-based undercoat

5 Colour coat (paint)

6 Dark wood stain (antiquing)

7 Spatter

3

4

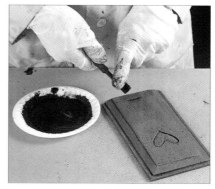

5

ABOVE AND LEFT: Painting an antique finish.

1a Dents, scratches and surface wear age a natural wood surface.

1b Wrap 100-grit sandpaper around a 25 mm dowel to make a tool for rounding edges.

2 The perfect aged look is only achieved by sticking to the steps.

3 Remove some of the colour coat with 320-grit sandpaper without sanding through the primer.

4 To simulate patina, leave traces of dark stain in crevices and areas prone to build up of grime.

5 After practising the spattering technique, give the project a uniform coat of fine speckles.

with 220-grit sandpaper. Apply one coat of a red oil-based undercoat. Once the undercoat has dried, sand lightly and apply your desired colour coat (earthy hues, as shown on page 280, look good on country projects). Satin-finish or semi-gloss-finish oil-based paints are ideal, or you could use acrylics.

3 Now roll back the years. Using 320-grit sandpaper, remove parts of the colour coat along the edges, corners and other areas where the paint would naturally have worn off through use. Change the abrasive paper often, as it will tend to clog. First, lightly sand the whole surface, then sand down to the undercoat around the heavily-worn areas, as shown. If you should accidentally sand right through the undercoat, the two coats of polyurethane should protect the stained wood. Because old wood is darker than new, be careful not to reveal the bare wood as you sand.

4 Patina in a few minutes. Apply a coat of a dark stain over the surface, then wipe off with a soft

BELOW: Colour washing is another technique used to create an antique finish.

ABOVE: Lime washing need not be limited to items of furniture. In this kitchen it has been used effectively on the floor to complement the pastel shades of the cupboard and shelves.

cloth as shown. Leave deposits in the crevices and other areas — the spots that would seldom have been cleaned over the years had this been a genuine antique or old piece of furniture. This residue simulates the sheen created by long use called 'patina'.

5 Add a bit more character by spattering the surface. Dip an old toothbrush into a shallow container of dark stain, then practise spattering the stain in a fine shower by holding the toothbrush 150 mm above a sheet of paper and running your finger through the bristles. When you have mastered this technique, add a uniform spattering of fine specks to the pro-

ject as shown. Don't overdo it. You will find a little spattering goes a long way. Allow the finish to dry thoroughly before using the item of furniture.

The crackled look

A crackled finish can be made by using acrylic paint over hide glue, or by covering the acrylic paint with an oil-based paint.

A crackled look can take decades to occur naturally, but this method needs only a few days.

Apply a base coat of paint to your project if you don't want the wood to show through the cracks. After this dries, brush on a thin coat of hide glue (animal glue simi-

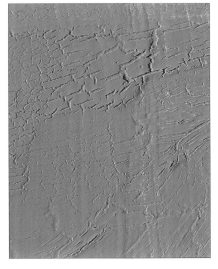

lar to gelatine). Hide glue pellets must be soaked in water overnight and heated in the top part of a double saucepan over hot water to prevent burning. The glue must dry thoroughly. This may take one or more days. Apply an acrylic paint in long, even strokes. In 20–30 seconds, the paint will begin to crack. To achieve the effect shown, skip the first coat of paint and apply hide glue to bare wood, followed by coats of white and green paint.

It pays to experiment to achieve the result you want. If you prefer a more subtle crackled finish, use the above procedure, but cover the acrylic paint with oil-based paint.

The limed look

In the past, furniture was often limed to prevent darkening with age. In addition, old furniture that has been chemically stripped will have a limed appearance. The result is most attractive. There are several types of limed interior stain available or you can simulate antique liming by using tinted white paint as shown in the side-by-side comparison of a pine door (above left). Open-grained timbers, such as oak, soak up more paint, making them appear whiter than others.

Use a shade of white in an oil-based paint that suits your taste. Experiment by mixing small amounts of black, green, yellow and/or other colours into the pure white base. Practise on scrap timber, sanded to a fine finish, before liming the piece you've selected. To start, brush tinted white paint all

over the surface and wipe it off before it dries, leaving paint in the crevices and corners. If you want to age the piece more, score around the knots and defects with a scalpel or sharp knife. Extra paint will accumulate in these crevices. Allow the limed surfaced to dry thoroughly before applying coats of satin-finish polyurethane.

Materials list

Sandpaper (100-, 150-, 220-, 240-, 320-grit); dark wood stain (two different shades); satin or semi-gloss-finish acrylic or oil-based paints; hide glue.

TOP LEFT: You can achieve a crackle finish like this by applying acrylic paint over hide glue.

TOP RIGHT: A crackled surface that is covered with an oil-based paint.

ABOVE LEFT: Liming, shown on the lefthand side of this pine door, gives a partially stripped look. The right half is finished without liming.

ABOVE RIGHT: Accentuate knots by cutting paint-retaining crevices around them with a sharp knife or scalpel.

Practical Matters

When you have made your plans, whether they are for a major house renovation or just a simple do-it-yourself project, it is time to address the practicalities. To make a piece of furniture or undertake a renovation, you will need a well-organised work space, usually in a shed or garage, where you can work without disturbing the rest of the household. As well as having a suitable work space, appropriate and well-maintained tools for the job are most important. This chapter itemises and illustrates the most commonly used tools and materials, and gives practical suggestions for how to go about organising them in your workroom.

Another important consideration is safety. While this is seriously addressed on any commercial building site, sometimes it is overlooked by the home handyperson. Safety is generally a matter of common sense, but it is worthwhile considering the useful pointers given here concerning the dangers of renovating, wearing protective clothing, and the correct storage and maintenance of tools and equipment.

Finally, don't forget environmental considerations. It is not always necessary to use toxic chemicals for cleaning, painting and finishing – consult the 'green' tips section for some useful pointers to help make your renovating project both a safe and enjoyable experience.

This well-equipped, well laid-out work space for the home handyperson occupies a section of the garage. Having a specific area such as this means you don't have to worry about creating a mess and you can work undisturbed.

The workroom

Whether you are undertaking major renovation work or a small do-it-yourself project, a designated work area will ensure the smooth running of the project.

Organising the perfect workplace

Smooth the path to successful, enjoyable and rewarding weekend projects by creating a well-equipped workspace. Even if the area for such a facility is not much bigger than a cupboard, organisation is the key. Establish a proper place for every piece of equipment, and remember that small items are more likely to go astray than large ones. Always keep the chuck key for changing a drill bit tied to the flex or body of your power drill, otherwise it will disappear. Tape measures and needle-nosed pliers also have a tendency to become elusive. In fact, any tool that is used regularly by different members of the family is likely to be misplaced. Equip yourself with duplicates of popular tools, and try to buy them in bright, even fluorescent, colours. With the work bench, the pivotal point of the workroom, never skimp on size and weight. It needs to be solid and very stable.

Make space for a workroom in the house where tools and materials can be stored. Floorplans of average homes rarely allow for such a space, so it is usually up to the resident

ABOVE AND RIGHT: Tools are within easy reach when hung on the wall.

home-maintenance and carpentry expert to find one. Such a workroom could be created in a spare bedroom or a roof space, or perhaps in a basement, if there is one. A large utility room could be sectioned off, while even the space under the stairs might be sufficient.

Ideally, a workroom should be dry, cool and reasonably soundproof, especially if it is located close to the living quarters of the house or the neighbouring property. It should also have excellent natural and artificial light; good ventilation (fumes from paints, finishes and various preparations can be not only unpleasant, but also dangerous); power points (preferably at bench height); a sturdy work bench at hip height for maximum efficiency; a practical floor finish, which won't be spoiled by inevitable spills; and suitable storage for all tools and materials. If the floor is concrete, lay a rubber mat over an offcut of underfelt in front of the work bench for comfort underfoot. Although the workroom is not supposed to be luxuriously appointed or a gathering place for wits and scholars, including a simple chair or stool (or two) will be a good idea for relaxing tea breaks or when a visitor drops in.

Common sense and safety in the workroom

- Develop the habit of wearing safety glasses in the workroom.
- Clean up at the end of every workroom session.
- Wear a dust mask when sweeping and vacuuming to get rid of sawdust and dirt.
- Read labels on preparations carefully. Some tasks involving potentially dangerous substances are best performed outside.
- Keep instruction books for equipment close at hand on a shelf or in a drawer.
- Service power tools regularly.
- Sharpen cutting edges of hand

tools; blunt blades are inefficient and dangerous.
- Keep sharp tools and poisonous preparations out of the reach of children. The latter, ideally, should be stored safely in a lockable cupboard
- When using tools, stay relaxed. Haste and bad temper are disastrous in the workroom.
- Unplug tools before leaving the workroom. Fit the door to the room with a lock.
- Clear the floor of obstacles. Carelessly placed extension leads can become dangerous tripwires in the workroom.
- Make sure you have a fire extinguisher close at hand.

ABOVE: The fire extinguisher should be close at hand.

BELOW: Screwdrivers and files are best stored on a hanging rail.

Workroom essentials

A work bench, a sawhorse, a basic set of hand tools and some power tools are considered the absolute essentials for the workroom. They can be added as your budget allows and your requirements change.

Work bench

No work bench? Use the dimensional drawing below as a guide to making one. Adjust the height to suit your own stature, and make the top flush with the front if a vice is to be installed.

Sawhorses

Essential to the serious handyperson, this pair (right) of sturdy sawhorses is made from inexpensive pine. They'll make the job of cutting timber much easier because their height is designed to allow your body to bend over the work so that maximum strength can be put into the job.

To saw the angles accurately, you will need a power saw that is set into its bench. If you have this

facility, cut all the angles at 75°. If you are not able to do this, cut the housing recesses in the top at 90° and allow the braces to set the legs at the correct angle.

If you have no power saw, cut the housings into the top with a saw, hammer and chisel, in the positions indicated in the diagram. Cut the legs about 25 mm longer than necessary and set them in the housings so that they protrude above the top. Saw them off level with the top last of all.

Screw through the braces into the edges of the legs, and through the legs into the housing, using 50 mm screws in the positions indicated in the diagram. The splayed legs will stop the sawhorses from toppling over, no matter how much weight may be applied to them.

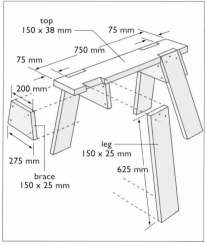

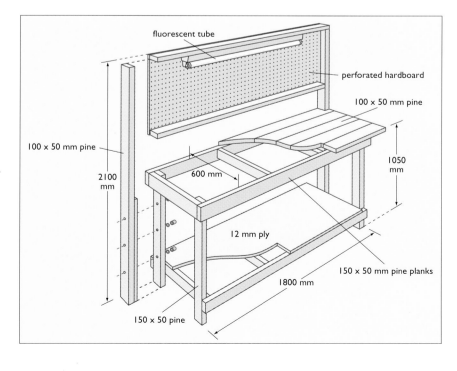

TOP: Pine sawhorses.

ABOVE: Sawhorse plan.

LEFT: Work bench plan.

FAR RIGHT: Power tools.
1 Drill
2 Circular saw
3 Orbital sander
4 Jigsaw
5 Router

Power tools

Although building tasks can be performed with hand tools, using electrical energy rather than the human variety will allow you to get the job done more quickly and, in most cases, more accurately.

These days, power tools are available in different capacities. Most manufacturers produce a light-capacity range, which is adequate for weekend projects. The main tools are listed here in order of priority.

A drill is essential. It is almost impossible to undertake any building project without drilling holes.

A circular saw is a must for work with any wood, apart from small-section timber.

An orbital sander is invaluable for giving work a professional finish. Most drills have disc attachments to take circular sheets of sandpaper and act as power sanders, but they tend to leave curved marks in softer surfaces.

The jigsaw allows you to perform a wider range of building activities, and in some cases it can also do the job of a circular saw.

The router, used to cut rebates in timber for stronger joints, should be your last purchase. Make do with simple or hand-cut joints until you become more experienced.

Drill (figure 1)

Most jobs call for holes to be drilled. Everything, from inserting screws to starting saw cuts that do not extend to the edge of the timber, is made much easier with a power drill and a good selection of drill bits. A variable speed control will enable drilling into materials of different densities, while a hammer facility and suitable bits will make drilling masonry easier.

Circular saw (figure 2)

Although most saw cuts can be made with a hand saw, a power saw will save a lot of time and energy, especially when using hardwoods. A saw with a 185-mm-diameter blade (approximately) will be sufficient for the amateur. While power saws are noisy and sometimes forbidding, their blade guards ensure that the cutting edge is covered when not in use.

Orbital sander (figure 3)

This is a wonderful companion when it comes to finishing any work. Any job is only as good as the finished surface, and using a sander is the quickest way to achieve a smooth appearance. It allows any blemishes in timber and plaster surfaces alike to be smoothed off with ease.

Jigsaw (figure 4)

This relatively modern invention opens up a whole new world to the home handyperson. It allows curved cuts to be made in just about any material. Also, because its blade is narrow and short, saw cuts can be made in places that otherwise would be too confined. Being able to saw circles and irregular curves allows a greater range of design options. Most models allow the blade to be adjusted to make angled cuts, too.

Router (figure 5)

The strongest joints incorporate rebates (a recess in one piece of timber into which the adjacent component fits). The router provides the only quick and accurate method of cutting a rebate. It has an adjustable guide at the side, which you set on the edge of the timber to maintain the position of the cutting tip.

Hand tools – A basic set

With the right tools, any job can be tackled. Basic hand tools haven't changed all that much through the generations, although plastic handles, retractable tape measures and

1

2

3

4

5

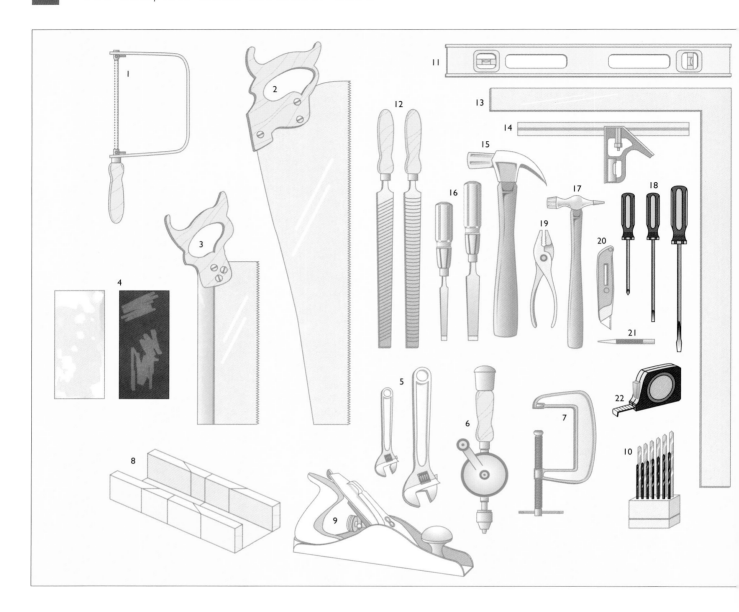

ABOVE: Hand tools.

planes indicate some signs of technological advance. Any old tools that are discovered in the course of cleaning out the workroom should be treasured. They are highly prized by collectors, and sometimes are of better quality than today's equivalents.

1 Coping saw. Ideal for cutting curves and intricate joints. Blades are replaceable.

2 Panel saw. For cutting larger pieces of timber to size. Use a small file to sharpen individual teeth when necessary.

3 Tenon saw. For cutting joints, such as mitres, and thin timber.

4 Oilstone. For sharpening chisels and plane blades.

5 Adjustable spanners. These ensure that you will always have a tool to fit a range of bolt sizes. Use bolts and nuts to join large timber pieces.

6 Hand drill. For small jobs, such as making screw holes.

7 G-cramps. For anchoring timber to the bench while it is being sawn. Also used to clamp timber during construction.

8 Mitre box. Sets saw blade at an exact 45° or 90° angle.

9 Plane. Finishes timber to any dimension. You can adjust the blade, depending on the depth of the cut.

10 Twist bits. Allow you to drill holes up to 15 mm in diameter. Flat and augur bits will drill larger holes.

11 Spirit level. For checking that all surfaces are perfectly horizontal or vertical.

12 Files. Handy for smoothing off corners and edges. Have at least one long, flat, fine-cut file.

13 Framing square. For marking out shapes on large sheets and checking large right-angles.

14 Combination square. Makes quick work of marking out 45° and 90° angles, and checking for accuracy with the integral spirit level at the same time.

15 Claw hammer. For general hammering jobs; claw head removes old or bent nails.

16 Chisels. Have one small and one large. Use for cutting recesses and grooves in timber. Bevelled-edge type is best.

17 Tack hammer. For small nails and panel pins in tight situations where a claw hammer is too large.

18 Screwdrivers. Buy these in different sizes as you need them, making sure that the blade fits the screw head exactly.

19 Pliers. For cutting wires and gripping or removing nails.

20 Trimming knife. Useful for cutting all materials, as well as fine adjustment to cuts in timber components.

21 Nail punch. Sets nail head below surface of material. It may be necessary to buy more than one to suit the different sizes of nail heads available.

22 Tape measure. Retractable type with locking facility is best.

Tips

• Don't be tempted to buy cheap tools on special offer in DIY stores – tips may break off screwdrivers, hammer heads could chip, and chisels blunt quickly. Invest a bit extra and buy reliable brand names.

• To prevent a new saw from rusting, wipe it over with an oily rag after use, and avoid cutting wet timber. Lubricate saws with candle wax and remove rust with turpentine and steel wool.

LEFT: This neat idea safely stores paint, hazardous materials and other workroom items behind roller doors in the garage while still allowing easy access to them.

Some simple how-tos

Learning how to assemble things properly will make any do-it-yourself job easier, and with the right finishing touch, you can achieve a professional look.

Joint techniques

Joining two pieces of timber together is the basis of most of the projects illustrated in this book. Here are some of the simplest joints, clearly drawn and explained. Try them out with scrap timber, using off-cuts of the same thickness for each one. All joints should be glued, nailed or screwed.

1   Butt. This is the most basic of timber joints and the most frequently used. Execute it simply by butting the two pieces of timber together and fixing one component to the other. Glue and screws, or nails, give the joint its only strength.

2   Rebated. You will achieve more strength if you cut a rebate into one piece of timber and insert the adjoining piece into it. Mark the rebate and cut down through the end grain first with a tenon saw (or circular saw if the wood is wide, or you have a lot of joints to make). Then cut across the grain to complete the rebate. You can also use a router to cut the rebate in one go.

3   Half lap. Cut this in the same way as a rebate. By cutting recesses into both components to a depth of half the thickness of the timber, you will make a very strong joint. This type is most often used for lengths of timber that are joined over their horizontal dimension.

4   Lap. Where two timbers do not have to finish flush with one another, this basic lap joint will suffice. It is vital that you position screws or nails diagonally across the joint, as this gives the joint its strength.

5   Brackets. Concealed steel brackets of different sizes and shapes may be used to reinforce any timber joint. You should also reinforce the joint itself with screws or nails.

6   Mitred. When you require a perfect finish and the joint is to be left exposed, you should use a mitred joint. You will need a tenon saw and a mitre box to ensure that the two cuts are exactly at 45°. A mitre cramp is useful to hold the two components in place while you glue and nail them together. Insert the nails at opposing angles to prevent the joint pulling apart.

ABOVE: The finishing touch is important if you are to achieve a professional look.

BELOW: Joint techniques.

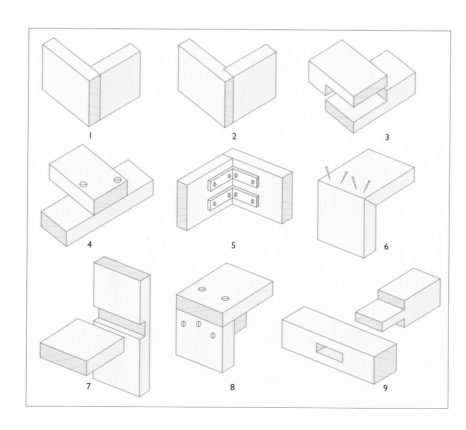

7 Housing. When making a T-joint (stronger than the butt), saw and chisel a groove, or housing, into one component to accommodate the end of the other. Start the groove by sawing downwards across the grain, making two parallel cuts through half the thickness of the timber. Chisel out the recess between the cuts.

8 Butt with block. If you don't think a basic butt joint will be strong enough for the job, you can reinforce it with a block on the inside of the angle. This makes a very practical joint, which you can use whenever appearance is not the main consideration. Screw or nail through both the components into the corner block.

9 Mortise and tenon. This is the strongest way to make a T-joint. Saw the tenon, or tongue, to fit into the mortise, or slot, of the other component. Both mortise and tenon should be one-third the thickness of the timber. You will have to use a sharp chisel to cut the mortise accurately.

The finishing touch

A professional standard of finish depends on preparing the surface properly before varnishing, waxing or painting.

Filling

Fillers vary from acrylic compounds (purely cosmetic cover-up fillers) to epoxy resins that bond with timber and take screws and nails.

Set nail heads and countersink screws with a countersunk drill bit, then use filler to conceal the heads. Smooth end grain by filling and sanding. Also conceal knots, splits and grain blemishes with filler. Despite claims to the contrary, all fillers shrink to some extent when drying. For deep cavities, build up layers, allowing each to dry before proceeding. Sand the filler flush with the timber surface.

Colouring may be difficult, as fillers often take up differing amounts of stain than timber. Although there are tinted fillers to match most common timber types, these won't always be a perfect match. It is advisable to test coloured filler on the underside of a project before proceeding.

Plugging

A plug allows you to conceal a countersunk screw with wood. After drilling the clearance hole for the screw, use an ordinary drill bit the width of the screw head and drill to a depth of 10 mm below the surface. (A countersunk drill bit cannot make a hole as deep as this.) Cut a piece of dowel of the same diameter, but a little shorter than the depth of the hole, add a dab of glue, tap it in place and sand flush.

A plastic cap is an alternative method of concealing a screw head, although the cap itself will remain visible.

Edging

Wooden edging strips can be used to conceal the end grain of timber or the sawn edges of particle board. Match their width to the thickness of the sheet material, or make them deeper for a more substantial look. Glue and tack the strips in place, filling and sanding the joints. Paint them to match, or finish with clear varnish to make a feature. Natural wood edging strips combine well with white or coloured plastic-laminated particle board.

Heat-bonded strips in a range of timber types and colours, for finishing veneered and plastic-laminated particle board, give professional-quality edges. A household iron provides the necessary heat source.

Sanding

Wrap sandpaper around a cork or wooden block and always sand with the grain. To smooth rough timber,

ABOVE: Stained timber has been given a sheen with polyurethane.

ABOVE: Timber and Boards

1	Pine	5	Hardboard
2	Red cedar	6	Plywood
3	Particle board	7	Hardwood
4	Plastic-laminated particle board	8	Dowelling

start with medium-grade paper and work through a couple of finer grades. Use fine-grade paper between coats of paint or varnish.

An orbital sander makes it easier to achieve a good finish. Work the sander along the grain, otherwise sanding marks will be apparent.

Staining

Work quickly and evenly, covering the entire surface with stain before it dries. Use a soft cloth or brush for applications and work in the direction of the grain. Wipe off the excess stain with a clean, dry cloth, and when it is dry, wipe again before applying a clear coat. It is always best to practise on a scrap of the same timber before you begin.

Choose a stain that is compatible with the finish you have in mind; check with the supplier before purchasing. Most stains produce denser, stronger colours than expected.

Timber and boards

The definitions of timber can leave the novice blinking in confusion. The words 'hardwood' and 'soft

wood' seem straightforward enough as descriptive terms, but the botanist and the woodworker have different opinions. Tradespeople use these terms literally to describe timber that is either hard or soft to work. In the field of botany, however, hardwood can include species such as balsa, which is physically soft, while softwood includes species that are physically hard, such as yew. The terms refer more to the structure of the tree and how it grows, than its actual hardness. True hardwood comes from broad-leaved trees, such as oak, elm and beech; softwood comes from coniferous trees that bear needles and cones, such as pine and cedar.

It is possible to buy timber directly from sawmills in widths and thicknesses limited only by the size of the tree, but standard sizes available in timber yards and DIY stores are more economical and easier to obtain. In the case of sheet materials, ask your local supplier about sheet sizes available so that you can minimise waste and maximise the purchase.

Although timber is cut, and sheet materials produced in an

astounding variety of thicknesses, widths and lengths, a retail outlet will only keep those sizes for which there is the most demand. Sometimes, it is worth going to a larger timber yard or sawmill to find sizes of materials suited to more specific requirements. Timber is sold by the linear metre, so estimate the length of each type needed before ordering.

Timber is sold in two forms: sawn and planed. Sawn timber has a rough texture left by the saw blade after initial sizing. It is ideal for structural work that will not be seen. Planed timber (sometimes known as prepared or PAR – planed all round) has a much smoother finish that only needs light sanding prior to painting or varnishing. Timber is sold in its nominal (i.e. sawn) dimensions. When it is planed, its dimensions are considerably reduced. For instance, a piece of sawn timber measuring 100 x 38 mm will be 90 x 30 mm when it has been prepared.

The amount by which the timber is reduced when it is planed smooth varies with different timber types and different milling equipment

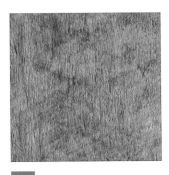
5

6

7

8

used. Bear this in mind if you are buying timber that must be of a specific size.

Pine

Several types of timber are grouped under the heading of pine. Normally, you will come across European redwood, also known as deal or Scots pine. Spruce (also known as white deal) comes into this category, as well. The nature of the grain makes these woods flex as well as splinter when sawn. The grain has very high contrast and often tends to be quite knotty. If you are buying pine, spend some time looking for pieces that are not warped or split. It is ideal for furnishings and shelving. Unless it has been treated with preservative, pine is not suitable for outside use. It is the most commonly available softwood. Standard nominal sizes range from 12 x 12 mm to 100 x 100 mm.

Fir

This timber is also known as British Columbian pine, Oregon pine and Douglas pine. Although prone to splitting, it is stronger than normal pine, is straight-grained and gener

ally knot-free. It is often used for structural work, window frames and interior joinery.

Parana pine

Available in large board widths, up to 300 mm, Parana pine is widely used for interior joinery, such as stairs. It is an even-textured wood, often free of knots and shakes, but it may warp or split as it dries.

Cedar

Also known as red cedar, this wood is quite expensive. However, it is durable in all exterior conditions. Its natural colour makes it even more appealing, and it will weather to a pale grey when left untreated. Its softness can be a disadvantage. For sizes available, check with your supplier.

Hardwood

Hardwoods vary widely in strength and weather resistance. Always consult a timber supplier to determine the most suitable wood for the job in hand. Oak and teak, for example are ideal for outdoor jobs, while beech isn't. The denseness of

hardwoods makes accurate work easier, but it also blunts tools quicker than working with softwood. They are more expensive than softwood, too.

Plywood

Plywood, which is made by laminating very thin layers of timber together, varies in quality, panel size and thickness. Because it is composed of layers, plywood comes in sizes wider than 300 mm. The layers impart strength to the sheets. Make sure to buy the right type for the job; if it will be subjected to damp conditions (indoors or out), specify exterior-grade or even marine plywood.

Common thicknesses for plywood range from 4 mm to 18 mm, while sheet sizes can range from 610 x 610 mm to 2440 x 1220 mm.

Hardboard

This dark composite board is a relatively dense material. It has no structural qualities and should be used only where it is supported by a frame. Hardboard forms an excellent underlay for floor coverings.

ABOVE: Parquetry is the most prestigious of floor finishes and can be laid in a variety of designs and types of timber. It is equally suitable for living areas and kitchens.

It should be fixed to the floor with panel pins 12.5 cm apart and 1 cm from the edges.

Thicknesses of hardboard are 3.2, 4.8 and 6.4 mm, sheet sizes being the same as for plywood.

Dowelling

This material has a round cross-section and is useful for making uprights and joining components in building projects. Thicknesses range from 6 to 44 mm, and lengths up to 2.4 m.

Particle boards

Also known as chipboard, this material is only suitable for interior use. A mixture of wood chips and glue is formed into sheets under pressure. The faces of the sheets are smooth, but the edges are rough and need concealing with timber edging. When fixing into particle board, special screws are required.

Thicknesses are 12, 18 and 25 mm, and can be bought in sheet sizes that vary between 1220 x 610 mm and 1220 x 2440 mm.

Melamine-faced particle board is ideal for use where a wipe-down surface is required. It is normally only available in white, and cut edges will need to be covered with wood or iron-on white plastic edging strips.

Medium-density fibreboard (MDF) is denser than standard particle board, allowing it to take normal screws. Cut edges can be finished by sanding and painting. Thicknesses range from 6 to 12 mm.

Making accurate measurements

Whether you're building a 50-room castle, a dog house or just a section of fencing, there's no such measurement as 'about'. Measurements must be exact. Learning this from the outset will save you a lot of time, money and frustration.

An equally important aspect of making correct measurements is starting from a square edge. This isn't automatic, by any means – most materials aren't square, especially the ends of boards and timber sections. However, most have a 'factory edge'. A factory edge is carpenters' vernacular for the milled edge of the material, which usually is true. Use this edge as a reference point for squaring the rest of the material.

To make truly accurate measurements, you'll need several tools, the most important of which is a rule or tape measure. This calibrated instrument is available in many forms, but your best bet is a 3, 5 or 8 m retractable steel tape.

You'll also need a pencil with a sharp point or, better yet, a flat carpenter's pencil (this has a flat lead rather than a round one) to transfer marks to the material. For even more accuracy, use an awl or a scriber to score cutting lines. Or you can use a trimming knife.

Another important marking tool, the chalk line, has many uses. Its chief function, though, is laying down long, straight lines. To use a chalk line, first make sure the string has plenty of chalk on it; don't skimp. Then, tie it to a nail at one end and stretch it taut. (You must have the string pulled tight to obtain a straight line.) To make the mark, pinch the string between your thumb and index finger, pull it away from the surface to be marked, then let it snap back on to the surface. Snap the line just once.

Using squares and levels

The words 'square', 'level' and 'plumb' are familiar to most people, but deceptively so. Before discussing how to achieve each of these desirables, let's define what they are. 'Square' refers to an exact 90° angle between two adjoining surfaces. In other words, a right-angle. When a material is 'level', it's perfectly horizontal; when it's 'plumb', it's truly vertical.

Never assume that any existing construction is square, level or plumb. Chances are, it won't be. To prove this to yourself, lay a spirit level along any floor in your home, plumb a wall section in a corner, or square a door or window opening. Don't be alarmed at the results.

Variation is normal in most construction, since houses usually settle slightly on their foundations, throwing square, level and plumb out of true. But when you make repairs or additions, you must compensate for the existing errors.

The three tools needed to establish square, level and plumb are a framing square, a spirit level and a plumb bob.

A framing square has two legs, set at right-angles. One leg is longer and wider than the other and is known as the blade. The other leg is known as the tongue. Usually marked in 1 or 5 mm increments, a framing square may also have a scale so you can align it for making angled marks.

A spirit level is used to determine level and plumb. When the work is level (horizontal) or plumb (vertical), the bubbles in the liquid-filled glass tubes on the spirit level are centred between the lines marked on the tubes.

How can you determine if a spirit level is accurate? Lay it on a horizontal surface and shim at one end if necessary in order to obtain a level reading. Now turn it around taking care not to move the shim. If you don't get the same reading, the

spirit level needs to be adjusted or replaced. With some models, you can compensate by rotating the vial.

A plumb bob is used to determine whether the upright elements of a building, such as walls and pipes, are truly vertical. It comprises a simple pointed weight suspended on a line.

Making a tool box

The simple and traditional-style tool box shown here is inexpensive and requires only a couple of hours of relatively easy work to make. Ours has a drawer in the bottom, which requires either a router or a bit of skill with a power saw to complete. You can leave it out and just build the basic box.

BELOW: Detail of tool box handle.

BOTTOM: The finished tool box.

You will need for the tool box (pine or fir, all dimensions are in mm):		
Components	Measurements	No.
A Ends	450 x 280 x 20	2
B Sides	900 x 225 x 20	1
	900 x 280 20	1
C Base rails	900 x 50 x 20	2
	180 x 50 x 20	2
D Floor supports	860 x 20 x 20	2
	200 x 20 x 20	2
E Drawer sides	220 x 52 x 20	2
F Drawer front	857 x 52 x 20	1
G Drawer back	857 x 42 x 20	1
H Handle supports	250 x 70 x 20	2
I Handle	860 x 50 x 40	1
J Drawer base	827 x 245 x 4 plywood	1
K floor	860 x 240 x 5 masonite	1

RIGHT: The tool box components.

BELOW: The slide out drawer of the tool box.

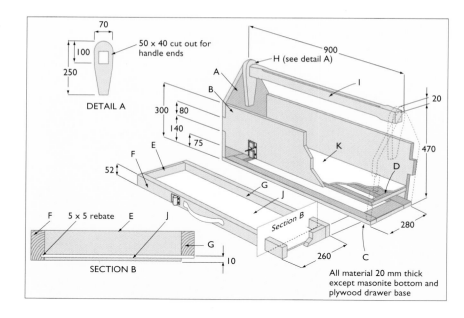

70
100
250
50 × 40 cut out for handle ends
DETAIL A

900
H (see detail A)
A
B
I
20
300
80
140
75
470
E
F
52
G
J
K
D
F
5 × 5 rebate
E
J
G
Section B
10
SECTION B
280
260
C

All material 20 mm thick except masonite bottom and plywood drawer base

1 Cut out the ends. If you have a jigsaw, mark the rounded top of each piece by drawing around a small paint tin or jar and cut along the marked line. Cut out the rebates to receive the tongues of the side pieces with a jigsaw or by making several cuts with a hand saw and knocking out the waste with a chisel.

2 Cut out the sides (making one shallower than the other if you intend to add the drawer) and screw them to the ends.

3 Screw on the base rails and the floor supports. Make the drawer to fit the opening. A drawer front that is 857 × 52 mm should fit, but measure to check. The same applies to the length of the drawer sides. Remember, measure twice, cut once.

4 If you don't own a router, two careful cuts with a power saw will do the trick for the drawer's bottom rebate. Set the first cut at 5 mm and the second parallel to it at 8 mm. This should give you a groove 5 mm wide.

5 Run a plane down the edges of the handle to bevel the corners, then fit it into the supports and screw them to the two ends. Drop in the masonite bottom, secure it with panel pins and you're finished.

The tool box can be as big or as small as you care to make it. Just remember that when it is fully loaded with all your tools, you need to be able to lift and carry it without the embarrassment of having to call for the help of a strong friend or two.

The dangers of renovating

When you renovate, you may need to climb into the roof or down a hole, use power tools and employ a variety of chemicals – all of which can present hazards.

The most common injuries on building sites are sprains and strains, back injuries, hand and finger wounds, and knee and leg injuries. Many of these are caused by falls that occur on slippery surfaces, ladders, steps, stairs and scaffolding. Always set ladders on level ground and secure them firmly at the top. The best angle is with the base one quarter of its height out from the wall. Scaffolding should only be put up by professionals. Keep all paths and access ways on your site clean and free of rubbish.

It's vital to keep a well-stocked first-aid kit on site. Special safety standards apply by law to all industrial sites, but do-it-yourselfers are on their own, so use common sense and take care.

Electrical safety

Keep electrical cables and flexes away from moisture. Make sure your tools are double insulated and that your electrical system incorporates a residual current device (RCD) to protect you against accidental electrocution, or use a plug-in RCD to protect tools you are working with.

If an extension lead is damaged, discard it. Don't use a lead that is too long; a coiled lead will cause a build-up of heat in the wires.

Chemical hazards

Renovators have to take special care with chemicals. Corrosive paint strippers, cleaners, gas and fuels, and even paints, can be sources of danger. Solvents can not only give off fumes, but they're also highly flammable.

Odour is not always a clue to danger; some gases are colourless and odourless. Remember to wear a respirator and work in a well ventilated area. Don't eat, drink or smoke in the work area, and clean up carefully at the end of the day.

It's worth using solvent-free materials whenever possible. These include water-based paints and floor finishes. Safe storage – out of children's reach – and proper labelling are vital with chemicals. When it's time for disposal, read the manufacturer's instructions or check with your local council.

Care with tools

Care is needed with any sharp tools. Don't overload a power tool so that it overheats. If a tool sparks, stops or behaves strangely, stop using it and have a qualified electrician inspect it. Let a tool's motor stop before putting it down, because it may kick back. Follow the maker's safety instructions.

Protective clothing

Protective goggles, thick gloves and tough clothing will protect you from spills and grazes. A dust mask may not be enough if you're using chemicals that produce harmful fumes; you should also wear a suitable respirator.

If you're using noisy machinery, ear protectors are vital. And be careful how you dress. Loose clothing or long hair can get caught in tools. Wear stout shoes with a good tread. Don't forget the risk of sunburn, either, if you're working outdoors; cover up and apply a sunscreen to exposed skin.

Tips
Where do I turn off the water?

Unless you are competent at working with pipes, all plumbing repairs should be entrusted to a qualified plumber, but you may prevent a lot of damage while you are waiting for a plumber to arrive if you know where to turn off the water.

- Do you know where the main stopcock (a valve within your property for turning off the water supply) is?
- Are you able to turn if off and on easily?
- Do you know where the water supply company's stopvalve is outside the property? (Normally, it will be under a hinged metal cover set in the ground somewhere near the boundary of the property.)
- Do you know where to turn off your immersion heater?

You should find out the answers to these questions.

Contacts

- For more advice on the disposal of hazardous chemicals, contact your local council, who will be able to provide you with details of sites that accept such materials, or may arrange for their collection.

'Green' do-it-yourself tips

- Wash brushes used in water-based paint in a bucket of water. Let the paint settle and tip the water on the garden. Dispose of hardened paint in the bin or at a toxic-waste tip. Do the same with white spirit, but pour the spirit back into its jar for re-use.
- When sanding, wear a dust mask and seal the area to contain dust.
- Don't wash filler down the drain. Tip it on to newspaper and leave it to dry. Then dispose of it in the bin or at a toxic-waste tip.

BELOW: In renovating this house the owners have made good use of recycled timber for both furniture and fittings.

'Green' renovating

For most of us, life becomes 'greener' every day. We're composting, recycling, buying products with less packaging, using unleaded petrol and so on. Now the 'green' revolution has even hit building.

Whether you're renovating or building from scratch, 'green' alternatives exist for many products you'll need. They're usually more expensive in the short term, but they can mean a more environmentally healthy home for your family. Ultimately, they can save you money, too.

Timber tricks

Recycle old timber in building to save money and resources. Once cleaned up, it can be used for a wide variety of projects, and damage such as nail holes can even increase its visual appeal. Check with local architectural salvage companies and demolition sites for timber that you can use again. You may not find the exact size you want, but remember larger pieces can always be cut or planed down to suit. Even buying secondhand wooden furniture, such as tables, or doors can provide sources of timber for new projects. If you have space, keep off-cuts for future use.

Green options

Solvent-based products regularly used in building and cleaning can cause health problems for some people, especially asthmatics.

Paint

Solvent-based paint can be dangerous during application and will continue to emit fumes that can affect some people. Use plant-based paint products instead. If removing lead-based paint, use a chemical peel so you don't breath in lead dust.

Polyurethane varnishes

Replace with hard oils made from plant oils and tree resin.

Steam cleaning

Instead of using solvent-based cleaning products, try steam cleaning areas of your home. Steam-cleaning machines are available from tool hire shops and will easily remove a remarkably wide range of substances.

Cleaners

There are 'green' alternatives to many solvent-based cleaning products. Check in your local supermarket or DIY store.

Index

This edition published for Index, 2000
First published in 1998 by Murdoch Books®, a division of Murdoch Magazines Pty Ltd,
GPO Box 1203, Sydney NSW 1045, Australia

CEO & Publisher: Anne Wilson
Associate Publisher: Catie Ziller
General Manager: Mark Smith

A catalogue record of this book is available from the British Library.

The Complete Home Makeover Book has been compiled from the resources of Murdoch Books ® and Better Homes and Gardens ®.

Project Manager: Sally Bird/Calidris Publishing Services
Text/Cover Design and Layout: Trevor Hood/*Anaconda Graphic Design*
Editor: Katie Millar
UK Consultant Editor: Ian Penberthy
Diagrams: Di Zign, Sydney
Printed by Toppan, China

© Text, design, commissioned photography and illustrations Murdoch Books® 1998

ISBN 1 89773 017 9

Acknowledgements:
Additional photography by: Philip Bier/View pp. 27, 30, 61; Jane Legate/Robert Harding Picture Library pp. 11 (top); Andy Payne pp. 10 (bottom), 27 (top), 87 (top), 123 (1, 2 & 3), 151 (top), 231 (bottom right), 232 (top left, top centre), 235 (top), 242 (bottom left), 291, 296; Rodney Weidland pp. 175 (bottom), 178, 191 (bottom), 286 (bottom), 287 (bottom).
The Publisher wishes to thank **RYOBI** for the use of the articles on the following pages: 84, 111 & 188.